Breaking Out of the Pink-Collar Ghetto

Breaking Out of the Pink-Collar Ghetto

Policy Solutions for Non-College Women

Sharon H. Mastracci

Foreword by Ray Marshall

M.E.Sharpe
Armonk, New York
London, England

Library of Congress Cataloging-in-Publication Data

Mastracci, Sharon H., 1968-
    Breaking out of the pink-collar ghetto: policy solutions for non-college women / Sharon
H. Mastracci.
        p. cm.
    Includes bibliographical references and index.
    ISBN 0-7656-1355-7 (cloth: alk. paper) ISBN 0-7656-1356-5 (pbk.: alk paper)
        1. Women—Employment—United States. 2. Working class woman—United States.
I. Title.

HD6095.M34 2004
331.4′11423—dc22
                                                                        2003061401

Printed in the United States of America

BM (c) 10   9   8   7   6   5   4   3   2   1
BM (p) 10   9   8   7   6   5   4   3   2   1

To Tony
... you'll never know, dear ...

Contents

List of Illustrations

Tables

Figures

Foreword

Breaking Out of the Pink Collar Ghetto: Policy Solutions for Non-College Women is important for policymakers, scholars, and labor market practitioners for a number of reasons.

Dr. Sharon Mastracci addresses the very important issue of how to change deeply institutionalized patterns of employment that have caused women, who constitute two-thirds of the growth of the American workforce, to be heavily concentrated in marginal, low-wage jobs. She demonstrates that women's employment conditions are due more to institutionalized practices than to overt discrimination—and that these practices are detrimental to women and the communities in which they live and work, as well as to the nation as a whole.

Mastracci also addresses an often neglected aspect of women's employment policy: how to get ordinary women into better-paying, more highly skilled jobs that not only enable them to support themselves and their families, but also improve the quality of their working lives.

And she evaluates important remedial interventions authorized by Congress and administered by the Women's Bureau. In so doing, Mastracci provides important insights into the work of the Women's Bureau, the only agency of government mandated to protect and promote the interests of women workers. *Breaking Out of the Pink Collar Ghetto* makes a credible case for the importance of (a) the Women's Bureau's, (b) effective training based on apprenticeship principles, which improves the wages of low-paid women; (c) community-based organizations as intermediaries between the Women's Bureau and women who need help; and (d) the factors that can enhance the effectiveness of these actors and processes.

Mastracci's research methods clarify the nature of the processes and institutions involved in improving women's employment opportunities and provide credible evidence for her conclusions and recommendations. Her bias was in the subject she studied, not in the way she conducted her research and analyses. She applied rigorous econometric analyses to the best data available. But, cognizant of the weaknesses as well as the strengths of quantitative methods, she supplemented her analyses with interviews, case studies, and a review of the literature. All of this supports the compelling story she tells.

Ray Marshall
U.S. Secretary of Labor, 1977–1981

Preface

In the absence of institutional supports and personal resources to chart a longer-term strategy, many young women and men can fall through the cracks and never realize their vocations and career aspirations. I fell into such a vocational void and would have remained there if one very influential person had not pointed me toward night classes at Owens Technical College in Toledo, Ohio, where I read and learned as if my life depended upon it . . . in many ways, it did; at least any second chance did. This initial "career change"—from nothing to something—allowed me the confidence and courage to take yet another leap later. In hindsight, I realize my great good fortune. What separated me from anyone else in that situation was simply luck. What of the cashier who tinkers with woodworking in her spare time, never considering that she could find a fulfilling career doing something she already loves? What of the adolescent tomboy, who may never realize her dreams of becoming a forest ranger, firefighter, or forensics expert, for she is told to "act like a lady"? Who intervenes for them? Must we all hope and wait for a lucky turn, for a guardian angel or two?

I believe government can serve appropriately in this role by establishing institutional supports where few or none exist. I wanted to focus on policymaking and program implementers, rather than on the targets of policy, to underscore government's important and appropriate role, its significant social function in helping individuals to discover their vocations when discrimination and other barriers prevent them from doing so. Public policy plays an extremely important role in providing opportunities for individuals to pursue rewarding career paths. While discovering one's vocation is a singular, selfish pleasure—and I am lucky enough to vouch for that—doing so serves a social function as well. Facilitating individuals' access to and entry into occupations and careers that engage them fully serves a larger public function and benefits whomever works with or is served by them.

Yes, I believe government very appropriately plays this role, although some will tell you that such efficient outcomes are naturally the result of rational decisionmaking. However, this position presupposes an absence of discriminatory beliefs about "men's work" and "women's work," as well as freer-flowing information and freer access to resources than what currently obtains for women looking for work or post-secondary training and educational opportunities— hence the appropriateness of government intervention. Some might protest that such intervention represents social engineering—again, allow individuals to pursue jobs, training, and education themselves, according to their tastes and preferences. The unseen hand shall guide each of us toward the best outcome. However, these critics fail to acknowledge that notions about "women's work" and "men's work" are *themselves* forms of social engineering. This study highlights the role of government intervention and the importance of doing so for non-college women who would otherwise end up in low-paying jobs with few long-term opportunities. Many women cannot afford to wait for luck to intervene.

Throughout the production of this book, many fabulous guardian angels and mentors have intervened over the years, and words cannot begin to express my thanks. I am indebted to Janice Hogan, the late Neal Hogan, and Maurice Hogan, to Larry and JoAnn Degnan for the timely push and their consistent support; and to Joyce Hallabaugh for giving me a chance when I needed one. Others to whom I owe many thanks for supporting me, providing advice, and keeping me sane include Bob Byrne, James K. Galbraith, Shama Gamkhar, Jerry Grammer, Dan Hamermesh, Kevin Isbell, Ray Marshall, Deirdre McCloskey, Roberta McKay, Michael Oden, and Brigid O'Farrell. Victoria E. Rodríguez righted my course early on, listened to my doubts and concerns, and continues to provide sage advice and insights: thank you, thank you, thank you. Moreover, my editor at M.E. Sharpe, Inc., Lynn Taylor, deserves all the gratitude in the world for her enthusiasm, keen eye, consistent belief in the project, and for eliciting my best work. Many thanks. Everyone at M.E. Sharpe has helped to develop this work, including Esther Clark, Elizabeth Granda, and Susan Rescigno. Some of the material in this book has been reviewed critically and some has appeared in print form elsewhere. Deborah Figart's comments, suggestions, and insights helped shape the book overall. The separate statistical analyses in Chapter 4 and Chapter 5 appear in the *Policy Studies Journal* and the *Review of Radical Political Economics*, respectively; and the case study analysis in Chapter 6 appears in *WorkingUSA*. Many thanks to the editorial staff and referees of these publications, whose suggestions improved the work a great deal. Other material has been critiqued by and otherwise inflicted upon audiences in various forums. All other chapters are original to the book, although arguments and ideas invariably appear here and there, given my tendency toward repetition and driving a point into the ground. Finally, I cannot begin to express my indebtedness to my best friend Tony, for his patience while enduring said repetitions, but, more importantly, for his unwavering love and support. You make me happy when skies are gray. In the end, however, although this text has benefited from the advice, expertise, insights, and support of each of these important people and many others, all errors and omissions found herein are mine alone.

We need not an unfettered and enfeebled private economy,
but a concerted partnership between a strong and determined
government and an energetic private sector, better regulated
but also more vigorous than we have had. It has been
done before. It can be done again. Success is not precluded
by laws of economics.
—*James K. Galbraith, 1998*

Breaking Out of the Pink-Collar Ghetto

Chapter 1
Pathways Out of the Pink-Collar Ghetto

Today, a woman earns just 74 cents for every dollar a man earns. Achieving equal pay is a major initiative of the U.S. Department of Labor. One of our primary strategies to reduce the gender wage gap between women and men is to increase opportunities for women in nontraditional jobs such as computer repairer, truck driver, and electrician.
—Women's Bureau of the U.S. Department of Labor, May 9, 2000[1]

Innovative partnerships between business, workers, and the government can help generate win-win investments for Americans.
—Secretary of Labor, Alexis Herman[2]

Working women earn less than men do for many reasons: head-to-head discrimination, where a woman is doing the same job as a man yet earning less for it; expectations and demands relating to unpaid work at home, where women are penalized for interrupting or postponing their educations and careers to care for children and parents, and assuming other such "private realm" burdens of the household; and occupational segregation by gender, where women tend to work in "women's jobs" and men tend to work in "men's jobs" and the former are remunerated far less than are the latter. The implications of this disparity are especially acute among women and men who do not earn four-year college degrees, a population that comprises the majority of the workforce. Although the proportion of the workforce earning a four-year college degree has increased over time, approximately three-fourths of the United States population has never earned one. Over one-fourth of the population never enrolls in formal schooling again after obtaining a high school diploma, an important yet overlooked trend examined by James Rosenbaum in *Beyond College for All: Career Paths for the Forgotten Half*.[3] Judging by the aspirations many parents have for their children and many individuals have for themselves, which commonly include a college education, earning a four-year college degree would seem to be a universal goal.

In many families, a college education is presumed, as it is part of a longer tradition of higher educational attainment. In other families, a college education is that brass ring, characterizing the accomplishment of one generation as well as of the preceding generations, whose members helped bring it about. Public policies aimed at making college more accessible assume that those who have not attended college want to go; that each person is in one of three states: attending college, already graduated, or aspiring toward college. This ignores a significant number of people. Many occupations essential to the U.S. economy do not require a four-year degree, including many service sector jobs and many in the skilled trades. Many workers in these jobs are not there temporarily while on their way elsewhere in their careers, either. What training and education options exist for the majority who will not graduate with a four-year degree, or those who will never attend college, many of whom aspire toward a higher-paying job, but perhaps not college?

In the pages that follow, this and several other questions are addressed. Is there more demand for post-secondary, non-college training and education options than what currently exists? Whether or not a job's functions require a four-year college degree, do employers demand a higher-educated workforce, resulting in an effective requirement if not an actual one? Have workers' demands for training and employers' expectations of educational attainment changed over time? Is the experience different for male and female workers? Do non-college women workers fare as well as their non-college male counterparts in the labor markets? Does a "college for all" policy presumption *really* hurt anyone? What kinds of programs might meet the needs of a non-college population while providing employers with a highly trained workforce?

This study addresses each of these questions, and its findings raise yet more issues. Yes, employment and training options fall short of the demand for them. Nearly two-thirds will not earn a four-year degree, yet skill requirements have increased. Some kind of alternative to college is necessary to meet the needs of a non-college population that still seeks high-paying, rewarding, and high-skilled careers, and occupations exist that offer these things, and do not require a four-year degree. Yes, workers' demands for training have changed over time, because employers' expectations of educational attainment have changed over time. Yes, the experience differs between men and women. Non-college women tend to hold lower-paying, lower-mobility "pink-collar" occupations compared to non-college men. Yes, a college-for-all assumption *does* hurt workers, especially female workers. College-for-all presumptions have precipitated program and funding cuts of non-college training and education opportunities. Because non-college women fare worse than non-college men do, such cutbacks end up limiting women's labor market opportunities. Presuming college-for-all results in fewer non-college options, which relegates many non-college women to careers comprised of a series of low-wage, low-mobility, low-skilled jobs. Programs *do* exist that have allowed some non-college women to break that cycle, on a pathway out of the "pink-collar ghetto."

The gender wage gap can be attacked on several levels, individually and in combination: comparable worth strategies force employers to acknowledge when men and women do the same job, whether or not their job titles are the same. Pay equity initiatives combat head-to-head discrimination, and policies designed to mitigate occupational segregation by gender combat the barriers women face to nontraditional "men's jobs." As the quotations at the beginning of this chapter indicate, the U.S. Department of Labor has attacked wage inequality on various fronts, including occupational segregation by gender: increasing "opportunities for women in non-traditional jobs such as computer repairer, truck driver, and electrician." Increasing the numbers of women in jobs that are nontraditional for them also happens to increase their economic welfare because these jobs pay more and involve advanced skills training, compared to many female-dominated jobs, as Chapter 4 demonstrates by revealing a statistically significant link between nontraditional occupations (NTOs) and the likelihood of earning higher wages.

Concerning policy solutions to occupational segregation by gender, former Labor Secretary Alexis Herman describes the programs analyzed here that have allowed many women to break free of the pink-collar ghetto as "innovating partnerships between business, workers, and the government," which this analysis shall demonstrate further. Indeed, when employers, unions, government, and nonprofits have worked together to train, place, and retain women in NTOs, the result has been a policy solution providing a pathway out of the pink-collar ghetto for many non-college women. The implications of these findings are significant not only for policymakers and the advocates, analysts, and scholars interested in the concerns of working women, but also for women seeking alternatives to the four-year college degree path to achieve their career objectives, some of whom may be transitioning from welfare to work. Working women support families, and improving their economic well-being remains an important policy objective. Combating occupational segregation by gender is a significant strategy for promoting gender pay equality.

The remainder of this chapter describes pink-collar jobs and underscores the reasons why public policy intervention is needed to provide non-college education and training options, insofar as supply falls short of demand for them. Moreover, this chapter discusses different theoretical explanations of differential labor market outcomes for women and men, and how policy interventions might alter labor market outcomes through education and training programs.

The Non-College Population

When workplace equity is dismissed as a nonissue, it is not the accomplishments of non-college women that are cited. The accomplishments of the few women often cited as "proof" of gender equality, usually high-profile female judges, doctors, lawyers, and business owners, may not be entirely relevant to women with different career goals and aspirations for themselves. Moreover, women in elite positions represent but a fraction of all working women, the bulk of whom are still in the same kinds of jobs they have always been in. In the U.S. economy, theirs are the original Invisible Hands; whether in necessary yet undervalued service-sector occupations, or in taking care of family members, particularly children and the elderly, which is even more necessary and not explicitly valued in the economy at all. In *Pink Collar Workers*, Louise Kapp Howe observes:

> But after you get through reading about all the historical changes, after you stop tracing all the twists and turns women's work has taken over the years, after you finish paying the necessary homage to all the exceptions and variations and tokens and models, this is what you always find: the vast majority of American women getting up in the morning, getting dressed, maybe grabbing a bite, and then going off to work at jobs (either within or without the home) where women form the bulk of the labor force; where pay is usually nil or low (in comparison to what men of the same or lower educational levels are making); where unionization is usually nil or weak; and where equal-pay-for-equal-work laws are of little or no meaning since if women are competing with anyone for these jobs they are competing with other women.[4]

The non-college population is important because the bulk of working women's careers can be characterized as Howe depicts them: low paying, weak or nonexistent unionization, and female-dominated. Sharon Harlan and Ronnie J. Steinberg assembled an unprecedented and unparalleled collection of works examining numerous aspects of numerous job training programs and their specific implications for women. In their introductory chapter to *Job Training for Women: The Promise and Limits of Public Policies*, the authors note:

> It has been difficult to focus scholarly and public attention on equal opportunity efforts directed explicitly at women without a college education.

Instead, most of the notice has gone to the minority of women who have, or who will obtain, a college degree. Much more has been published on how women prepare for and get professional and managerial jobs.[5]

Indeed, Beyer and Finnegan surveyed undergraduate students and conclude "that undergraduates had low awareness of occupational segregation and the gender gap in wages and they consistently underestimated segregation. Both males and females tended to believe that gender equity has been achieved."[6] From an undergraduate student's perspective, gender inequity may seem an artifact of a bygone era, and if these are the young women and men who might exert more influence on policy and research than may their non-college counterparts, then the non-college majority becomes ever more invisible. Most scholarly research and policy development commits this error and perpetuates the "pioneering myth": that the accomplishments of a handful of pioneering women and minorities represent gender and race equity in the general case. Chapter 2 describes the college bias in detail. As more and more is written from a college-for-all standpoint, a self-perpetuating cycle ensues: managerial and professional positions are considered appropriate for young women to aspire toward, inspirational stories of women's achievements in these areas are emphasized at the expense of equally inspirational stories of women in skilled trades, and in fact the absence of images and stories of tradeswomen suggests that they do not represent appropriate career goals for young women. Indeed, as Harlan and Steinberg also note:

> The rising educational attainment of the labor force in the United States and, in particular, women's increasing share of bachelor's, graduate, and professional degrees sometimes obscures the fact that the job training needs of ordinary women will place the greatest future claim on public educational and training resources. Most of the women in the labor force today, as well as most of those who will enter it in the future, *are not* and *will not be* college graduates.[7]

The non-college female population simply represents "ordinary women." Ordinary men and women seek alternatives to the four-year college degree path to advance themselves in the labor markets, but options are few relative to their demand, due in part to the research and policy bias described above. Without an awareness of training alternatives, or without alternatives altogether, many women neither seek nor receive any formal post-secondary education at all, and are therefore most likely to default into pink-collar occupations. With so many women responsible for all or part of their families' economic welfare, it is necessary to alter this trend and facilitate women's entry into different fields. The Bureau of Labor Statistics' Employment Cost Index (ECI) survey categorizes occupations as blue-collar, white-collar, and services. Blue-collar jobs are those in the skilled trades including carpentry, masonry, welding, pipefitting, as well as other manual-labor occupations like truck driving, agriculture, mining, and manufacturing. As the reader may be envisioning as she reads this, blue-collar jobs tend to be held by people who completed apprenticeships or vocational training, usually men. White-collar jobs are highly skilled jobs involving law, medicine, and business and held, for example, by lawyers, doctors, managers, administrators, and sales workers, as well as other jobs involving clerical work, that do not require extensive academic training. White-collar jobs can be held by people who have completed extensive schooling (like attorneys and surgeons) or vocational training (like secretaries, dental assistants, and legal assistants). Services include various occupations from firefighters to janitors and cleaners. (Appendix Table A.1 lists the major groupings as defined in the ECI.) Pink-collar jobs are those where women dominate in terms of overall employment, and can be blue- or white-collar, or in the services. While manufacturing is classified as a blue-collar industry, automobile manufacturing is male-dominated while textile and apparel manufacturing is female-dominated, and the latter can be considered "pink-collar." Similarly, while Finance, Insurance, and Real Estate is classified as a white-collar industry, stockbrokers tend to be male and bank tellers tend to be female and therefore their job can be considered "pink-collar." Again, as the reader may be envisioning already, the jobs classified as "pink-collar" tend to be lower-paying ones, and women's concentration in them is a significant factor in the gender pay gap.

Why Occupational Segregation?

Despite women's gains in educational attainment compared to men, women still hold the same jobs they always have. In fact, fully *50 percent of all working women are concentrated into approximately 5 percent of all occupations*. Of the 496 occupations in the 2001 Current Population Survey (CPS), half of all women work in only 28 of them, and this differs little whether one includes college-educated women or not. Table 1.1 below lists these 28 occupations and the proportions of women employed in each.

As Table 1.1 shows, 4 percent of all working women work as secretaries. This may not seem like a high percentage until one considers that *there are more women working as secretaries than there are women working in 300 other occupations*. Not only are women concentrated in a handful of occupations, but also the jobs they are concentrated in pay less and involve skills that are not remunerated in the labor markets, as even a cursory glance at this

Table 1.1

**Concentration of Female Employment: The 5.6 Percent of
All Occupations Where 50 Percent of Women Work, 2001**

	Occupation name (three-digit Standard Occupational Classification code)	Percent of women's total employment
1	Secretaries (313)	4.00
2	Cashiers (276)	3.93
3	Managers and administrators (022)	3.54
4	Registered nurses (095)	3.41
5	Teachers, primary school (156)	3.17
6	Nursing aides, orderlies, and attendants (447)	3.13
7	Supervisors and proprietors, sales occupations (243)	2.72
8	Bookkeepers, accounting, and auditing clerks (337)	2.18
9	Waiters and waitresses (435)	1.77
10	Receptionists (319)	1.72
11	Sales workers, other commodities (274)	1.56
12	Accountants and auditors (023)	1.54
13	Investigators and adjusters, except insurance (376)	1.49
14	Cooks, except short order (436)	1.47
15	Teachers, secondary school (157)	1.32
16	General office clerks (379)	1.27
17	Janitors and cleaners (453)	1.27
18	Administrative support occupations, nec (389)	1.26
19	Teachers' aides (387)	1.25
20	Teachers, pre-kindergarten, and kindergarten (155)	1.12
21	Health technologists and technicians, nec (208)	1.01
22	Managers, medicine and health (015)	0.99
23	Data entry keyers (385)	0.97
24	Social workers (174)	0.96
25	Managers, food serving and lodging establishments (017)	0.90
26	Maids and housemen (449)	0.90
27	Administrators, education and related fields (014)	0.85
28	Typists (315)	0.81
	Total proportion of female employment in these occupations	50.51

Source: Author's tabulations of annualized and weighted Current Population Survey (CPS) data; "nec" = "not elsewhere classified."

list would suggest. As in the CPS itself, in Table 1.1, each occupational title is accompanied by a three-digit Standard Occupational Classification (SOC) code. SOC codes are not random or alphabetical according to job title, but rather, are organized into Major Occupational Groups (MOGs) according to job function: 000s, 100s, 200s, and 300s, up to 800s. As the list in Table 1.1 shows, women are not only concentrated into a handful of occupations, but tend to hold jobs in certain MOGs. While employment in these groups is not evenly

Figure 1.1 **Concentration of Female Employment, Occupational Groups Where Women Work, 2001**

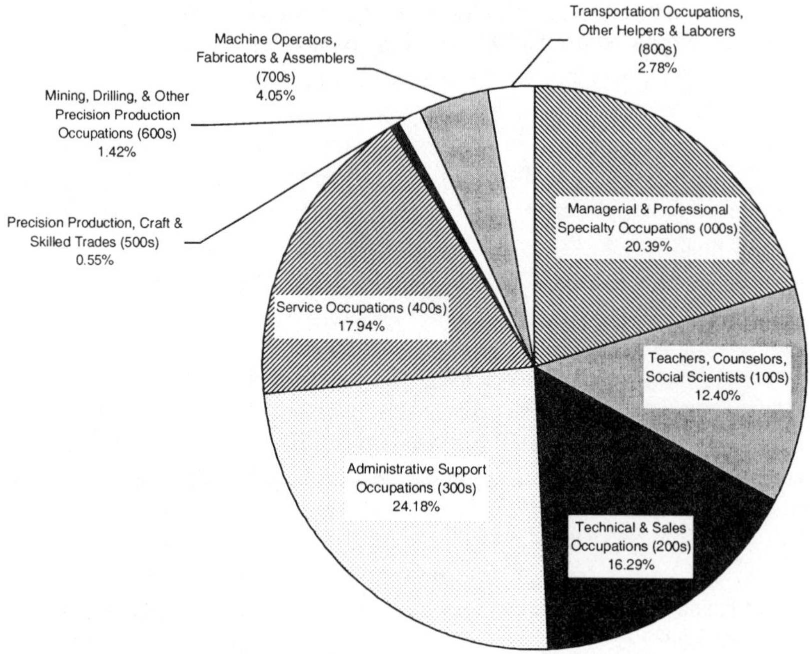

Source: Author's tabulations using data from the U.S. Census Bureau.

distributed—there are fewer workers in the 500s, say, than in the 300s—women are not only concentrated in a handful of occupations, but also are over-represented in a few occupational groups. Figure 1.1 depicts the distribution of women's employment among occupational groups by three-digit SOC code.

Occupations are grouped according to three-digit SOC code and women's representation in each is calculated in Figure 1.1. Occupations in the Managerial and Professional Specialty MOG include, for example, managers and administrators, registered nurses, dentists, pharmacists, and engineers. Women's representation in these jobs mirrors that of women and men overall, at approximately 20 percent. Occupations in the 100s include primary and secondary teachers, college teachers, and social workers, among other similar jobs. Women are over-represented in these jobs; while comprising only 9.43 percent of total employment, 12.40 percent of all women work in these jobs. Examples of Technical and Sales Occupations (200s) are radiology technicians, sales workers, and cashiers. Again, women are over-represented in this occupational group, as well: while comprising 14.92 percent of employment in 2001, 16.29 percent of women worked in these jobs.

Administrative Support Occupations (300s) include clerical workers. As the reader might expect, women represent the bulk of employment in this group. While this group represented about 14.81 percent of overall employment in 2001, nearly one-quarter of all working women held jobs in this MOG in 2001. Service Occupations (400s) include many different service occupations, from childcare workers to firefighters, police, and waiters and waitresses. About 15 percent of all workers held jobs in this category, while nearly 18 percent of working women did. Women are underrepresented in the remaining occupational groups. While less than 1 percent of working women worked in Precision Production Occupations (500s), for example, as mechanics, in construction trades, as plumbers, and as pipe fitters, this MOG comprised 7.52 percent of employment in 2001. Similarly, while women comprised only 1.42 percent of employment in Mining, Drilling, and Other Precision Production Occupations (600s) such as machinists, tool and die makers, upholsterers, tailors, and seamstresses, employment in this group was about 3 percent in 2001. The group Machine Operators, Fabricators, and Assemblers (700s) includes occupations like woodworking, metalworking, routing, and textile cutting machine operators, and comprised 5.36 percent of overall employment in 2001, and 4.05 percent of women's employment. Finally, Transportation Occupations and Other Laborers (800s), which includes truck drivers, construction helpers, and manufacturing assemblers employed 8.59 percent of the workforce overall in 2001, but only 2.78 percent of women.

As the data show, not only are women concentrated in a small number of jobs and occupational groups, but also the jobs they tend to hold pay less and offer fewer opportunities for career advancement. Because women support families either as parts of dual-earner households or as single heads of households—indeed, women head the vast majority of single-headed households with children—they are not *choosing* to hold low-paying, dead-end jobs, but rather, are prevented access to higher-paying, NTOs for women due to a lack of information, outright sex discrimination, and a combination of these and other factors. However, prominent and significant schools of thought maintain that market forces ought to govern the distributions of women and men across occupations, because rational women supporting families will seek out higher-paying, higher-skilled jobs.

The Failure of Market Forces and the Need for Policy Intervention

If a woman holds a low-paying pink-collar job, whose responsibility is it that she cannot support her family, hers or yours? In their examination of labor market outcomes by levels of education and training, John Tyler, Richard J.

Murnane, and Frank Levy note "there is always a lower tail to any distribution."[8] There are always labor market winners and losers, and the "bottom tail" somehow ensures success and prosperity for the bulk of the population in the middle of the distribution. Should government intervention via policy interfere with this process? Does it really matter that men hold some jobs and women hold others?

Yes and no.

Differences in "men's jobs" and "women's jobs" are not benign. Women's jobs oftentimes pay less, involve less training, and afford workers fewer opportunities for promotion. Unskilled women workers who might prefer a different career path can easily fall into a "traditional" occupation like domestic worker, cashier, or waitress. Low-wage jobs tend to be female-dominated ones, and as Barbara Bergmann observes, wages fall when a job becomes "more female," as women are "overcrowded" into jobs.[9] Women are limited to certain occupations by their overall levels of education and experience, which are lower than men's are on average, but more important, women face barriers to entering male-dominated fields. Bergmann finds that the overcrowding of women in certain jobs has a significant negative impact on wages and employment growth, and Jeremy Bulow and Lawrence Summers find that changing the distributions of women and men in jobs reduces pay inequality.[10] Along with other scholars, Donald Treiman and Heidi Hartmann note that the wage gap is due to occupational segregation more so than it is due to head-to-head sex discrimination.[11] Chris Tilly and Charles Tilly go further and state flatly, "The great bulk of male-female wage differences has long resulted from the fact that most men and women work in differentially-rewarded sex-segregated jobs."[12] Despite consistent evidence that women's jobs pay less and provide fewer opportunities for advancement, women still flood the same fields year after year, as both Chapter 3 and Appendix Table A.3 demonstrate.

Rational Actors or Creatures of Habit?

Given the existence of female-dominated and male-dominated jobs, and given the difference in wages and upward mobility between the two, both of which are investigated further in the following chapters, many scholars and policymakers predict that a rational economic actor would avoid such jobs and seek out better ones. As fewer and fewer workers are willing to take the lowest-paying jobs, so the thinking goes, demand will increase and the wages paid to attract workers, male or female, would have to increase over time. Theoretically, this is appealing. However, not only are plenty of women willing to accept the lower pay that accompanies pink-collar occupations, but the supply of women workers remains consistent, so no employer need raise wages to attract workers, either now or over time. If non-college women workers behaved more rationally and avoided lower-paying, low-mobility pink-collar jobs and entered higher-paying, high-mobility jobs, market forces would prevail and even out the distributions of men and women across occupations, thereby minimizing gender pay disparities. Government policy, from this point of view, ought *not* be developed and implemented to cure for widespread irrationality.[13] But, which is more likely, widespread irrationality or barriers to entering other occupations or training programs in preparation for other jobs? Is it possible that many women who are fully or partially responsible for the financial support of their families, and whose career paths are not relevant to seeking a four-year college degree, would prefer *not* to hold low-paying pink-collar jobs, but overt and implicit barriers exist preventing some non-college women not only from avoiding low-paying, low-skilled jobs, but also from getting into the better-paying jobs? Most likely, barriers to entry impede women's progress toward training for and obtaining nonpink-collar jobs, and neither employers nor workers continually calculate utility-maximizing and cost-minimizing functions to determine their actions. Employers and workers, male or female, make decisions much more on the basis of habit and custom than on optimizing functions. An economic actor is neither an instinctual creature nor "a lightening calculator of pleasures and pains."[14] One might refer to the nature of an economic actor's decision making process as "bounded rationality":[15] optimizing, yet within one's habits of action and habits of thought.

While this explanation seems plausible, it still appears to contradict what an economic actor, acting in her best interests, should do. Former Labor Secretary Ray Marshall reconciles the predictions of theory with observations of actual behavior by acknowledging that, yes, market forces *should* bring about the dynamics predicted above, nobody willingly remains in low-paying, low-mobility jobs, and there ought not to be a reserve labor force for low-paying, low-mobility jobs.[16] Over time, the supply of workers to these jobs should dry up as they seek better jobs, which increases demand for the one type of job and decreases demand for the other. Wages should even out over time, wages for the one increase while those for the other decrease, and this would constitute the larger economic impact on labor markets overall.[17] According to Secretary Marshall, the key is "over time." Market forces do not act to resolve inequalities *in an acceptable period of time*, given changes in culture and society.[18] He questions what is meant by "over time": in five years, in a lifetime? From this point of view, the orthodox theory is not specific enough about the *when*, and since economic actors are also political and cultural and social actors, economic forces must be responsive to changing ideas on equality and economic justice, as characterized by landmark pieces of legislation and court decisions favoring a more equitable workplace. As it stands, many economic outcomes lag behind economically just outcomes. For economic outcomes to respond to social, cultural, and political contexts, oftentimes, policy intervention is required. James K. Galbraith acknowledges this "respectable liberal dissent" from the market forces argument, "that although the price mechanism may work eventually, it doesn't work fast enough."[19]

Unfortunately, many hear the first part of the dissent, "yes, theory predicts correctly," but ignore the second part, "not in a realistic timeframe," and therefore policy is needed to accelerate the process and spur change that is more consistent with the political, societal, and cultural contexts that have made gender pay equity an important objective. Labor markets themselves are social structures that cannot be analyzed separately from their contexts, and therefore, are far more than the sum of individuals' investments in their human capital. Individual workers exercise only so much agency in determining their labor market outcomes; decisions of employers and workers have a lot more to do with the prevailing structures of labor market institutions and the habits and customs therein, rather than series of isolated individual decisions rooted in maximizing utility and minimizing cost. Government intervention has been viewed as inefficient and impractical, when it has been the stickiness and inflexibility of market forces to respond to contextual changes in an acceptable period of time that have contributed to the current state of inequality. Indeed, if certain expectations of progress are not met, then market forces are inefficient and impractical, as betrayed by the disclaimer "not in an acceptable period of time." Although Galbraith notes the liberal dissent from the market forces position, he doubts that simple skills training, or greater investments in workers' human capital, is enough to bridge the inequality gap in wages or resolve entrenched patterns of occupational segregation. The structure of economic outcomes such as persistent occupational segregation of non-college women in low-wage, low-opportunity jobs, or overt pay discrimination between women and men in the same jobs, however, *can* be changed through policy intervention. Opposing theoretical explanations concerning the type of policy intervention necessary to do so are discussed in the paragraphs that follow.

Theories Explaining Pink-Collar Persistence and Prescribing Remedies

Akin to the rational actor approach, a human capital approach predicts that any training and employment program would be effective because such programs allow workers to upgrade their education and skill set, or human capital, making them more qualified for whichever occupations they target. Rational employers hire the most qualified workers to maximize productivity and minimize costs, so if these training programs produce well-trained candidates, it would not matter whether they were women or men. However, this assumes an environment where barriers to entry and sex discrimination should not exist in the long run. Just as workers are not consistently "rational actors," nor are employers. Employers operate according to bounded rationality, as well, and oftentimes seek to maintain workplace stability as a means to optimizing productivity.

Systematic imbalances in the distribution of men and women across jobs should not endure over time, even with an assumption about an employer's "taste for discrimination,"[20] which, according to theory, should become too costly to sustain over time. But both pink-collar jobs and male-dominated ones exist and persist. Again, the rational actor or human capital approach would prescribe *time*: the labor market simply needs time to clear and return to equilibrium. Neither tastes for discrimination nor occupational segregation persist over time. Employers would not be able to afford their discriminatory tastes over time, as the discriminated-against groups would accept lower wages and unbiased employers could operate with lower costs and drive biased employers out of business or at least away from their tastes. Occupational segregation would not persist because workers in low-wage, low-mobility jobs would increase their human capital endowments to qualify themselves for the better jobs and refuse to accept the jobs they used to hold before increasing their levels of human capital. From this point of view, policy intervention is unnecessary, but if policy were proposed, the only appropriate intervention would be one that simply facilitates what would occur via market forces in time. Policy can come in the form of training programs to facilitate skills acquisition, for instance. Is *this* enough to alter patterns of discrimination or occupational segregation? Galbraith challenges the assumptions surrounding an affirmative answer to this question:

> Yet the notion that equalizing *skills* will equalize *incomes* rests on a confusion: a confusion between equity in access to lottery tickets and equity in the value of the prizes. It is one thing for a program to hold out, subsidize, and support new chances for individuals to compete on the educational and career ladders. It is something different to promise that the ladder itself will become shorter and wider as a result of an increase in the numbers crowding their way up the rungs. It is something entirely different to suppose that each new entrant and reentrant in the educational sweepstakes will enjoy a chance of success equally high as those who have already entered and won. It is something entirely different, something bold and ingenious, to promise that we can return to the middle-class solidarity of

three decades ago, entirely by diffusing knowledge through the population and by allowing free labor markets to work.[21]

As one who is skeptical of the so-called wisdom of the markets, it is clear to me that the "bold and ingenious" scenario is also the least realistic and least likely one. Galbraith observes that the increasing access approach appeases "education activists" while not wholly offending "free-market purists,"[22] but this political palatability comes at a price. The price comes in the form of the great leap in logic one must make when putting one's faith in the wisdom of the markets. Ironically, it is the faint-hearted access approach that involves "bold and ingenious" assumptions to make it work: presuming that equal access to education and training will equalize labor market outcomes is naive at best. Unfortunately, the "bold and ingenious" approach has guided much of the thinking surrounding policy to address workplace inequities. Although Galbraith dismisses the free-market approach, he does not share the perspective of other heterodox theorists—that the labor markets are divided into different segments, or tiers. Segmented Labor Market (SLM) theory is part of the larger Institutionalist critique of orthodox theory, and an alternative approach to explaining labor market dynamics. In SLM, "emphasis . . . is placed on the roles of class struggle, institutional forms and processes, and the sphere of reproduction in labor market structurization, representing an increasingly credible and nuanced alternative to the orthodox paradigm."[23] Explaining labor market outcomes cannot involve simple human capital endowments or discriminatory employment practices, but must incorporate class, race, and gender, as well as institutional arrangements that can also perpetuate the status quo. Excellent anthropological analyses focusing on working women such as those done by Vivian Price,[24] Louise Kapp Howe,[25] Susan Eisenberg,[26] Molly Martin,[27] and Barbara Ehrenreich[28] have emphasized the roles of culture and norms influencing labor market outcomes, while this book adopts more of the SLM lens in its analysis by emphasizing information flows and structures of training and employment and the institutions involved, including government and nonprofits.

SLM theory explains the occurrence and persistence of occupational segregation by gender by observing that there is no such thing as a single, freely-competitive labor market; no big pot where all workers compete with one another and the only thing differentiating them is their human capital endowments, or education, experience, and skill sets, which provide employers information about their workplace productivity. In addition to primary and secondary labor markets in individual industries and even individual firms, there are internal and external labor markets in industries and firms. A firm's internal labor market is its own hierarchy where individuals can apply for and obtain positions from inside the company. Therefore, people not already employed there really cannot compete for job openings, unless the firm decides to expand its search to the external labor market. In many cases, if a firm does seek applicants outside its internal labor market, it is for entry-level positions, because the higher-level openings have been filled internally. Success breeds success, but if a person cannot break through to an internal labor market, whether in a firm or an industry, then she cannot compete for job openings because she does not even know about them. In this way, SLM theory does a much better job of depicting actual labor market dynamics compared to free-market assumptions and predictions of orthodox theory.

In their influential book, Peter Doeringer and Michael Piore [29] describe the dual labor market based on qualitative aspects of individual jobs, where different norms apply in coexisting labor markets, and workers in each do not compete with one another. Primary sector workers enjoy greater upward mobility, higher pay, and fringe benefits, have more training, and more security than secondary sector workers do. Primary sector jobs tend to be autonomous, higher-ranking, white-collar jobs. Instability, lower pay, and inferior working conditions characterize secondary sector jobs; labor skills are lower and more exchangeable among other low-skilled workers. Career opportunities and the ability to ascend the ranks are not characteristic of secondary sector jobs, which include pink-collar jobs.[30]

David Gordon, Richard Edwards, and Michael Reich [31] identify primary *subordinate* and primary *independent* to denote the differences in working conditions between, say, craftsmen and lawyers. Craftsmen and other blue-collar skilled trades workers have specialized skills and higher pay, fringe benefits, and the ability to collectively bargain, but they do not have the entrepreneurial and managerial skills of the banker, salesman, or other white-collar workers. Besides that, the differences between primary and secondary are basically the same under Gordon, Edwards, and Reich: workers are virtually exchangeable and skill requirements are low in the secondary sector, while workers in the primary sector are specialized and highly trained. Capital-intensive industries, such as manufacturing, and larger firms provide higher wages and opportunities for advancement, while labor-intensive ones, such as service industries, do not. Capital-intensive firms and industries tend to be in the primary sector. Labor-intensive firms are commonly in the secondary sector, and they are more likely to devote resources to monitoring and supervision than are firms in the primary labor markets.[32] Craftsmen and bankers are more autonomous than assemblers and tellers are. Accordingly, the terminology differs between the two: people have "jobs" in the secondary sector and "occupations" in the primary labor market. The SLM approach calls to mind Galbraith's fundamental observation that the experiences of workers depend on the industry they work in, which segmentation theorists would characterize as the tier. Again, Galbraith does not go so far as to assume a tiered structure.

Compared to human capital theory or discrimination models, SLM models lend themselves to explaining occupational segregation by accounting for *structural* differences between workers and jobs. SLM theory predicts that the workers in the secondary sector will not be able to enter the primary sector, despite increases in training and education.[33] SLM theory is consistent with the empirical evidence, and it provides a theoretical basis for the long-term, persistent, and systematic unevenness in the distribution of women and men over occupations. However, SLM theory is less promising for programs intended to reduce occupational segregation. Women do not gain access to NTOs in the primary sector because they *cannot*; workers are not perfectly mobile; they must "queue up" for available positions but are largely stuck in the secondary labor market. This is consistent with what is observed: the empirical evidence on occupational segregation provides a theoretical basis for long-term, persistent, systematic separation of workers and jobs. In *Job Queues, Gender Queues*, Barbara Reskin and Patricia Roos specify a model of the dual-queuing process that formalizes how certain workers are ranked by employers and must wait to gain access to primary labor market occupations, and how those same workers have nearly free access to other kinds of jobs, secondary tier occupations.[34]

SLM theory suggests that a policy intervention may not have *any* impact unless the fundamental structures of the primary and secondary labor markets are altered. This approach leaves much more for the policy developer to go on: undermine the processes, cultural, sociological, and economic, that led to the current noncompetitive structure in the first place, and policy intervention can have an impact.[35] Cultural and sociological processes can be altered through outreach and raising awareness about discriminatory practices and with educational materials demonstrating women's abilities. Economic reinforcements to the *status quo* can be mitigated by enforcing affirmative action and equal opportunity laws, which would force discriminating employers and coworkers to pay for their prejudices. On the flip side, showing women the economic and psychological benefits to working in certain nontraditional fields can also undermine the economic, cultural, and sociological processes that result in persistent occupational segregation.[36] Some have noted a potential shortfall in SLM theory: its suggestion that if a policy intervention does not undermine the processes surrounding the current structure of labor markets, altering habits of thought and habits of action, then it probably will not have an effect. In this way, short-term, targeted policy proposals will not work, which is a daunting prospect for the oftentimes resource-poor area of employment and training policy for women. Similarly, Chris Tilly and Charles Tilly observed that this, as well as other Institutionalist approaches, has "not worked out anything like the range of applications that neoclassical analysts have proposed and have assumed the validity of neoclassical accounts in many respects."[37] However, recent research provides evidence to contradict this charge.[38] Indeed, criticisms of the Institutionalist critique give short shrift to the impact of heterodox approaches that are based in sound theory and demonstrate the effectiveness of policy interventions that bring about specific labor market outcomes.

Targeted employment and training programs can also produce a negative result that fuels critics' arguments against them. Daniel S. Hamermesh discussed the effect that increasing one group's labor costs relative to another group's lowers demand for the former, as well as the effects of policies on firms' ability to hire and fire at will. Reducing occupational segregation of women workers into lower-paying jobs may outweigh the costs of reducing employer flexibility, however. The increased cost of training and retaining women workers, relative to men, will decrease employer demand for women workers. The increased costs of employing women are detailed in later chapters on program implementation, but generally involve the additional services necessary to prepare them for some workplaces and provide ongoing support to ensure retention. In terms of a firm's flexibility in making hiring decisions, spurring demand for women workers through use of what Hamermesh defines as "Q-policies," if successful, effectively removes some of the employer's control over whom to employ. Such a disruption results in an increase to the firm's internal costs of adjustment.[39] Hamermesh notes that while these kinds of policies "may achieve the goals of increased diversity of employment within the workplace and of more equal distribution of earnings by race or sex, [t]hey also generate the (at least short-run) economic cost of reduced flexibility of the labor market."[40] Therefore, programs that successfully train and spur demand for women workers also could raise the price of the latter, relative to male workers, which may create some employer resistance to participating. If an employer responds to these changes, increased labor costs of women workers and decreased flexibility, by favoring male workers, the firm may not be acting in a deliberately prejudicial manner necessarily, but rather, may be responding to competitive pressures to minimize costs. Tilly and Tilly interpreted this higher cost of certain workers as a choice between maintaining the stability of the workplace and hiring or promoting a qualified worker whom the others would reject. They noted:

> The tradeoff is delicate. In many jobs, the productivity of any particular worker depends on the cooperation of workers in connected jobs; to what extent do facility in a common language, personal acceptability, the sharing of tacit knowledge acquired outside the workplace, and solidarity based on common origin or acquaintance directly affect cooperation, hence productivity?[41]

To what extent, indeed? Employers' choice of a less-qualified worker who does not "disrupt" the workplace smacks of discriminatory labor practice, but again, cost minimization pressures may be operating, as well. There is a fine line between the two. Tilly and Tilly precisely describe the socialization that a policy intervention must address according to SLM theory, in addition to that which allows women to believe they are incapable of doing certain jobs in the first place. Hamermesh interpreted this as increasing the costs of nontraditional workers by reducing employers' flexibility in hiring and firing decisions. Institutionalists interpret this cost decision as a tradeoff between maintaining stability and increasing overall productivity, whether in response to competitive pressures or not. The result is a discriminatory barrier to entry for women seeking employment in NTOs, which any worthwhile policy must address. Other recent work on the minimum wage has sought to stem the growth and influence of anecdote in debates surrounding labor market policy interventions on behalf of low-wage workers, and much of it has not supported the standard neoclassical predictions.[42] A theory of labor demand creates a typology of policies that can be effective in evaluating aspects of the labor market.[43] Specific policies that seek to change the quantity of labor supplied to an occupation can be effective in doing so by spurring demand for female workers. The different kinds of policies defined in this typology work on both the supply side and the demand side. On the supply side, policies can increase investments in human capital and therefore increase one's chances of improving one's labor market position. On the demand side, policies can spur demand for certain types of workers in specific occupations, and could possibly change the structure of that particular labor market. According to this approach, therefore, modest targeted employment programs *can* be effective in increasing opportunities for non-college women, but they may increase the cost of the newly integrated worker. SLM best explains the reasons why pink-collar jobs exist and persist, and prescribes a way to alter concentrations of women and men in jobs by attacking the socialization surrounding them, and labor demand theory predicts the potential impact of smaller programs that operate on both the demand and supply sides of labor markets, and recommends ways to provide incentives for employers to alter concentrations of women and men in jobs.

Overview of the Book

Sources of Information

This study sheds new light on the non-college female population and their employment and training options, along several different dimensions and using several sources of information. In addition to extensive interviews and site visits underpinning the case study analyses of community-based organizations and state program implementers highlighted in later chapters, this study takes advantage of several administrative data sets, the primary one being the CPS annualized data from merged outgoing rotation groups (MORGs). The CPS is administered monthly to approximately 60,000 households, and MORGs are extracts of the basic monthly CPS during a household's fourth and eighth month in the survey, when the usual weekly hours and earnings questions are asked in addition to the regular workplace and demographic questions. Every household entering the CPS is interviewed each month for four months, ignored for eight months, and interviewed again for four more months. Usual weekly hours and earning questions are asked only at households in their fourth and eighth interview. These outgoing interviews are the only ones included in the MORGs. Because new households enter each month, only one-fourth of all households are in an outgoing rotation each month.[44] A risk of including the same household in consecutive years exists. To ensure against double counting in the present analysis, estimations using consecutive years are avoided.[45]

Because the MORG data used here focus on working women aged sixteen and older, and women's career paths often take them out of the formal workforce, two additional significant sources are employed to capture employment, training, and job search information on women: the CPS Job Training Supplemental conducted in January 1983, 1991, and 1992, and the National Longitudinal Survey of Youth, 1979 (NLSY79), in which several series of questions were asked about education and training activities and respondents' perceptions of education and training as parts of their overall careers.

The National Longitudinal Survey of Youth is a continuing survey, and was conducted first in 1979 and repeated about every other year through 1999. Employing the longitudinal survey allows this analysis to track education and training decisions over time for individuals both in and outside the labor force. Although women's workforce participation rates continue to increase over time, their careers are more likely to be interrupted due to life events than men's careers are. Women's perceptions of the payoffs of post-secondary education and training, along with their expectations about their roles as workers, wives, and mothers are very important to trace over time. The cohort covered by NLSY79 is relevant to this study, as the current labor market context is covered, and the decisions made by women embarking on their careers and those who may be considering a middle-life career change or who have a need to become more financially self-reliant reflect the current social and political context within which two training programs are evaluated in subsequent chapters. Isolating a non-college population from a longitudinal survey will help demonstrate the long-term labor market effects of any post-secondary training and employment opportunities respondents pursued. Finally, analysis of women's education and career decisions when they are out of the formal workforce allows this study to include differently situated women and their career-related decisions in a holistic manner.

Chapter 2 also employs evidence from the CPS Job Training Supplemental, which was conducted in January 1983, 1991, and 1992, and provides an additional source of specific information on education and training decisions. Both individuals in and outside the labor force are included, and specific questions on respondent's training availability, access, and usage inform this study further. Chapter 2 makes use of the CPS Supplement to demonstrate that the kinds of jobs non-college women tend to hold also tend to involve informal training, whereas the jobs non-college men tend to hold involve formal skills training that is both portable and valued more highly than the training non-college women tend to receive via female-dominated jobs. The CPS Supplement found that the demand for training is the same for women and men, but the kind of training they receive differs.[46] Chapter 3 employs MORG data to track male- and female-dominated occupations over time. Chapter 4 uses these data to show that a particular subset of the overall non-college population is an appropriate and interesting subset on which to focus policy because higher-wage, higher-skilled occupations are targeted by doing so. As in Chapter 4, the statistical analysis in Chapter 5 uses the annualized MORGs, and replicates the analysis with even- and odd-numbered years to avoid the remote yet potential problem of double counting households. An additional significant source of information comes through the case study analyses, which rely on primary data collected through interviews, archival analysis, and site visits. Liberal use of extended quotations, which the reader may have observed already, also extends throughout the text. This allows each individual to speak in her own voice, the importance of which Shulamit Reinharz demonstrates in *Feminist Methods in Social Research* and other scholars have noted as well.[47] The final chapter relies on the body of evidence assembled in this study to point toward directions for further research and a call for action.

The Remainder, Chapter by Chapter

Chapter 2, "Training Policy and Alternative Career Paths" illustrates the presence of a college-for-all bias; implicit but very real incentives exist to support the traditional four-year college degree route, alternatives are ignored, and ignoring alternative career paths has particular consequences for women workers. This chapter ends with a call for training and education resources that are responsive and relevant to alternative career paths, especially for women.

Chapter 3, "A Pattern of Decline and Its Ramifications" demonstrates how women without training end up in low-paying, low-mobility jobs, and that non-college jobs for women are less rewarding than are non-college jobs for men.

Chapter 4, "Past and Current Alternative Programs: Evidence of Promise in Nontraditional Occupations" introduces a subset of the non-college female population, women in nontraditional, male-dominated occupations. This subset of the non-college female population is interesting and important for several reasons, not the least of which being the amount of policy attention paid to it. Specific policies have been developed to train and place women in high-skilled NTOs because, as stated earlier, non-college men fare better in the labor markets than non-college women do. Facilitating access to high-wage, high-mobility, non-college occupations is essentially to train women for male-dominated jobs. Therefore, programs that do this are important to further our understanding of programs that could provide pathways out successfully. Two such programs are described in detail, specifically, how they incorporate predictions of Institutionalist and SLM theory to make a dent in the imbalanced distributions of women and men in certain jobs. The cultural and social factors underlying occupational segregation should also force the reader to understand that, despite the positive impact of these programs, this small success story, however surprising, clearly does not suggest that the very broad and intransigent dynamics resulting in pink-collar ghettos in the first place could not possibly have been upended by these two modest grant programs. While these are small steps toward rearranging male and female concentrations, they are just that, small steps. Much can be learned, but this is not the end of the story.

Chapter 5, "A Little Goes a Long Way: Statistical Evidence of Small Program Effectiveness" presents the statistical analysis of these programs and the implications of its findings. This chapter reports the results of statistical analysis evaluating two programs that have trained and placed women in high-wage, high-mobility occupations. Two non-college training and employment programs successfully increased the participation of women in high-paying, high-skilled occupations over the past few years.

Chapter 6, "Nuts and Bolts I: Why and How States' Programs Worked" and Chapter 7, "Nuts And Bolts II: How and Why Nonprofits' Programs Worked" build upon the statistical analysis and illustrate how states and non-profit organizations, respectively, were successful in increasing women's participation in high-wage, skilled jobs. These chapters examine grant recipients and their projects, their political advocacy, and their level of expertise, to determine whether grant-funded projects benefited women workers or not. Also demonstrated is how grant-funded projects were *not* successful where grantees had no track record, where they were not politically involved, or where they did not possess policy expertise. The focus of these chapters lies with the program implementers themselves.

Chapter 8 "A Call for Action" raises significant issues concerning the implications of these findings, and where research and policy must go from here. An important question is: if non-college women were integrated into these occupations, did incumbent workers lose their jobs? Or did the economy grow at such a rate that the newly trained and placed workers were absorbed without displacement? Moreover, if these programs provided pathways out of pink-collar jobs, yet these jobs are important to the economy, who took them? Do programs to train and place non-college women into better jobs serve only *some* women? Do women of color remain in low-wage, low-mobility occupations while white women gain from government programs aimed at improving their labor market opportunities? The last chapter raises significant issues concerning the implications of these findings, and where research and policy must go from here. The final chapter also discusses the potential effect of the booming economy of the 1990s on the employment outcomes found here. In this chapter, I also assess the findings from both the statistical and case study analyses as well as revisit the research questions and hypotheses, and the predictions from theory.

Three significant directions for future analysis exist. First, further analysis must determine whether the economic downturn affected the female recent hires in NTOs to a disproportionate degree; whether employers suspended their prejudices and dipped down further into job queues to employ women workers to meet their demands for labor, and, once economic growth declined, fired or laid off those women workers. Further analysis would also broaden the current study and estimate the impact of targeted skills training programs on labor market institutions overall. Were workers displaced as a result of training women workers and placing them in NTOs? If so, where did these displaced workers end up? In addition, who filled the pink-collar jobs that these women *would* have entered, had they not completed an NTO training and job placement program? Is there evidence of a race-substitution effect, are nonwhites or new migrants to the United States ending up in the dead-end pink-collar jobs that these women worked to avoid, and, if so, is that acceptable in terms of overall economic welfare? These are the more interesting larger issues that would necessitate an understanding of the dynamics of U.S. labor markets that lie beyond the scope of the current analysis. A third and final significant direction for further research is to question the factors influencing wage structures fundamentally. Are occupations and occupational segregation the relevant dimensions along which to classify and analyze labor market experiences, as the present study presumes, or are industrial categorizations more telling, as Galbraith finds? If industrial performance is the appropriate dimension to study, then the successes of the programs analyzed here will only prove to be short-lived, because they did not upend the dynamics determining wage structure. Perhaps the most important direction for further research based on this analysis is to question the fundamental presumptions of targeted policies. As the present analysis attests, alternative employment and training programs have provided non-college women with employment opportunities in high-wage, high-skilled occupations. However, while important in the absence of any prior statistical analyses, like any interesting study, this one only opens the door to more questions.

Before these significant endeavors are pursued, however, several points must be established: the importance of non-college employment and training options, how such options have been reduced or eliminated in recent years, how the absence of such options is especially harmful to non-college women's labor market opportunities, and the successes of two programs and how they worked, who they affected, why they are important components in the overall range of post-secondary options for women, and what they did to alter some training and hiring practices to provide some women with a pathway away from their likely alternative: the pink-collar ghetto.

Chapter 2

Training Policy and Alternative Career Paths

> We need to publicize the fact that, while college takes a minimum
> of four years, so do most apprenticeship programs. The big
> distinction between the two is that during the apprenticeship, the
> learner is continuously earning a steadily increasing living, and at
> the conclusion of training, with the journeyman's certificate, is not
> looking for an entry-level job. She or he either already has a secure
> position, or can readily get one through the union hall at top pay.
> —*Robert McAndrews, Coordinator of the*
> *Associated General Contractors Apprenticeship Program*[1]

Training and education beyond high school are fast becoming prerequisites
to careers with good and better pay, increased upward mobility, and a reduced risk of unemployment in the United States. But college is only one
path. Alternatives to this path are overlooked more and more as U.S. policy
and culture elevate one post-secondary approach over all others. Yet, even as
the numbers of college entrants increases, the majority do not graduate with
a four-year degree, nor do most occupations require a four-year college degree. High-wage, high-mobility, skilled, non-college occupations exist, but
without post-secondary alternatives, many young people take on the expense
of a few years of college and end up on unrewarding career paths. This chapter demonstrates that the lack of alternatives is especially detrimental to non-
college women, as non-college jobs for women are less rewarding than are
non-college jobs for men. This chapter also illustrates the presence of a college-for-all bias; and that implicit but very real incentives exist to support
the traditional four-year college degree route. Evidence also suggests that
targeted, specialized, post-secondary education and training can translate into
better-paying, higher-skilled occupations than a few years of a general college education can.

Non-College Women at Work

Non-college women represent a significant portion of the workforce, insofar
as women comprise about half of all workers, and the majority of those in

the workforce do not graduate with a four-year degree. Moreover, not only do women participate fully in dual-earner households, but they are far more likely than men are to be the sole income earners as single heads of households and to support families on their own. Given the importance of this population, it is critical to understand their experiences in the labor markets: what kinds of jobs non-college women tend to hold, what kind of training is involved, and the rates of pay non-college women tend to earn. In brief, non-college working women represent a significant portion of the workforce, the majority of single-headed households are headed by women, and these female-headed households are far more likely to be poor than are other types of households; yet, despite all the incentives to pursue high-paying careers, non-college women tend to hold low-skilled, low-paying, "pink-collar" occupations that do not provide many opportunities for advancement.

Populations of Interest to the Current Analysis

Thus far, the non-college population has been defined ambiguously to include individuals without four-year college degrees. The data allow for more specific populations to be defined, and allow this analysis to feature workers with some post-secondary training, as well as workers who ceased their formal education once they earned their high school diploma or General Equivalency Diploma (GED). In all, four populations are defined according to their educational attainments, with merged outgoing rotation group (MORG) data over a twenty-year period. See Table 2.1.

The population of interest to the current study includes principally the "High school/GED" group, but also the "Some college" population. While the data do not allow for a parsing of the "Some college" population into subgroups to isolate those who intend to complete a four-year degree but are not finished yet, it is possible to isolate those who have earned associate degrees in occupational and vocational programs, and those with "some college but no degree." Again, whether the "no degree" population *intends* to finish or not is impossible to determine with the data. The non-college population comprises the majority of the workforce; indeed, nearly two-thirds of the working population never earns a four-year college degree. Using 2001 data from the Census bureau, Figure 2.1 was created to illustrate the share of the workforce comprised by non-college workers.

Compared to the overall averages shown in Figure 2.1 above, women are less likely to drop out of high school, and slightly more likely to pursue some post-secondary education and training. However, women are also slightly less likely to complete a four-year college degree program or earn a postgraduate degree. Over the past two decades, women have pursued education

Table 2.1

Population Definitions by Educational Attainment

Population	Definition
Less than high school	Individuals who either dropped out of school before earning a diploma, those who have not earned a GED, or those who are currently in high school (the Current Population Survey includes individuals aged sixteen and above)
High school/GED	Individuals who have earned a high school diploma or GED, and have not pursued formal education at the time of the survey
Some college	Individuals who have taken college courses but left school before earning a four-year college degree, those who have earned a two-year degree including an associate's degree or certificate, or those who have taken college courses and continue to do so, with the intention of completing a four-year program
College graduate	Individuals who have already earned a four-year college degree, including those who are currently enrolled in graduate programs, as well as those who have already earned advanced degrees (JDs, MBAs, PhDs, MDs, etc.)

and training after high school to a greater degree than men have, as the following figures show. Using data from the Census bureau covering the period from 1979 to 2002, Figure 2.2 illustrates that, while women and men were as likely to pursue post-high school education and training in the beginning of the period, women continued to enter post-secondary programs at a higher rate than men did.

As Figure 2.2 shows, women have pursued post-high school education and training far more than men have over the past two decades. While men have more lucrative labor market opportunities with or without college degrees, women do not. As other scholars have indicated, increased educational attainment has played a significant role in improving women's career opportunities and earnings power over the past several years. Moreover, women's increased post-secondary participation has also allowed them to narrow the gender gap among college graduates, as Figure 2.3 illustrates.

The numbers of women and men earning four-year college degrees has increased over time, and researchers have indicated that the numbers can be expected to increase in the future. Indeed, as Jennifer Cheeseman Day and

Figure 2.1   **The Non-College Population, Educational Attainment of Women and Men by Highest Grade Completed, 2001**

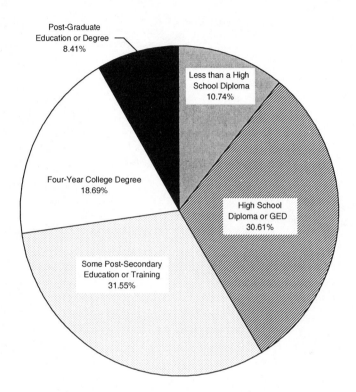

Source: Author's tabulations using data from the U.S. Census Bureau.

Kurt Bauman find in their study, *Have We Reached the Top? Educational Attainment Projections of the U.S. Population*, not only will more and more people pursue post-high school education and training, but "the greatest contrast is that between high-educational-growth females and low educational-growth males. Any policy designed to address educational growth needs to be flexible enough to address the particular challenges facing various groups."[2] More and more women are pursuing post-secondary education and training, and as this book argues, alternatives to the four-year path are especially critical to women, because women comprise nearly half of the workforce. Women comprise approximately half of both the workforce and the non-college population. As Figure 2.2 shows, women's share of the non-college population

Figure 2.2 **Numbers of Women and Men with Some Post-Secondary Education and Training, 1979–2002**

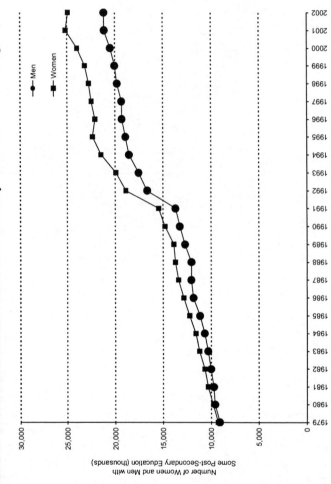

Source: Author's tabulations of data from the Bureau of the Census Table A-1, "Years of School Completed by People 25 Years Old and Over, by Age and Sex: Selected Years 1940 to 2002 (estimated)." Internet release date March 21, 2003. Available at www.census.gov/population/socdemo/education/tabA-1.pdf.

Note: Data for 2001 and 2002 are from the expanded CPS sample and were created using population controls based on Census 2000 data.

31

Figure 2.3 **Numbers of Women and Men Earning at Least a Four-Year Degree, 1979–2002**

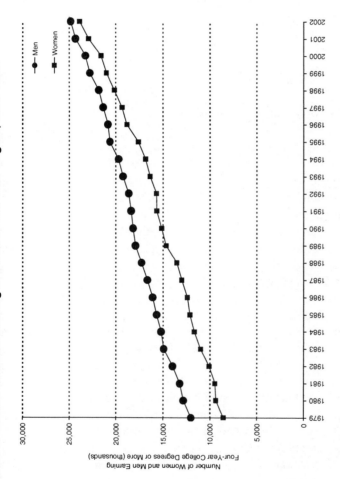

Source: Author's tabulations of data from the Bureau of the Census Table A-1, "Years of School Completed by People 25 Years Old and Over, by Age and Sex: Selected Years 1940 to 2002 (estimated)." Internet release date March 21, 2003. Available at www.census.gov/ population/socdemo/education/tabA-1.pdf.

Note: Data for 2001 and 2002 are from the expanded CPS sample and were created using population controls based on Census 2000 data.

has decreased over the years, but since the non-college population remains the majority of the workforce, non-college women remain a large subpopulation of the workforce. The non-college female proportion of the workforce is a highly significant population that policy cannot ignore. Indeed, as is demonstrated throughout this book, without targeted policy interventions, non-college women end up in the same dead-end pink-collar jobs, despite their continued education and training. Not only are targeted post-secondary programs important to non-college women's careers, but these programs must target high-wage, high-skilled occupations and not only train women for them, but also place them in quality jobs and provide support to retain them there. This book examines two such programs that assist non-college women escape the pink-collar ghetto.

Non-College Women and Pink-Collar Jobs

Barbara Ehrenreich's profile of low-wage working women unable to make ends meet in *Nickel and Dimed* was preceded by Louise Kapp Howe's in-depth profiles of women in pink-collar jobs in 1977.[3] Even a cursory reading of these texts underscores how little has changed for low-wage working women in the quarter century or so that had elapsed between the two studies. Howe's frustration with the glacial pace of progress on equal employment and equal opportunity even at that time is palpable throughout the book. Unfortunately, although women have advanced in many white-collar fields, not much has changed elsewhere. Howe lists "pinkest of the pink collar occupations" for 1962 and 1975, which are repeated and updated with 2001 data in Table 2.2.[4]

Slight decreases exist in all of the jobs listed in Table 2.2, except for hairdressers, a job that is essentially as female dominated as it was in 1975, and more female dominated than forty years previously. Some occupations exist in 2001 that were not specified in earlier periods, and some of these are highly female dominated including childcare-related occupations such as family childcare providers (98.7 percent female), prekindergarten and kindergarten (97.8), childcare (97.0), and early childhood teachers' assistants (94.7). Also consider the drastic employment declines of many female-dominated occupations like typists, telephone operators, bank tellers, stenographers, private household workers, billing, posting and calculating machine operators, and data-entry keyers, and one has a better idea of the employment environment faced by women whose educational attainment did not extend past the high school diploma. The rub is that men of similar educational attainment have always had access to higher-paying skilled trades that involve job mobility and advancement as well; the skills learned

Table 2.2

The Pinkest of the Pink-Collar Occupations, 1962, 1975, and 2001

	Percent female		
	1962	1975	2001
Registered nurses	98.5	97.0	93.1
Elementary school teachers	86.5	85.4	82.5
Typists	94.8	96.6	95.0
Telephone operators	96.3	93.3	83.3
Secretaries	98.5	99.1	98.4
Hairdressers	88.1	90.5	90.4
Waiters and waitresses	88.1	91.1	76.4
Nursing aides and attendants	75.2	85.8	90.1
Sewers and stitchers	94.1	95.8	74.2
Private household workers	97.3	97.4	96.2

on many of these jobs are valued and transferable, and are well remunerated. Although many crafts and trades occupations are also on the decline, many others have positive employment prospects, and most enjoy union representation.

Every other year, the Bureau of Labor Statistics (BLS) conducts ten-year projections of growth trends across occupations and industries. Table 2.3, "Occupations with the Largest Projected Job Decline, 2000 to 2010" lists these occupations and indicates the amount of training usually required and the general level of pay. Table 2.3 is directly from the BLS projections published in the November 2001 *Monthly Labor Review*.[5] Shading is added to highlight the clerical and other pink-collar jobs where non-college women are concentrated traditionally. The occupations where non-college women tend to work are precisely those projected to suffer significant declines in the coming decade. It is *precisely* these women whom alternative training programs can benefit; to train and place them in higher-skilled occupations where their risk of unemployment, low wages, and fewer opportunities is reduced.

Not only does inequality remain in the labor markets, but the results of employment growth projections alongside occupational segregation by gender, the formal term for what produces pink-collar jobs in the first place, are especially harmful to women's economic well-being. Alternative training paths are crucial. Schmidt and Denhert go even further to state, "Until women working in all skilled trades becomes an everyday occurrence, career and school counselors owe it to all women to make the participation of women in the trades a top priority."[6] Evidence from the Current Population Survey (CPS) Supplement is consistent with what Table 2.3 illustrates: female-dominated occupations disproportionately involve only short- or moderate-term on-the-job training. This is further underscored by the table's counterpart:

Table 2.3

Occupations with the Largest Projected Job Decline, 2000 to 2010

Occupation	Employment (in thousands)		Change		Quartile rank by 2000 median hourly earnings[a]	Education and training category
	2000	2010	No. (1,000)	%		
Farmers and ranchers	1,294	965	−328	−25	2	Long-term on-the-job training
Order clerks	348	277	−71	−20	3	Short-term on-the-job training
Tellers	499	440	−59	−12	3	Short-term on-the-job training
Insurance claims and policy processing clerks	289	231	−58	−20	2	Moderate-term on-the-job training
Word processors and typists	297	240	−57	−19	3	Moderate-term on-the-job training
Sewing machine operators	399	348	−51	−13	4	Moderate-term on-the-job training
Dishwashers	525	483	−42	−8	4	Short-term on-the-job training
Switchboard operators, including answering service	259	218	−41	−16	3	Short-term on-the-job training
Loan interviewers and clerks	139	101	−38	−28	2	Short-term on-the-job training
Computer operators	194	161	−33	−17	2	Moderate-term on-the-job training
Dining room and cafeteria attendants and bartender helpers	431	402	−29	−7	4	Short-term on-the-job training
Electrical and electronic equipment assemblers	379	355	−24	−6	3	Short-term on-the-job training
Machine feeders and offbearers	182	159	−22	−12	3	Short-term on-the-job training
Telephone operators	54	35	−19	−35	2	Short-term on-the-job training
Secretaries, except legal, medical, and executive	1,864	1,846	−18	−1	3	Moderate-term on-the-job training
Prepress technicians and workers	107	90	−17	−16	2	Long-term on-the-job training
Office machine operators, except computer	84	68	−16	−19	3	Short-term on-the-job training

Occupation					Training
Cutting, punching, and press machine setters, operators, and tenders, metal and plastic	372	357	−15	−4	3	Moderate-term on-the-job training
Postal service mail sorters, processors, and processing machine operators	289	275	−14	−5	2	Short-term on-the-job training
Railroad brake, signal, and switch operators	22	9	−13	−61	2	Work experience in a related occupation
Wholesale and retail buyers, except farm products	148	135	−13	−9	2	Bachelor's degree
Meter readers, utilities	49	36	−13	−26	2	Short-term on-the-job training
Butchers and meat cutters	141	128	−13	−9	3	Long-term on-the-job training
Parts salespersons	260	248	−12	−4	3	Moderate-term on-the-job training
Inspectors, testers, sorters, samplers, and weighers	602	591	−11	−2	3	Moderate-term on-the-job training
Eligibility interviewers, government programs	117	106	−11	−9	2	Moderate-term on-the-job training
Door-to-door sales workers, news and street vendors, and related workers	166	156	−10	−6	3	Short-term on-the-job training
Procurement clerks	76	67	−9	−12	2	Short-term on-the-job training
Railroad conductors and yardmasters	45	36	−8	−19	2	Work experience in a related occupation
Barbers	73	64	−8	−12	4	Post-secondary vocational award

Source: Daniel E. Hecker, "Occupational Employment Projections to 2010," *Monthly Labor Review* (November 2001): 81, www.bls.gov/opub/mlr/welcome.

ªThe quartile rankings of Occupational Employment Statistics annual earnings data are presented in the following categories: 1 = very high ($39,700 and over); 2 = high ($25,760 to $39,660); 3 = low ($18,500 to $25,760); and 4 = very low (up to $18,490). The rankings were based on quartiles using one-fourth of total employment to define each quartile. Earnings are for wage and salary workers.

BLS also projects the *fastest*-growing occupations to 2010, which can be found in Appendix Table A.2. The fastest-growing occupations that tend to be held by women are commonly in the service sector and involve informal, on-the-job training. The sole higher-skilled, fast-growing occupations listed by the BLS that tend to employ disproportionate numbers of women are health care related, such as nursing aides and registered nurses. Other occupations projected by BLS to experience fast growth through 2010 are highly skilled jobs involving information technology.

The previous chapter spelled out the reasons why we cannot wait for "the market" to resolve the concentrations of high-school educated women workers in low-wage jobs with few opportunities for advancement, but rather, must craft policy to intervene and alter the status quo and to assist women interested in obtaining employment in high-wage jobs that provide career ladders for women. The previous chapter also discussed different theoretical approaches to how such an intervention ought to be crafted, different theories explaining labor market dynamics predict various outcomes and prescribe particular features for an intervention to realize its desired effect.

Policy intervention is necessary because the market has not addressed sex-segregated training and employment in an acceptable period of time. Incentives favoring the traditional, white-collar, four-year degree path remain, which results in alternative paths being overlooked. Emphasizing one path to the exclusion of the other has particularly damaging implications for women, as they are far more likely to end up in low-wage pink-collar jobs when the education and training system has failed them or they have failed out of their educational programs. Jobs that men in similar situations end up in do not have the bleak futures that pink-collar jobs do.[7] Any attempt to change patterns of occupational segregation by gender must tackle the sex-role socialization surrounding male-dominated occupations, which affects employers and male coworkers, as well as women workers themselves. Because similarly situated men do not face the same dead-end employment outcomes, and the market cannot be relied upon to address this problem in a reasonable amount of time, policies providing alternative employment and training programs are necessary to increase the numbers of women in occupations dominated by men. This is demonstrated by the data presented later in this chapter.

Two distinct intervention sites exist: the training site and the employment site. Any given policy or program can address one or both of them. Policies designed to intervene and alter sex-segregated hiring patterns increase the numbers of women in male-dominated occupations and acknowledge the barriers to entry women face even when they have the skills required for the job. Placement assistance must be coupled with retention efforts to ensure that competent and capable women are not pushed out of jobs due to workplace sex discrimination. This is consistent with the assertion in the previous chapter that human capital theory is flawed, insofar as differences in skills and education cannot account fully for occupational segregation by gender, and that, for many women, it is not enough just to have the right "human capital endowments." Robert Glover also notes the internal and external barriers to entering nontraditional occupations (NTOs): external involves skills and overt sex discrimination in hiring, and internal involves sex-role socialization of women workers and/or their coworkers.[8] Intervening in both training and placement and retention sites triggers a learning process that can address the internal and external barriers to entry. As more women demonstrate their abilities in training programs and workplaces, educators, career counselors, employers, coworkers, and women themselves, set in motion the process of changing their own minds and the minds of others regarding notions of sex-role socialization. Both sites must be altered to address the larger problem of women's concentration in low-wage pink-collar occupations and underrepresentation in higher-status, male-dominated occupations.[9] In acknowledging that training is both a cause as well as an effect of gender inequality, Harlan and Steinberg note:

> On the one hand, the training system is a *source* of occupational segregation. Training programs influence the occupational preferences of millions of women who participate in them each year . . . and prepare most of them in a few traditional female-dominated occupations. On the other hand, the training system *reflects* the demands of the labor market by providing the skills it requires. Training programs respond to the high labor demand in low-paying clerical and service occupations with the result that women (and men) are channeled into the paths of least resistance.[10]

Again, policy interventions must address both intervention sites to alter occupational segregation by gender. Through such policy interventions, individuals experience what former Labor Secretary Ray Marshall called cognitive dissonance, which can mitigate gender discrimination through a learning process by which individuals can, if they choose to, overcome prejudices by observing evidence that contradicts their biases.[11] In this case, observing women who successfully complete training programs and work effectively in occupations dominated by men can allow discriminators to overcome their biases by accepting contradictory evidence. Secretary Marshall admits that the discriminators must be *willing to see* this evidence, and it must be repeated in order to be effective in mitigating discrimination. Women entering and succeeding in college classrooms, working side by side on worksites as apprentices and as students in vocational education and training programs have gone a long way toward changing minds about women's capabilities. As the case studies will demonstrate, however, follow-up monitoring is needed to ensure job retention after placement through zero-tolerance sexual harassment prevention policies; assuming male coworkers will simply accept a tradeswoman's presence once they observe her succeeding on the jobsite is unrealistic, as Cora's testimony reveals:

> I am a Millwright. We are the ones who dismantle, move, install, change layout, set up, repair, overhaul and maintain all machinery and heavy mechanical equipment including power shafting, pulleys, conveyors and hoists. We work from plans and blueprints. We are able to install the equipment and align parts or components of the equipment using hand or power tools or hoisting equipment if necessary. This work is dangerous, noisy, busy and dirty. This is one of the most diversified of the skilled trades. I am giving this very brief summary of this trade so women interested can get a feel for what they would get into. While this has been economically good on one hand I have been through the mill with harassment. It also interrupts your home life. For every man fired for harassment five more take his place. Any women going into the trades should be mentored not once or twice but continually.[12]

Similarly, Maurita, a heavy equipment operator, cautions, "You can't say, 'I can't do that, I'm just a girl,' or be afraid you're going to break a nail . . . you have to be willing to get dirty, disgustingly dirty. You're going to sweat." And when she arrived on the jobsite, she observed, "You should have seen their faces . . . I mean it looked like they hated me."[13]

Women pursuing nontraditional fields face barriers that are not overcome by simply demonstrating competence on the job. Post-secondary training and education is important to anyone seeking to further her career, and tradeswomen have had to seek out opportunities in the college-for-all environment, and stick with their career choices in the face of significant challenges. Education, mentoring, and continued support are needed. However, these and most other women have had to seek out not only their nontraditional training and education resources, but their support and mentoring resources as well.

A college education remains relevant only to a minority of working women. Although the proportion of women attending and graduating with four-year degrees has increased substantially over time, that proportion remains a minority. Presuming all women will or should attend college is a disservice to the significant portion of working women supporting themselves and families, either as single heads of households or as parts of dual-earner households. This assumption remains a disservice, yet the four-year college path is prioritized over other forms of post-secondary education and training, and policy presumes individuals have either already graduated, are in college, or are preparing to attend college. The next section traces this bias in policy and culture, and its particular detrimental effect on working women.

The College Bias

Political responses to increasing labor market inequality have taken the college-for-all approach on an increasing basis, particularly since the end of World War II and passage of the GI Bill. That program made a college education accessible to thousands of young men for whom such an experience would never have been available. However, for much of the postwar period, the influx of GIs into college degree programs coincided with U.S. labor markets that still employed significant numbers of non-college workers, mostly men, in high-wage, high-skilled, upwardly mobile occupations with collective bargaining protections, union representation, and job security.[14] Over recent decades, as labor market institutions such as these have deteriorated, the political will supporting policies aimed at maintaining full employment has faded, and immigration has increased, the non-college working population has been affected to a far greater degree than has the college-educated population. Not only has political support for full employment policies faded, but as balanced-budget objectives increasingly eclipse other fiscal strategies, tax incentives and other policies to increase access to a college education become more politically palatable than government spending on employment and training programs. Such hands-off market-focused strategies remove government supports for full employment and direct interventions into labor markets and the four-year college path become the government-sanctioned career goal for all. This is reflected in John Bishop's and Shani Carter's analysis producing the following policy recommendation, which characterizes much of the literature in this area: "Education is a public function, and a public policy response to the shortage appears to be in order. Cost-effective ways of stimulating a substantial increase in the supply of college graduates are needed."[15]

Education *is* a public function, but increasing the numbers of college graduates is only one way to provide this public good. The following paragraphs demonstrate the presence of a college-for-all bias along several dimensions. One result of this bias has been that alternatives to the four-year path are increasingly overlooked, leaving individuals seeking post-secondary training and education to pursue the four-year path whether it is appropriate for them or not. An exploration of the ramifications of this shows that women are made worse off than men are by a college-for-all presumption.

Incentives Supporting the Four-Year Path

Academic courses of study are emphasized over vocational ones in two important ways: decreased funding of vocational alternatives decreases the number of programs available, and cultural attitudes against vocational programs discourage the distribution of or search for information about whatever options are left. Prepaid college savings plans and the tax advantages they enjoy are but two examples of policy-specific incentives favoring the four-year, full-time white-collar college degree path. Others include federally funded and federally guaranteed higher education student loan programs and state-level support for higher education, while loan programs and direct funding for vocational education have experienced cuts regularly for several years, even during the budget surplus years of the 1990s.[16] In addition, cultural attitudes about vocational training programs and two-year colleges that are "sometimes dismissed as the poor relations of higher education," have caused them to be overlooked as viable alternatives to career preparation.[17]

Another aspect of the preference of academic career paths over vocational ones may also be due to the predilection of society and policymakers toward more free market and competitive approaches to determining outcomes. Traditional academic courses of study are considered more freely competitive than are targeted employment and training programs, if a student fails out of her college courses, then she has merely experienced her "just deserts," and this is in fact an indication that competitive forces are working, the student rises or falls due to her own endowments of discipline and ability. From this point of view, the resulting academic degree is, then, truly *earned*. Vocational programs, especially government-funded ones and those targeted toward a particular population, are not market-driven environments and the resulting degree or certificate is not earned, but rather, given. Moreover, additional services targeted toward women in these programs make them even less "fair." Particular features of outreach, training, and placement programs such as providing childcare services and transportation are detailed later in this chapter, but as Harlan and Steinberg observe:

> The negative implications of designing narrow training programs are especially strong for women. With an emphasis limited to getting a job, or even to job skill development, the provision of these other training functions and support services is either devalued, or worse, prohibited by training institutions. Too often, women are simply regarded as less desirable

participants than men for conventional programs because they require costly "special" services that are not "legitimate" training functions. Quick turn-around and cheap placements are allowed to substitute for a chance of longer-term stability and higher earnings capacity for women.[18]

This is similar to the tradeoff between higher productivity and workplace stability relating to employer hiring decisions mentioned in the previous chapter. The choice is between doing what is expedient and what might be beneficial in the long run: bring women in, incur the costs of these "special" services, and risk disrupting the male-dominated workplace, or preserve the male-dominated workplace and maintain sex segregation. Constant messages in contemporary U.S. society and funding decisions by federal and state governments betray the partiality toward college degrees over vocational approaches. In high-technology electronics manufacturing, for example, Nance Goldstein finds that employers preferred that their workers had more of an academic background, resulting in the "para-professionalization" of otherwise technical training programs. In the fast-growing field of high-tech electronics manufacturing with its promise for continued employment growth, she concluded, "The opportunities for gaining a qualification in a program shorter than a two-year associate's degree dwindled."[19] Even non-college mainstays like DeVry Institute of Technology now tout their baccalaureate degree programs. The demands of the job did not change so much as the preferences of employers shaped the manner in which training was delivered. Another example of this is the decline of apprenticeship opportunities in the United States, which is described in detail below. The emphasis on four-year, full-time academic programs and the lack of funding for alternative vocational programs and apprenticeships limit the career options of both poor and working-class women.

Alternative employment and training programs are relevant for two populations of women: working-class women and women in poverty receiving public assistance. While there are clear implications for either important group individually, the current study takes a broader focus that includes both. The so-called "work first" emphasis of current public assistance programs and discriminatory notions of "self sufficiency" prevent women on public assistance from continued training and education. The current philosophy of welfare programs is to decrease enrollments, not to train and educate women for career ladder occupations.[20] As Bloomer, Finney, and Gault find, "the types of jobs that welfare recipients can get without higher education or nontraditional job training do not pay adequate wages to lift women and their families out of poverty."[21] Nontraditional training opportunities for women are essential for helping women who are transitioning from welfare to support their families in the long term. Welfare reform strategies have been criticized for emphasizing the short-term objective of reducing welfare rolls to the detriment of pursuing any long-term economic self-sufficiency objectives. Indeed, sexist notions of "self sufficiency" underlie current welfare policy, as well: while self sufficiency for men connotes obtaining a job with a wage sufficient to support a family, for women, it is interpreted strictly as getting them off the public dole.[22] Despite that half of the nearly 6.5 million families under the poverty level, the conventional wisdom surrounding economic self sufficiency for women focuses on getting them off the public dole, rather than helping women earn a wage sufficient for supporting a family. Impatience to reduce welfare rolls pushes these women directly into pink-collar jobs without much chance that they will ever be able to take the time for training and education toward a different career path, even if they had information about alternative training and education programs.

In addition, education and training alternatives are relevant for working-class women for whom poverty is not an immediate threat, and for those who have earned a high school diploma. For these women, the lack of outreach does not permit them to make fully informed career decisions. Although the pressure to get off welfare is not there, if the messages suggest, and the available options appear to be, only the four-year college path or remedial adult basic education, these women may also fall through the cracks and end up either earning far less than they could, not using their skills, not discovering their potential interests, or becoming stuck in jobs they do not really care for because alternatives were never made known. At some point, then, poverty may be a very real possibility.

Family socioeconomic status (SES) has a significant link to the choice to end one's education after high school or not. Citing U.S. Department of Education statistics, Harlan and Steinberg state that nearly half of all young women from middle-SES families, and 63 percent of women from lower-SES families did not continue their education right after high school.[23] Moreover, among the same groups of middle- and lower-SES families, young women and men who did not perform well in high school were even less likely to continue their schooling. Again, the implications of this for young women are worse than they are for men because the jobs that similarly situated men end up in are better paying than pink-collar jobs are. Opportunities to follow alternative career paths would be especially beneficial for young women and men in middle- and lower-SES families. Tax incentives and government programs supporting the four-year college degree path, coinciding with decreased public funding of vocational programs result in a disjunction between women who might be interested in alternative training and education programs and the providers of such services.

Institutional Deterioration: Alternatives Are Overlooked

Decreased funding and the lack of information about available alternatives are very real determinants of women's educational choice. A sense of inevitability regarding her choices channels a woman into the same pink-collar jobs regardless of where her own career interests may lie. Without information on alternatives, a woman may never realize her own interests in nontraditional fields unless options are presented to her, and, as Elizabeth Giese discovers in her analysis of vocational options in Michigan, "According to administrators, the majority of counselors inform students about opportunities in non-traditional jobs only if students request such information."[24] Specific best practices of programs are detailed later in this chapter, but, again, women cannot make informed choices about their careers without full information, and many may not even know what they fail to ask for. From their analysis of post-secondary training and education programs, Louise Haignere and Ronnie Steinberg note, "Many job counselors have told us that without an explicit focus on non-traditional occupations, women almost invariably choose traditionally female careers."[25] For women without networks that might give them information that a career counselor may not, the lack of awareness of different training programs is the same as the lack of these programs altogether. The *perception* of available alternatives is as influential as the actual number of alternative training programs in determining women's occupational outcomes. In a study of vocational-technical programs in Wisconsin, women "experienced barriers to enrollment as a consequence of the limited number of programs which they *perceived* as available to them."[26]

The point of any outreach program is to provide information so that a woman can make a fully informed career choice, whether or not she ends up in nursing or welding. The point is *not* to shuttle women into the trades for the sake of increasing their numbers, but rather, to redress problems of sex-role socialization of women themselves and of the individuals in their support systems, as well as the problems of sex bias in career counseling and education and training so that women are in the best positions to make career choices, given the full range of options, as articulated by Haignere and Steinberg:

> We emphasize that the purpose of outreach and career exploration is *not* to get as many women as possible to sign up for nontraditional training programs, but to enable them to make the most informed career choice they can on the basis of more complete knowledge. Ultimately, a woman's career longevity is the crucial test of program effectiveness, and herding

women into NTOs [nontraditional occupations] for the sake of EEO [Equal Employment Opportunities] statistics or other reasons will *not* contribute to longevity.[27]

In some job-training centers and employment offices, and only until recently in others, women were shuttled into traditionally female jobs, whether they expressed interest in different jobs or not. Haignere and Steinberg find that this is no more economically efficient than shuttling women into NTOs whether they are interested in them or not. Like many others who have analyzed these programs, they further note that once women are given the information on a variety of training and job opportunities, particularly about the potential to advance, obtaining highly marketable skills, and higher pay and the ability to work autonomously, "the number willing to enroll in NTOs is usually impressive."[28] Withholding information, intentionally or not, only reinforces sex-role socialization and incentives toward the four-year degree path, and the potential bias in career counseling that channels women into the same jobs.[29] Apprenticeship provides a practical and valuable alternative to the four-year degree path, but the concept has never taken hold in the United States as it has in Europe. Apprenticeships formalize a combination of in-class and on-the-job training; that is, it is not the individual student's responsibility to pursue her own on-the-job opportunities, but rather, her employer and educator combine in a formal relationship to provide a comprehensive learning experience that results in high degrees of job placement and higher earnings than either on-the-job experience or in-class learning could on their own. As Olivia Crosby notes:

A child development apprentice, for example, might spend the day as an assistant teacher, helping to supervise children, lead activities, and make arts and crafts materials. That evening, in class, the apprentice might learn safety procedures and theories of child development.[30]

Although apprenticeships are most closely associated with blue-collar skilled trades, many occupations involve them, including cooks, carpenters, machinists, firefighters, patrol officers, and heating and air-conditioning installers and repairers. As the quote at the beginning of this chapter notes, apprenticeships average about four years, depending upon the occupation. For instance, most carpentry occupations involve four-year apprenticeships, but a carpentry apprentice works for six years before completing her program. If apprenticeships can last as long as a college education can, and positive career outcomes result from each, why emphasize college over apprenticeships? Moreover, women and men completing apprenticeships do not seek entry-level positions, while many if not most college graduates seek and take jobs at the entry level. Well-paid, rewarding careers are found via a range of means. Apprenticeships may represent the most marked examples of the effects of college bias in the United States. Compared to European countries, apprenticeship has failed to become the significant vehicle for hands-on training and placement of young women and men in the United States because, among other reasons, continued land availability and a constant supply of immigrant labor made alternatives to apprenticeship cheaper for both workers and employers, trade unions were not consistent in linking membership with the completion of an apprenticeship, employers did not agree on market-wide standards for employment in the skilled trades, and apprentices who dropped out of their agreements with their masters were never consistently barred from gaining employment in their trade of choice anyway.[31] Today, apprenticeships attract nearly four applicants for every one opening,[32] so they are not plentiful for men *or* women, but the scarcity presents an even greater barrier to entry for women. Susan Eisenberg reveals that "while the sons of construction workers knew when and how to apply for apprenticeship programs, women had to make extraordinary efforts to submit applications."[33] Indeed, a woman identifying herself only as "D." sought assistance from other tradeswomen via the Internet in the following bulletin board posting, for even though she is obviously talented and from a "construction family," she nevertheless lacked the social capital necessary to navigate the application and qualification process for apprenticeships and trades work:

> I am 39 years old, grew up in a construction family, learned enough to build my own house including doing the dirt work, all carpentry, cabinets from scratch, wiring and plumbing it myself. I find myself in need of changing careers (am now a clean room worker in a chip plant) I would like to become an electrician. Would like to know how to go about this, what the educational requirements are and how I go about finding someone who will take me on and train me. My brother, the owner of a residential electrical company seems to believe there are no women in this field and refuses to help me at all. Thought perhaps one of you might be able to point me in the right direction.[34]

Given the barriers faced even by a woman who is knowledgeable about the trades and who should be able to draw on her family connections, it should come as no surprise that men outnumber women in apprenticeships by six to one.[35] In addition to lacking informal networks that lead to job matches more than formal networks do, women often come to a training and education program at a later age than do men, as a consequence of having and raising children or realizing that they lacked valuable skills training after a few years of working in dead-end, pink-collar jobs. In this case, because many apprenticeships involve age limits, older women are excluded outright.

Similarly, Robert Glover notes, "apprenticeship is underutilized in America for several reasons [but] can offer limited promise for women."[36] He posits an interesting explanation for the internal barriers: the sex-role socialization affecting women's employment in trades. He suggests that, although many jobs in the skilled trades pay well, their status in American culture remains low due to an "anti-manual" bias. This is felt by the men working in skilled trades, leading them to "draw dignity from pride in their craftsmanship." Entry of women into these occupations can be threatening to incumbent male workers, as their craftsmanship becomes more "closely associated with manliness."[37] Policy interventions must be sensitive to the potential sources of workplace sex discrimination, particularly placement and retention policies that seek to maximize women's longevity in the fields for which they have been trained. Entrenched biases rooted in sentiments like these will not fade quickly, if ever. However, Glover observes that women viewed the benefits in terms of pay and valuable training as worth the effort, despite the difficulties in successfully obtaining and completing apprenticeships for employment in skilled trades. In fact, women are more likely to complete their apprenticeships, as they "have a stronger attachment to their apprenticeship training than do men."[38] Overall, he recommends the greater use of apprenticeship for skilled trades and other occupations, which would benefit all workers, particularly women.

Leslie McCall notes other institutional changes that affect the non-college population: minimum wage, unemployment, immigration, and collective bargaining.[39] Examining wages in local labor markets and macro- and micro-level data, McCall finds that increasing employment insecurity leads to the greatest differential between wages for college-educated women and women who dropped out of high school. Employment insecurity is when a worker cannot be confident that her job is long term or not threatened, and is generated by local unemployment, immigration trends, unionization, and trends in flexible or casual employment. High unemployment depresses wages as more workers are available to work at lower wages than incumbent workers; higher rates of immigration have similar effects on wages; decreasing unionization removes job tenure protections that workers enjoyed when they were covered by a union contract or collective bargaining agreements; and increasing use of temporary workers reflects the trend of contracting out business functions. Increasing outsourcing diminishes some employees' long-term employment expectations, and oftentimes, contract-company employees are not covered by collective bargaining agreements or represented by unions.

McCall finds all these factors to be influential in explaining wage differentials among college and non-college women. As other studies have shown, the educational attainment of workers does not dictate labor market outcomes; rather, changes in local labor market institutions have an impact in determining the jobs women hold. With these findings in mind, it is appropriate to wonder why more and more women enter four-year college degree programs every year, given that so many do not graduate, and that the returns to education are determined by local labor market phenomena and not wholly by one's human capital investments. This analysis suggests that the lack of post-secondary alternatives channels increasing numbers of women into traditional, four-year degree programs. Women expect to gain from four-year degree programs because many women have experienced increasing returns to education, but they also suffer more severe labor market penalties by not completing their four-year degree programs. Women with some post-secondary education work in jobs with less pay and fewer opportunities for advancement, compared to male workers. Alternatives to the four-year degree path are important for women workers, but alternatives to the four-year path are few and on the decline.

Returns to Education and Perceived Returns to Education

Given the institutional deterioration of opportunities for the non-college population, it stands to reason that the numbers of college entrants would increase over time, if post-secondary education and training is expected to pay off in the workplace. Has the demand for post-secondary education and training increased over time? Have labor market opportunities kept pace with an increasingly educated workforce? In the paragraphs to follow, the increased demand for post-secondary education and training is, indeed, demonstrated, using the CPS Supplemental Survey on Job Training and other information sources. Findings of other analyses demonstrate that, on average, increased human capital investments do pay off in terms of higher wages and improved labor market opportunities. However, evidence suggests that the *type* of education and training matters: in some instances, workers fare better with specific post-secondary training that is not part of a four-year college curriculum compared to workers with a general college education. Moreover, it is also shown that the supply of four-year college graduates has exceeded the demand for them. College graduates increasingly accept jobs that do not require a four-year college degree. Evidence suggests that college graduates queue up for jobs requiring a college degree, just as secondary-tier workers queue up for primary-tier occupations. However, in spite of increasingly limited labor market opportunities, a wage premium still exists for college graduates. Despite the wage premium, a bias favoring the four-year college path remains harmful to many workers because that premium accrues to individuals who have *earned* a four-year degree, and many of them do not finish four-year college degree programs. Couple that with the evidence that a few years of general college training can actually penalize some workers, compared to those who also have less than four years of college but whose post-secondary training is targeted to a specific occupation or field, and the potential harm to non-college women and men is clear.

The harm is exacerbated by the trend demonstrated above that alternatives to the four-year college path are increasingly overlooked. Young women and men entering labor markets and considering post-secondary options tend toward four-year degree programs in the absence of explicit alternatives. These alternatives are not made explicit because a four-year college degree is increasingly favored as the sole pathway toward upward mobility. About two-thirds will either not complete a four-year degree program, or will never have enrolled in the first place. Many of them would have benefited from an alternative post-secondary education and training option, because not only do specific post-secondary programs accrue greater benefits than less than four years of a general college education does, but even among the one-third who graduate from college, an increasing proportion must take jobs that do not require a college education and queue up for more appropriate jobs, insofar as the supply of college graduates increasingly exceeds the demand for them.

Increased Demand for Post-Secondary Education and Training

Increased educational attainment is well known to afford individuals higher incomes, lower risk of unemployment, and greater job opportunities. Earning a college degree remains a goal of most parents for their children because of the opportunities further education affords. As this analysis has argued, however, policy ought not to adopt a one-size-fits-all approach to promoting further educational attainment because a significant portion of people will not complete a four-year degree program. In addition to the reasons cited earlier, interesting evidence exists to suggest that not only are some college graduates failing to obtain jobs that require their skills, but also, that other forms of non-college post-secondary education and training brings greater benefits to workers than a four-year degree does. While information on workers' sources of training and their perceptions on whether their jobs require them to have obtained certain types of training is limited, the evidence on increased demand for post-secondary education and training is not just anecdotal.

The CPS conducted supplemental surveys on job training in January 1983, 1991, and 1992. Between 1983 and 1991, the number of respondents indicating that they needed training for their current position increased by approximately 20 percent, "roughly equivalent to employment growth over the 1983–91 period."[40] The supplemental surveys distinguished qualifying training from skills training; the former is training needed to qualify for their job and the latter is training taken once a job was obtained to improve skills. For example, one must have graduated from law school to obtain a position as an attorney, and practicing attorneys commonly take continuing legal education courses to sharpen their skills. The law degree represents qualifying training and the continuing education courses represent skills training. Any individual respondent could have indicated one or both types of training.[41] Alan Eck finds the difference in earnings was greatest for workers who took both types of training, compared to those who took neither. More important, Eck finds that the *requirements* of the job dictate the levels of earnings and opportunity, more so than does the educational attainment of the worker:

> There may be a need for a better match between educational programs and the requirements of the workplace. . . . For example, many workers with college degrees indicate that they are employed in jobs that do not require special skills or education and that their earnings are lower than earnings of college graduates in jobs that require special skills. And workers with less education, but who are employed in jobs that require special skills or training, earn as much as college graduates who do not require training to get their job.[42]

Jobs that require fewer skills pay less than skilled jobs do. Workers with less education in skilled jobs earn as much as graduates in nonskilled jobs do; the college premium is offset by the skill level of the job. Furthermore, there are many skilled jobs that do not require a four-year degree, so demand does exist for non-college workers.[43] What is more, increasing numbers of college graduates take jobs that do not require a college education and queue up for jobs that do. In that case, evidence suggests that the supply of college-educated workers exceeds the demand for them. The following section describes the college-educated queuing-up phenomenon in detail.

Queuing Up for Jobs Requiring a Four-Year College Degree

In separate analyses, both Kristina J. Shelley and Daniel E. Hecker find that an increasing number of college graduates hold jobs that they feel do not require a college degree.[44] Hecker finds that the proportion of underemployed college graduates increased since the early 1970s to about one in five graduates, and Shelley projects that this trend could increase to about one in four over the 1990 to 2005 period. Tyler, Murnane, and Levy find contrary evidence by comparing workers with no more than a high school diploma with those holding at least a four-year college degree in "high school jobs."[45] This approach ignores a significant portion of the non-college population with some post-secondary education, and the distinction between jobs *not requiring* a college degree and jobs requiring *no more than* a college education makes their analysis very different from the others. Indeed, as Bernhardt, Morris, Handcock, and Scott find, the earnings and labor market opportunities of workers with strictly high school diplomas declined so much over the past decades that analyses consistently find positive effects of educational attainment if "high school only" is used as the reference group.[46]

One very interesting difference between the Hecker and Shelley analyses and the Tyler, Murnane, and Levy analysis and projections like those found in the *Occupational Outlook Quarterly*, is that the former rely upon the CPS Job Training Supplement, and the latter examine actual employment patterns by educational attainment. Specifically, the Job Training Supplement asked workers whether they felt their jobs required a college degree, while the *Quarterly* uses "the proportions of occupations usually filled by college graduates [as] the basis for analyzing the demand for college graduates."[47] From the point of view of this analysis, equating where a worker works with where they ought to be based on their skills and training places more faith in the wisdom of the market than is warranted. That is to say, this analysis departs from the "rational actor" approach that assumes an individual holding a four-year college degree holds a position that requires a four-year college degree. This analysis examines actual flows of workers, as well, but does not assume that labor market outcomes correspond to human capital endowments. Workers often hold positions that do not require the education and training they possess, temporarily or not, by choice or not. This is not to say that four-year college graduates experience widespread unemployment; in fact, data over time demonstrate the opposite.[48] The interesting trend is not that college graduates are unemployed, which they are not, but that they are *under*employed, which they are, on an increasing basis, as Hecker demonstrates. Hecker also shows that the abundance of college graduates available for jobs requiring a college degree suggests that college graduates accept non-college jobs and queue up for jobs demanding their education and training: "An increasing number of college graduates were employed in jobs that did not usually require a degree; and employers had little difficulty hiring a sufficient number of college graduates to fill jobs that required a college degree."[49]

Indeed, neither Hecker nor Shelley suggests that college graduates *permanently* hold jobs that do not require a college degree. College graduates appear to queue up for "better," more highly skilled occupations, and temporarily hold jobs not requiring a college degree. None of these analyses refute the financial rewards of increased educational attainment; in fact, the impetus for Hecker's 1992 study was to reconcile the conflicting information on graduates' earnings and their labor market outcomes. Although Eck finds that workers without college degrees can earn more than college graduates, given other types of training and education endowments, his research does not refute the college wage premium either. Graduates appear to queue up for occupations requiring college degrees based on the promise of higher earnings, lower risk of unemployment, and greater job mobility, which in fact accrues to the majority of college graduates. What does this trend have to do with the non-college population? This analysis asserts that a bias favoring the four-year college path, as well as overlooking the shrinking alternatives to the four-year path, has contributed to this trend. Shelley articulates the effect of this trend:

> The expected increase in the number of college graduates, versus fewer college-level job openings in the future will have an effect on opportunities for workers with fewer years of education as well. The prospect of underemployed college graduates crowding out others who would normally fill positions that do not require a college degree means more careful career planning will be necessary for persons who are not college graduates.[50]

Although Shelley properly points out the ripple effect of this crowding-out trend, the present analysis takes a different approach: rather than placing the onus on the non-college population to engage in "more careful career planning," greater and greater emphasis on the career planning needs of the non-college population are recommended. The following chapter demonstrates how ignoring the needs of the non-college workforce is more detrimental to women than it is to men, based on the types of jobs non-college women tend to hold.

Chapter 3
A Pattern of Decline and Its Ramifications

> This is a critical time for women and girls in vocational programs . . . [i]f the trends discussed here continue, drop-outs are likely to increase, supportive programs will continue to disappear, and many women will be locked into traditionally female, low-wage occupational categories. Students, educators, advocates, and policymakers must work together to support these students and make sure they continue to have an opportunity to prepare for the world of work and economic independence.
> —*National Coalition for Women and Girls in Education, 2001*.[1]

The previous chapter demonstrated the presence of a college-for-all bias in an environment where a minority of workers graduates with a four-year college degree. This chapter illustrates not only that the college-for-all bias has accompanied a decline in post-secondary alternatives, but also that these trends have particularly harmful consequences for non-college women workers. This conclusion is reached by revealing intransigent patterns of occupational segregation by gender over time: non-college women tend to hold the same low-paying pink-collar occupations; therefore, policy intervention is needed to alter these patterns. Clearly, market forces cannot be relied upon to break the pink-collar cycle for non-college women.

Vanishing Post-Secondary Options

Incentives favoring the four-year full-time academic approach allow alternatives to be overlooked and are especially harmful to women whose career paths do not involve the four-year full-time plan. First, due to the real or perceived lack of alternatives, women without plans for college tend to end up in low-wage, low-mobility pink-collar occupations, while non-college men do not. Second, non-college men commonly receive skills training informally by working with relatives or friends, and oftentimes can translate their skills into employment via informal networks to which women tend not to have access.[2] Third, because women often apply to post-secondary employment and training programs at a later age than men do, apprenticeships with age restrictions remain out of reach. Fourth, "special" services and inflexibility in hiring and promoting decisions can make women trainees and workers seem, at least to some, to be more costly than their male counterparts. Fifth and finally, although integrating training programs and workplaces may be the right thing to do, educators and employers often choose to preserve stability rather than risk disrupting the *status quo*. What is more, each of these things individually and in combination with one another further preserve sex-segregation of training sites and workplaces by not allowing women and men to witness women's success in training programs and jobs in nontraditional occupations (NTOs), only reinforcing the notion that women cannot and should not participate in these fields. Indeed, overlooking alternative training and education programs continues to overcrowd women into pink-collar occupations and fortify the existing male concentrations in certain skilled blue-collar occupations. Not only are alternatives overlooked, but policy remedies, such as gender set-asides in vocational education programs, have been drastically reduced or eliminated altogether. Gender set-asides are resources targeting women in education and training programs, employment opportunities, and government contracted work. Race and gender set-asides have come under fire in several high-profile court cases, including *Metro Broadcasting v. FCC, Adarand v. Peña, Hopwood v. Texas*, and the recent Supreme Court case challenging admissions criteria of the University of Michigan. Popular sentiment has shifted dramatically away from supporting gender and race set-asides, prompting some to criticize them as "reverse discrimination" against whites and men. Such critics point to the achievements of several high-profile women and members of race and ethnic minority groups and declare affirmative action approaches like set-asides as no longer needed. Again, this perpetuates the pioneering myth discussed earlier, particularly as articulated by Louise Kapp Howe: that the achievements of a few very successful individuals have been allowed to act as proxies for working women throughout the economy, when in fact, while some have made gains, many, particularly non-college women, have not. Reverse discrimination rhetoric has resulted in significant and severe cuts to vocational and technical education sex-equity programs and to affirmative action initiatives overall.

The Women's Bureau of the U.S. Department of Labor administered Women in Apprenticeships and Nontraditional Occupations (WANTO) and NEW, but other federal-level gender-specific employment and training programs have been funded through the Carl D. Perkins Vocational and Applied Technology Education Act, administered by the U.S. Department of Education. The National Coalition for Women and Girls in Education

(NCWGE) conducted an analysis of the impact of policy changes, specifically, the reauthorization of the Perkins Act in 1998 (Perkins III), on the administration and level of gender equity services; a follow-up to their 1995 study.[3] Through their survey of more than 1,500 service providers, NCWGE found that Perkins III eliminated many gender and sex-equity set-asides, decreased funding for targeted programs overall, and decreased funding from state and local education agencies, leading to a decline in the level and quality of services to students and an accompanying increase in unmet student needs.[4]

In their 1995 study, NCWGE found that the Perkins sex equity efforts helped women attain economic independence and that such measures should not be eliminated. In 2001, they sought to determine whether states continued to target women in education and training programs without any requirement to do so and with less funding, and found that most have not. In addition to their survey results, NCWGE ranked state efforts according to eleven criteria to gauge the extent to which they "Promoted" and "Protected" their gender-specific programs, whether their programs were "Losing Ground," whether program support was "Disintegrating," or whether there had been a complete "Failure" to continue any gender-specific education and training programs. Of forty-nine states ranked according to these criteria, NCWGE found that, because of the absence of sex-equity requirements and the decreased funds due to Perkins III, none of the forty-nine states promoted their gender set-asides and sex-equity programs; twelve states protected their gender-specific programs; programs in nineteen states were losing ground; programs in fifteen states suffered disintegrating support; and three states failed to continue their gender set-aside and sex-equity programs altogether.

With less funding from the federal Perkins program, states have to use their own monies to promote or protect their gender-specific education and training programs. Moreover, a state would have to voluntarily make sex equity in education and training a priority, because Perkins III eliminated those goals. As NCWGE found, none used their own funds and made sex equity a priority in their education and training programs. Few states were able to protect their existing programs, but the vast majority, 75 percent, was unable or unwilling to make sex equity a priority and continue funding their programs in the wake of Perkins III. Many states eliminated their programs in anticipation of legal challenges to affirmative action, as well.

Piedmont Works, a Program of Piedmont Virginia Community College (PVCC), was funded by the Perkins Sex Equity Set-Aside program and Temporary Assistance for Needy Families (TANF). Piedmont Works serves single parents, displaced homemakers, and single pregnant women, particularly low-income workers and welfare recipients, and provides a percentage toward tuition, books, supplies, uniforms, childcare, and transportation for those pursuing Associate of Applied Science degrees, career studies certificates, job skills training at PVCC, vocational training at other post-secondary institutions, and GED or high school diploma programs at area adult education programs. In addition to small tuition stipends, Piedmont Works provides career exploration, planning, and counseling; assessment; personal counseling; job readiness training; job search; monthly life management skills workshops; and tutoring.[5] Because Piedmont Works targets women and is funded with Perkins Sex Equity Set-Aside dollars, it will no longer be able to operate unless other funding sources are found. The loss of Piedmont Works is but one example of the effects of diminishing alternatives on low-wage women workers represented by Perkins III cuts.

The Outlook for Post-Secondary Education and Training Alternatives

The prospects for future gender-specific employment and training efforts are not favorable. The recent economic downturn further exacerbates this problem. States cannot run deficits the way the federal government can. Without a mandate to prioritize these programs, one could expect them to suffer further cuts and be eliminated altogether. In an economic downturn, social services are always vulnerable. Economic stimulus efforts, especially those intended to prop-up state budgets, could help states restore or protect state and local level programs. But again, in lean economic times, other domestic policy issues are prioritized over adult education and employment policies. An indeterminate and ill-defined war on terrorism has distracted policymakers from focusing on domestic policy issues, as well. Finally, to the extent that domestic policy issues are attended to *at all* in a congressional election year, primary and secondary education issues will draw the attention, rather than adult and vocational education.

Finally, the "work first" emphasis of welfare programs has had the effect of limiting adults' employment and training opportunities in favor of placing them in jobs and reducing welfare rolls. Overall, with less federal funding and without a federal mandate to make sex equity a priority in education and training programs, states are left to support such programs on their own, and most have been unable or unwilling to do so. In lean economic times, states that have supported their programs have even fewer incentives to continue, particularly given balanced-budget requirements. State budgets have been hit hard by the nationwide economic downturn, national security issues have taken priority over issues of domestic policy within the federal budget, and different industries experience different levels of growth, which could influence the types of jobs NTO programs train women for. Although vocational education and employment and training programs have been cut throughout federal and state budgets, gender-specific set-asides have been all but eliminated, and women's participation in NTO-related vocational education and employment programs is low without targeted initiatives.

The chances for women to gain economic self-sufficiency are lower than men's are in the absence of policy interventions because, given similar levels of training and education, the blue-collar jobs men end up in are better paying and involve more marketable skills than do the lower-level pink-collar clerical and service jobs women end up in. Other things being equal, things remain unequal: outcomes for women without targeted policies to get them into training and employment programs are worse than they are for men. The next section illustrates how non-college women tend to hold the same occupations over time, as do non-college men, but women's jobs tend to be lower-paying, lower-skilled jobs, whereas men's tend to involve higher wages, higher skills, and opportunities for advancement.

Non-College Women Are Worse Off Than Non-College Men

At all levels of educational attainment, women tend to earn less and work in jobs with less upward mobility and less union representation, and in jobs that involve fewer transferable skills, compared to men with similar levels of educational attainment.[6] Moreover, these trends have been persistent over time. In fact, Marlene Kim finds that "nearly two out of five women work in jobs that pay low wages. Women are more likely to be low paid if they are young, single, or less educated, *or if they are employed in certain jobs.*"[7] That is, regardless of educational attainment, holding "certain jobs" relegates women workers to poverty and near-poverty status. Current Population Survey merged outgoing rotation group (CPS-MORG) annualized data for working women and men in the United States illustrate how non-college women have held the same kinds of jobs over the past twenty years, jobs that tend to be the same as Kim's "certain jobs" of low-wage women workers. Non-college men have held many of the same occupations over the past twenty years, as well. The differences between the jobs women have tended to hold and those men have held involve the levels of training, pay, and transferable skills in each. Tables 3.1 and 3.2 show the top ten occupations held by non-college women and men, respectively, ranked by the number of people employed in each occupation. Refer to Appendix 3 for detailed tables that show how little the occupational mix has changed over the twenty-year period from 1979 to 1999. Indeed, these tables show how occupational segregation by gender has resisted changes over time, including increased automation and computerization, and increased educational attainment.

Table 3.1

Where Women Work: Top Ten Occupations by Percent of Total Employed, Women with a High School Education, 1979 to 1999

Rank	1979	1984	1989	1994	1999
1	Secretaries	Secretaries	Secretaries	Cashiers	Cashiers
2	Sales clerks, retail	Cashiers	Cashiers	Secretaries	Nursing aides
3	Cashiers	Nursing aides	Nursing aides	Nursing aides	Secretaries
4	Bookkeepers	Waiters and waitresses	Waiters and waitresses	Waiters and waitresses	Waiters and waitresses
5	Waiters and waitresses	Bookkeepers	Bookkeepers	Bookkeepers	Receptionists
6	Assemblers	Sales workers	Sales workers	Cooks	Bookkeepers
7	Nursing aides	Cooks	Cooks	Sales workers	Sales supervisors
8	Typists	Typists	Managers and administrators	Receptionists	Cooks
9	Miscellaneous clerical	Sewing machine operators	Receptionists	Sales supervisors	Retail sales occupations
10	Sewers and stitchers	Assemblers	Assemblers	Assemblers	Assemblers

Table 3.2

Where Men Work: Top Ten Occupations by Percent of Total Employed, Men with a High School Education, 1979 to 1999

Rank	1979	1984	1989	1994	1999
1	Truck drivers	Truck drivers	Truck drivers	Truck drivers	Truck drivers
2	Miscellaneous machine operators	Janitors and cleaners	Janitors and cleaners	Janitors and cleaners	Janitors and cleaners
3	Heavy equipment mechanics	Carpenters	Carpenters	Laborers, not construction	Laborers, not construction
4	Carpenters	Laborers, not construction	Laborers, not construction	Misc. machine operators	Misc. machine operators
5	Welders and flame cutters	Miscellaneous machine operators	Miscellaneous machine operators	Carpenters	Carpenters
6	Auto mechanics	Welders	Assemblers	Assemblers	Construction laborers
7	Foremen	Assemblers	Construction laborers	Cooks	Assemblers
8	Assemblers	Electricians	Freight handlers	Freight stock handlers	Cooks
9	Construction laborers, not carpenters' helpers	Industrial machine repairers	Welders	Production occupations supervisors	Freight stock handlers
10	Machinists	Machinists	Production occupations supervisors	Stock handlers and baggers	Stock handlers and baggers

Using 1998 CPS data, Marlene Kim concludes that those most likely to be low paid include food service workers, workers in cleaning and building services, health and household services, and administrative support and clerical workers such as clerks, receptionists, bank tellers, and copy machine operators. The overlap between Kim's low-wage jobs and those listed above is clear. The following table demonstrates persistent occupational segregation by gender for men, although male-dominated jobs tend to accrue greater benefits than female-dominated ones do.

Both women and men with no more than a high school education are employed as cooks and assemblers; however, the remaining top occupations for this group differ in their training and the industries in which each tends to fall. The top occupations for high-school educated women tend to be in the service sector, including clerical jobs, retail sales, and health care, while the top jobs for men tend to be in construction, transportation, and manufacturing. Men's average annual earnings are higher than women's are, at all levels of educational attainment, as depicted in Figure 3.1. Consistent with Eck, Figure 3.1 shows how, depending on the type and source of qualifying and skills training, workers with some post-secondary training can fare better than those with a few years of college do.[8]

For most of the twenty-seven years covered in Figure 3.1, women earned less than men did, regardless of educational attainment; the returns to gender are greater than are the returns to education. Only in 1990 did female college graduates' earnings eclipse male high-school graduates' earnings; until then, men with no post-secondary education or training earned more than did women with four-year college degrees. By 2001, women with four-year degrees finally earned as much as men with some post-secondary education and training.

Traditional non-college post-secondary alternatives like apprenticeships have been less accessible to women than men, for reasons stated earlier. Because women can expect lesser returns to post-secondary, non-college education and training, and because of their limited access to post-secondary, non-college alternatives such as apprenticeships, women comprise a larger portion of both the some-college and college-graduate populations. Over the twenty-year period covered by the CPS-MORG data, higher percentages of women seek post-secondary education,[9] as Figures 2.2 and 2.3 illustrate. The disparity between men's and women's earnings despite educational attainment levels provides further evidence to doubt the human capital prediction: although more women than men pursue continued education and training, they continue to work in the same lower-paying occupations and earn less than men earn. This evidence further underscores the importance of post-secondary education and training options because

60

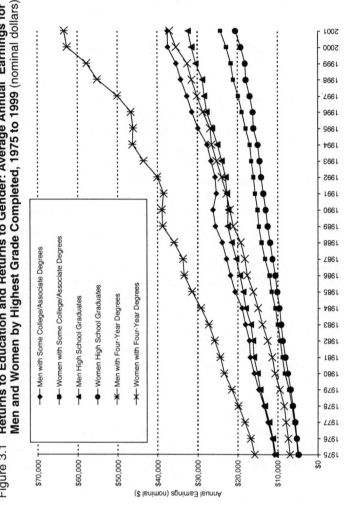

Figure 3.1   Returns to Education and Returns to Gender: Average Annual Earnings for
Men and Women by Highest Grade Completed, 1975 to 1999 (nominal dollars)

- ◆ Men with Some College/Associate Degrees
- ■ Women with Some College/Associate Degrees
- ◄ Men High School Graduates
- ● Women High School Graduates
- ✻ Men with Four-Year Degrees
- ✕ Women with Four-Year Degrees

Annual Earnings (nominal) ($)

Source: U.S. Census Bureau, Current Population Survey, Education and Social Stratifica-
tion Branch, Table A3, "Mean Earnings of Workers 18 Years Old and Over, by Educational
Attainment, Race, Hispanic Origin, and Sex: 1975 to 2001." Press release, March 21, 2003;
available at: www.census.gov/Press-Release/www/date.html.

post-secondary education and training continues to be demanded by both women and men.

As Figure 3.1 shows, women with high school diplomas and even those with some post-secondary education earned far less than did any other group, with the gap between high school-educated women and men widening significantly from the early 1980s on. Women with high school diplomas tend to hold low-paying service-sector jobs, oftentimes at the prevailing minimum wage. In examining the extent to which workers spend significant portions of their careers in minimum wage jobs, Carrington and Fallick conclude that, although the incidence of minimum wage careers is low, it is not insignificant: "Blacks and women are more likely than white males to spend significant portions of their career in minimum wage jobs" but more important, that "the presence of children is positively correlated with minimum wage job holding for women, *but negatively correlated for men.*"[10] Women's childbearing and childrearing responsibilities result in more frequent career interruptions, part-time work, and job changes, resulting in more time spent in entry-level positions. Similarly, Presser and Cox examine the effects of women's responsibilities as mothers on their labor market experiences, and add an interesting perspective to the "Top Ten" tables above. They find that, except for secretaries, receptionists, and other clerical positions, the jobs lower-educated women tend to hold force them to work during nonstandard hours such as evenings and overnights, and nonstandard days such as weekends. Nonstandard work schedules increase mothers' demands for childcare during evenings and weekends, which can be more expensive than daytime childcare.[11] Moreover, Presser and Cox find that low-educated women are working these schedules not by choice, in order to make arrangements with relatives or friends to coordinate childcare, but because of a lack of labor market options. Revisiting Table 3.1, among the top occupations for women with high school diplomas or less, nursing aides and other health care positions often involve evening, weekend, and third-shift work; cashiers, waitresses, cooks, and retail sales jobs often involve evening and weekend work; only clerical positions follow a more first-shift daytime schedule. Therefore, not only are high-school educated women more likely to have "minimum wage careers" because of their greater caretaking roles, but they also have fewer childcare options, given the work schedules of the types of jobs they tend to hold.

Increased educational attainment benefits women as well as men in terms of earnings as well as in job mobility and labor market opportunities. Unfortunately, as Barbara H. Wootton finds, real gains have been made only by college-educated women earning four-year degrees or more.[12] Women with some post-secondary education have made small gains, in the absence of targeted employment and training programs to improve their labor market opportunities. As stated earlier, the "some college" definition not only includes women and men with two-year degrees, but also those with *any* formal post-secondary training. Increasing the amount of training or schooling for women increases their average weekly earnings, but the disparity between women and men remains because women with some college education largely end up in the same occupations anyway. Recall the discussion of human capital theory in the previous chapter. Training and education alone do not resolve pay disparities or occupational segregation by gender because the structures of labor markets remain the same. Whether one is swayed by the segmentation explanation or the gentler assumption that, although a tiered structure may or may not exist, barriers to entry keep certain classes of workers from gaining access to occupations despite their human capital endowments, the empirical evidence suggests that levels of education and training do not dictate labor market outcomes. Appendix Table A.3b features detailed information over the twenty-year period for workers with all levels of educational attainment: high school, some college, and college degree. The top-ten occupational mix changes slightly over time only for college-educated workers, and the changes reflect changes in the economy. For instance, computer-related occupations begin to appear in the list for college-educated men in the late 1980s, as do health care-related occupations such as registered nursing and social work. For college-educated women workers, health care occupations remained their top employers over the twenty-year period, as did education-related occupations. Management and administration jobs are top employers for college-educated women, as well.

It is important to note that, for women, the top-ten list for workers with a high school diploma does not differ much from the "some college" list, suggesting that a policy intervention must do more than just provide skills training; it must also provide placement and retention assistance. Further education and training alone do not appear to alter the patterns of job placement; women tend to hold the same kinds of jobs whether they have pursued further training or not. For instance, some post-secondary schooling allows many women workers to hold positions as registered nurses and as adjusters, but otherwise, the jobs they hold are the same as if they had a high school diploma. Their pay may increase for attaining an advanced certificate or two-year degree, but the jobs working women have access to remain largely the same.[13] For men, some post-secondary education appears to make certain occupations available that were not available to them with only a high school education, including positions as electricians, managers and administrators, and sales supervisors. To transcend barriers to employment in high-wage, high-skilled occupations with upward mobility, any policy intervention must do more than simply provide skills training. Table 3.3 lists the top ten occupations for women and men with some college education, the average hourly earnings in 2000, and the earnings rank of each occupation.

Occupational segregation by gender persists over time for non-college women and men, but the jobs men tend to hold pay better than women's jobs do, as Table 3.3 shows. The average hourly pay rate for all jobs in 2000 was $16.61. Only one of the "women's jobs" earned more than this average, and indeed, three of them were ranked in the bottom 10 percent of all occupations. Out of 427 jobs, eight of the "women's jobs" ranked in the bottom half. Of the ten "men's jobs," four ranked in the top half, three earned more than the overall average, and eight of them averaged more than $10.00 per hour. What is more, at least two of the "men's jobs"—carpenters and electricians—involve highly skilled, apprenticeable work and oftentimes union representation. Moreover, consistent with Presser and Cox, many of the "women's jobs" in Table 3.3 involve nonstandard work schedules, as well.

Summary and Implications for Policy

Women support and raise families either on their own or as parts of dual-earner households, and have long since ceased working for "pin money," if indeed women ever worked for any other reason besides financial support. The previous chapter demonstrated that a bias favoring the four-year path exists, that institutional factors such as unemployment, immigration, collective bargaining, and a tendency toward four-year programs have resulted in the overlooking of alternative education and training programs, and in college graduates' crowding out of non-college workers for jobs that do not require a college degree, This chapter shows that non-college women end up in jobs with lower wages and fewer benefits than non-college men do. Given these various influences, plus the evidence that the inherent justice of the market is slow, if it exists at all, the need for policy intervention is great. Prior analyses have resulted in varying recommendations: Alan Eck's analysis suggested that a policy to reduce skill mismatches ought to increase the skill demands of jobs, not just the skill endowments of workers; in other words, policy ought to intervene to alter the structures of labor markets; to "widen the ladders" and perhaps multiply them.[14] Marlene Kim

Table 3.3

Top Ten Occupations by Percent of Total Employed, for Women and Men with Some College Education, Average Hourly Earnings and Earnings Rank of the Occupation, 2000

	Women			Men		
Top ten occupations by numbers employed	Average hourly earnings, 2001	Earnings rank (out of 427)		Top ten occupations by numbers employed	Average hourly earnings, 2001	Earnings rank (out of 427)
Secretaries	$14.46	255		Truck drivers	$12.96	300
Registered nurses	21.69	119		Electricians	19.81	150
Cashiers	8.26	413		Managers and administrators	32.64	41
Nursing aides and attendants	9.11	399		Sales supervisors	16.59	211
Bookkeepers	11.96	327		Cooks	8.82	406
Receptionists	10.43	369		Laborers, not construction	10.17	378
Waiters and waitresses	3.99[a]	427		Janitors and cleaners	10.25	375
Sales supervisors	16.59	211		Cashiers	8.26	413
Investigators and adjusters (not insurance)	13.28	287		Carpenters	17.28	197
Sales workers	12.52	310		Stock handlers and baggers	10.28	373

Sources: Top occupations were calculated by author's tabulations of Current Population Survey annualized data; average hourly earnings and earnings rankings come from Table 1, "Hourly Earnings of Full-time Workers and Weekly and Annual Work Hours, National Compensation Survey, 2000," in John E. Buckley, "Rankings of Full-time Occupations, by Earnings, 2000," *Monthly Labor Review* (March 2002): 46–61.

[a]Tips are not included in earnings for waiters and waitresses.

and Barbara Wootton recommend altering labor market structures to get women out of the jobs they traditionally hold, to reduce occupational segregation.[15]

The next chapter demonstrates why programs for women in "nontraditional occupations" provide the most interesting and appropriate locus for analyzing programs to provide pathways out of low-wage, low-skilled occupations with few opportunities for advancement. Chapter 4 also describes two employment and training programs targeted toward non-college women, to increase their participation in high-skilled occupations.

Chapter 4

Past and Current Alternative Programs

Evidence of Promise in NTOs

> Women can earn two to three times as much as they can in the
> more traditional fields like clerical or sales . . . occupational
> segregation accounts for most of the reason why women still
> earn 73 cents for every dollar men make. But with the
> population of single mothers growing, women . . . can no
> longer afford to pass up jobs that start as high as $12 an hour,
> to stick to more traditionally "female" careers.
> —*Michelle Simko,* Hard-Hatted Women[1]

The previous chapter demonstrated that non-college women end up in jobs with fewer benefits and less pay than non-college men do, and that these trends in occupational segregation by gender have been accompanied by drastic cuts in post-secondary vocational programs and sex-equity programs. Policy intervention is needed to alter patterns of occupational segregation. This chapter shows that policy interventions targeting nontraditional occupations (NTOs) provide non-college women with high-wage, high-skilled career opportunities because NTOs are linked to higher wages, marketable skills training, and opportunities for advancement.

To train for NTOs *is* to train for higher-wage, highly skilled, non-college careers.

To train for NTOs truly provides a "pathway out" of the low-opportunity jobs non-college women tend to hold. Moreover, this chapter surveys the career counseling literature, which illustrates how such policy interventions can be effective in altering workers' perceptions of their abilities and can allow them to succeed in post-secondary education and training programs. Finally, two post-secondary education and training programs are introduced: Nontraditional Employment for Women (NEW) and Women in Apprenticeships and Nontraditional Occupations (WANTO).

A statistical model is used to determine whether a policy intervention that focuses on women's participation in NTOs provides women with career pathways toward higher-paying, high-skilled, upwardly mobile occupations, by illustrating that NTOs increase women workers' likelihood of earning higher-than-average wages. Therefore, to train women for NTOs is to prepare them for rewarding, remunerative careers. The next section, Job Counseling and Sex-Role Socialization in the Workplace, recalls the predictions of Segmented Labor Market (SLM) theory: policy interventions that fail to address sex-role socialization and labor-demand structures will not alter patterns of occupational segregation. Research in career counseling has addressed sex-role socialization in the workplace, and labor-demand theory addresses demand-side factors. Findings from the career counseling literature lend insight into ways to tackle the insidious messages consciously and unconsciously accepted and furthered by women and men regarding women's work-related abilities. The literature reveals that a woman's career-related self-efficacy can be developed in four ways: performance accomplishment, vicarious experience, verbal persuasion, and addressing physiological states. In many studies, these four activities have been found to alter sex-role socialization in the near term as well as over longer periods of time.[2] Segmented Labor Market theory is less clear about the longer-term impact of policy interventions. Queuing-up processes may remain to exclude women from primary labor markets over the long run. Labor demand theory provides a framework predicting the effects of even small policy interventions that seek to operate on both the supply and demand sides of labor markets. These approaches coupled with findings from career counseling studies provide the means for *explaining* sex segregation in training programs and employment, as well as *identifying* ways to change patterns in both individuals and institutions to increase the numbers of women in male-dominated training programs and jobs over the long run.

This chapter demonstrates why programs for women in "NTOs" provide the most interesting and appropriate locus for analyzing programs to provide pathways out of low-wage, low-skilled occupations that offer few opportunities for advancement.[3] This chapter also describes two employment and training programs targeted toward non-college women to increase their participation in high-skilled occupations, WANTO and NEW, and surveys career counseling best practices that inform the approach taken by them. The goal of WANTO and NEW has been to increase the numbers of women in jobs that do not involve the four-year college career path.

Job Counseling and Sex-Role Socialization in the Workplace

In this section, the best practices of NTO employment and training programs are described through the framework of four activities found to develop career-related self-efficacy, and how these best practices conform to the findings of effective career counseling studies. In addition, this section discusses that, although best practices are known, they are not always parts of employment and training programs. It is important to note, however, that even the best program is no panacea; follow-up retention efforts are as important as placement and training efforts, if not more so. Policies must involve interventions into both sex-segregated training programs and sex-segregated employment processes, and placement initiatives cannot exist without long-term retention. Moreover, low- and middle-income women remain at a far greater risk of not completing NTO courses of study compared to the men in those programs. Training and placement programs for women without continued support services cannot be relied upon to remedy deeply entrenched sex-role socialization and sex discrimination in nontraditional courses of study and workplaces. This chapter concludes with detailed descriptions of WANTO and NEW, and the following chapter contains the statistical analysis that demonstrates the significant and positive impacts of these programs.

Developing Career-Related Self-Efficacy in Women and Program Best Practices

Given the emphasis of academic programs to the exclusion of vocational ones, and the especially harmful implications of this for women's economic self-sufficiency, alternative education and training programs for women are of critical importance. Many studies on career counseling for women have produced evidence that policy interventions work, too.[4] Sex-role socialization and attitudes about women in NTOs present significant barriers to women seeking training and employment in these fields. Segmented Labor Market theory underscores the importance of challenging sex-role socialization in addressing occupational segregation by gender in training programs and employment outcomes. Sex-role socialization is observed even in very young children, which suggests that ideas of what is appropriate for women and men are developed very early.[5] One very important, perhaps the most important, means for tackling sex-role socialization is to empower women and change their own perceptions of their abilities and appropriate roles for women in the workplace, akin to Ray Marshall's predictions of cognitive dissonance in workplace discrimination. Sullivan and Mahalik, studying career-related self-efficacy, found:

> Low career self-efficacy expectations constitute an important psychological barrier to women's choice, performance and persistence in career decision making. Therefore, reducing cognitive barriers for women or more specifically, increasing women's career-related self-efficacy . . . should facilitate women's career development.[6]

The four activities found to help develop career-related self-efficacy, in order of their importance[7] include, focusing on successful performance accomplishments; participating in vicarious/observational learning exercises; addressing physiological states; and finally, receiving verbal persuasion and encouragement.[8] These activities address much of what Haignere and Steinberg classified as "past inequalities" or the culture and socialization leading up to the current state of affairs. Their "future inequalities" refer to workplace discrimination, which placement and retention strategies are designed to address. Focusing on these self-efficacy activities, moreover, is not to imply that it is up to individual women to make changes in order to adapt to the male-dominated workplace. While these activities will help women make fully informed career decisions from a position of high self-efficacy, policies must also address the structures of the labor markets that these women will enter. However, because individuals affect institutions just as institutions affect individuals,[9] these four activities can play a role in ultimately altering the labor markets that these women will enter by changing the women themselves, their employers, and coworkers, and theoretically, the wage structures and supply of workers in the pink-collar jobs they leave behind. Other aspects of policy development and implementation are targeted toward changing labor market institutions specifically. Best practices for employment and training programs are discussed below in terms of these four activities.

Performance Accomplishment

Effective NTO employment and training programs involve hands-on skills training in addition to classroom instruction. Participants in Sullivan and Mahalik's experimental groups shared stories of past accomplishments with peer-group members and conducted other positive self-assessment and goal-setting exercises. Nontraditional employment and training programs with hands-on skills training include shop classes that teach the exact skills a woman will need on the job, whether drilling, welding, or machining. Other forms of direct skills training leading to performance accomplishment include seminars on workplace vocabulary and protocol, tool familiarity and tool identification, strength and fitness training, blueprint reading, and other hands-on activities. Reinforcing accomplishments fosters continued success.

Vicarious or Observational Learning

Vicarious learning to increase career-related self-efficacy is done through mentoring relationships, shadowing, or any other activity that allows a new female entrant into an NTO training program to share and be inspired by the experiences of a female role model. This activity increases self-confidence by providing positive examples for a new trainee or employee to aspire toward. Participants in experimental programs have interviewed and conducted case study analysis on successful women, and observed others in their own groups as they negotiate challenges in their own career development processes. Mentoring and role modeling are significant components in effective NTO programs, and were found to be critical success factors in Idaho's NTO programs.[10] In addition, many programs incorporate long-term links with business and industry to maintain mentoring relationships with women in occupations across firms and fields. Clearly, tradeswomen's advocacy organizations play a critical part in facilitating and maintaining role models and mentoring relationships for women in the trades.

Addressing Physiological States

This is a complex way of stating that women seeking nontraditional career paths need to pay particular attention to and receive specific instruction in stress management techniques, anxiety management, conflict resolution, dealing with discrimination and harassment, and relaxation techniques. Anxiety management also includes addressing math anxiety, which has kept many women away from nontraditional skills training. Negative self-talk and self-defeating thoughts derail women from their objective of developing greater self-efficacy, and these activities help manage negativity. Overcoming these obstacles can involve specific workshops or taking refresher math courses to employ performance accomplishment to address math anxiety. Childcare services, flexible training schedules, and training stipends may also be included under this category; providing financial and childcare resources for women who otherwise could not afford to enroll in training over several weeks and relaxing rigid training schedules address significant sources of stress women must face that most men do not.

Verbal Persuasion and Encouragement

Persuasion and encouragement come in the form of both recruiting women into the trades and maintaining their confidence once they are there. To build confidence from within, women in NTO training programs routinely give and receive verbal feedback and encouragement because they may only rarely receive it on the job.[11] This positive environment goes along with combating the negative self-talk described above, as well as the focus on performance accomplishment. Recall Cora's assertion (Chapter 2) that tradeswomen must receive mentoring throughout their careers.

Effective NTO programs include specific outreach messages to attract women candidates as well; filling information gaps through targeted career counseling and women-specific promotional materials to allow women to make fully informed career decisions play the greatest role in generating interest in nontraditional fields. In this vein, it is very important that program administrators and career counselors maintain a high level of sensitivity to sex bias in educational and outreach materials, as well as in the messages they send themselves. Concerning outreach techniques, in her case study of NTO programs in Oregon and Washington, Barbara Byrd noted their use of career fairs and especially of tradeswomen advocacy groups, which provided "some of the best examples of sophisticated, strategic, ongoing recruitment efforts."[12] Haignere and Steinberg highlighted the following specific outreach messages that focused on women, and the NTO literature consistently underscores how important it is for program administrators and career counselors to use these types of outreach tools: "Women: become an auto mechanic and earn good money; There's no such thing as a man's job; High paying jobs in the skilled trades for women."[13]

Concerning the messages sent by career counselors and program administrators themselves, research has shown that sex-biased information maintains current patterns of sex segregation in training and employment programs. However, the research also shows that, for women clients who are not interested in working or learning in NTO fields, receiving such information from career counselors or NTO program administrators does not alienate them.[14] That is, women and men who heavily favored traditional career choices "rated the counselor as being no less effective when he suggested an NTO than when he suggested a traditional occupation; they were equally willing to work with him in either case."[15] Widespread use of NTO outreach materials and messages, therefore, is not likely to alienate women searching for career guidance, so there is little harm in employing these techniques to generate interest in diverse learning and working opportunities. The cost of abandoning sex stereotypes in career counseling is low or nonexistent, while the cost of perpetuating them is high.

Programs Often Do Not Incorporate These Activities

In their analysis of federally funded programs, Haignere and Steinberg found that although the components of effective programs are well known, federal "guidelines contained many structural barriers both to women's being trained and to the proliferation of NTO training programs."[16] Ironically, although NTO programs and the activities listed above are aimed at changing patterns of discrimination and therefore labor market institutions, the structure of labor market and policymaking institutions can hinder changes by failing to address two important components of employment and training programs: eligibility and accountability measures. For instance, Haignere and Steinberg identified barriers to women's participation related to eligibility requirements and measures of program success, which were both related to federal budget constraints. Affirmative action programs have been eliminated routinely because of the current political reaction to quotas, set-asides, and timetables. Cutbacks in Perkins III demonstrated a political aversion to quotas and sex-equity set-asides. But without such milestones, NTO employment and training policies can and have underserved women. Veteran preference in all federal employment and training programs tends to benefit men because so few veterans are women. Age limits on apprenticeships disproportionately exclude women, and, sometimes, income limits disqualify women if they have been newly divorced or separated and their former spouse's income is included.[17]

Outcome measures in employment and training programs can disproportionately exclude women if job placement is overemphasized. Given federal budget constraints, as already noted, these programs are very small, programs are commonly under pressure to demonstrate their effectiveness, and, for employment and training programs, effectiveness is measured by job placements. Furthermore, given the services that have been shown to benefit women in addition to skills training, childcare, mentoring, transportation, and all the self-efficacy activities described above, women become less attractive as program participants because they are considered costlier by some and take more time to place in jobs, compared to potential male participants. This tension between good and good enough should sound familiar: like employers, NTO program administrators must choose between making the right decision to incorporate more women participants who may involve more costs and time to place in NTOs and the very real, unsympathetic restrictions on time and money imposed by state and federal budgets and the policymakers who make budget decisions each year. Unfortunately, prospective program participants are either underserved or not served at all, given these constraints. Incentives to select men over women for NTO training remain, because of the higher cost of services associated with female participants and the increased amount of time and follow-up activities accompanying placement of women in NTOs.

To Train for NTOs Is to Train for Career Opportunities

Nontradtional Occupations as a Pathway Out

To determine whether NTO training programs are appropriate policy instruments for increasing the likelihood of earning higher wages in higher-skilled jobs, and therefore increasing women's economic self-sufficiency, the following model was estimated using Current Population Survey merged outgoing rotation group (CPS-MORG) data:

P /High Wage/ $= \alpha + \beta_1$ Age $+ \beta_2$ Age Squared $+ \beta_3$ NTO $+ \beta_4$ Race $+ \beta_5$ Ethnicity $+ \beta_6$ Educational Attainment $+ \beta_7$ Marital Status $+ \beta_8$ Year $+ \varepsilon$

The likelihood of falling into the high-wage category is a function of age and its square, whether the worker holds a nontraditional job or not, a worker's race, ethnicity, educational attainment, and marital status, and the survey year. The probability of earning a high wage is defined as 1.25 times median real weekly earnings, and is a function of a worker's age, whether or not they hold an NTO, race, ethnicity, and educational attainment. High wage includes roughly all workers earning near the top one-quarter of median real earnings,[18] and is a dichotomous variable equal to one if the observation earns at least 1.25 times median real earnings and zero otherwise. This definition of high wages is consistent with other analyses.[19] On average, approximately 36.49 percent of all workers are in the high-wage category, about 22.66 percent of female workers fell into the high-wage category, and 50.14 percent of male workers earned at least 1.25 times median real weekly earnings. These are the baseline probabilities against which the results of estimation are compared. Commonly, age is used as a proxy for one's level of experience; older workers have more work experience than younger workers do. Both age and age squared are included to capture the nonlinear effects of age on wages; the oldest workers earn comparatively less than workers in middle age, during peak-earning years. Year-fixed effects and demographic variables are included as controls.

The key coefficient of interest is on the variable "NTO." NTOs for women are defined as those where women comprise 25 percent or less of total employment, and this has been the definition used by the Women's Bureau of the U.S. Department of Labor for more than twenty years.[20] The dichotomous variable "NTO" equals one if the observation holds a job defined as NTO, and zero otherwise. Table 4.1 lists the top thirty NTOs for women by total employment.

Many of these occupations, including those in construction, transportation, the crafts and trades, and public safety occupations, enjoy extensive training involving transferable skills, have union representation, and involve health benefits and pensions. To train women for these occupations is to provide them with opportunities for career advancement and with marketable skills. But, do these occupations afford women better earnings along with skills, employment, and advancement opportunities? The next step is

Table 4.1

Top Thirty NTOs for Women by Total Employment (in thousands) **and Percent Female Employment, 2001**

Occupation	Total employed	Percent female
Operators, fabricators, and laborers	17,698	23.3
Precision production, craft, and repair	14,833	8.7
Construction trades	6,253	2.5
Transportation and material moving occupations	5,638	10.4
Handlers, equipment cleaners, helpers, and laborers	5,326	20.5
Construction trades, except supervisors	5,266	2.4
Mechanics and repairers	4,807	4.9
Mechanics and repairers, except supervisors	4,547	4.7
Motor vehicle operators	4,356	12.2
Precision production occupations	3,641	24.6
Farming, forestry, and fishing	3,245	20.8
Truck drivers	3,156	5.3
Protective service	2,478	20.4
Engineers, architects, and surveyors	2,360	11.6
Engineers	2,122	10.4
Other agricultural and related occupations	2,004	19.1
Freight, stock, and material handlers	2,003	24.1
Vehicle and mobile equipment mechanics and repairers	1,795	1.5
Sales representatives, commodities, except retail	1,511	23.4
Carpenters	1,486	1.7
Sales representatives, mining, manufacturing, and wholesale	1,480	23.7
Related agricultural occupations	1,269	17.8
Laborers, except construction	1,252	21.2
Material moving equipment operators	1,111	4.8
Supervisors	1,076	19.7
Police and detectives	1,066	17.8
Construction laborers	1,024	3.6
Engineering and related technologists and technicians	1,007	21.3
Supervisors	986	2.5
Electrical and electronic equipment repairers	984	11.4

Source: Author's tabulations of Current Population Survey annualized data, 2001.

to determine whether NTOs are also linked to higher earnings. Using the model specified above with CPS-MORG data from 1979 to 1999, the likelihood function is estimated and the results are pressented in Table 4.2.[21]

As Table 4.2 shows, several variations of the model were run. Insofar as the dependent variable is a yes/no variable—either the observation falls into the high-wage category or not—maximum likelihood estimation allows one to determine which of the independent variables increases, decreases, or has no effect on the probability of falling into the high-wage category. Each value

Table 4.2

The Effect of Holding an NTO on a Worker's Probability of Earning at Least 125 Percent of Median Weekly Earnings, Using Weighted Current Population Survey Annualized Data, 1979–1999

	(1) All observations	(2) Women workers	(3) Men workers	(4) All non-college workers	(5) Non-college women	(6) Non-college men
Holding a nontraditional occupation	.3192[a]	.1276[a]	.1551[a]	.2975[a]	.0960[a]	.1429[a]
Demographic control variables included?	Yes	Yes	Yes	Yes	Yes	Yes
Year-fixed effects included?	Yes	Yes	Yes	Yes	Yes	Yes
Number of observations	2,087,525	1,047,386	1,040,139	1,886,793	932,990	953,803

Notes: The effect of holding an NTO on one's probability of earning at least 1.25 times real median weekly earnings = f [age, age squared, NTO, race, ethnicity, educational attainment, marital status, year].

[a]Significant at the 0.01 percent level.

in Table 4.2 is a probability associated with each independent variable on the likelihood of being in the high-wage category, and each is interpreted roughly as a percentage-point change in that likelihood. The key variable of interest here is the NTO independent variable: does holding an NTO increase, decrease, or have no effect on being in the high-wage category, and does this differ for men, women, non-college men, or non-college women? The findings in Table 4.2 indicate that, for all groups, holding an NTO increases the likelihood of falling into the high-wage category. Interestingly, however, holding an NTO increases non-college women's chances of earning higher wages, and this finding is not only statistically significant but also economically significant: because non-college women tend to hold low-wage jobs with fewer opportunities for advancement, as Table 3.3 showed, finding that an NTO significantly increases women's earnings is an important indicator that NTOs represent pathways out of the pink-collar ghetto. These findings are economically significant for another reason: women support families and they need productive careers and career opportunities to do so. In Chapter 7, the reader will meet Tonya, a brick mason, who is well aware of the importance of holding an NTO: "I am not just supporting myself I have two children to think of . . . I have to work harder for them." The reader will also note based on Table 4.2 that the impact of holding an NTO on wages is less for non-college women than it is for all other groups. Figure 3.1 demonstrated that women at all levels of educational attainment earn less than men do, so it should come as no surprise that the magnitude of holding an NTO on non-college women's earnings is less than it is for men and all women workers (some of whom have higher levels of educational attainment and hold nontraditional jobs such as physician and engineer).

The baseline probability of female workers in the high-wage category is 22.66 percent, and the magnitudes of the probabilities listed in Table 4.2 should be compared to this baseline probability to determine whether the impact is "a lot" or "a little." Column (2) indicates that holding an NTO makes all women workers almost 56.31 percent more likely to fall into the high wage category: holding an NTO increases any woman worker's chances of earning higher wages by 12.76 percent, from 22.66 to 35.42, a 56.31 percent increase. These findings simply underscore the fact that NTOs for women pay more than the jobs in which women tend to be concentrated, especially pink-collar ones, because many NTOs are professional positions. However, does holding an NTO increase a non-college worker's chances of earning higher wages as well?

Compared to college graduates, non-college women and men are less likely to fall into the high-wage category because occupations that require post-graduate and professional degrees, including physicians, lawyers, engineers, and many finance industry jobs, which are among the highest-paying occupations. Therefore, the interesting results are found in columns (4) through (6): the positive and statistically significant estimates reveal that holding an NTO increases the likelihood of earning at least 125 percent of median earnings for *non-college* women and men, too.[22] Moreover, because the likelihood of earning high wages is less for women than it is for men, the *magnitude* of the impact of holding an NTO is greater for women than it is for men. The likelihood of any non-college woman falling into the high-wage category is 19.73 percent, which is lower than the 22.66 probability possessed by any woman, regardless of educational attainment. The effect is less for men because at all educational levels men tend to earn more than women do, and men also tend to hold these kinds of jobs to a far greater extent than women do.

Examining the effects of the other independent variables, the results of which are not reported in Table 4.2, also provides interesting evidence of differences between the ways men and women experienced the labor markets over this twenty-year period. Based on the age squared independent variable, for both women and men, the chances of falling into the high-wage category are lower for both very old and very young workers, although the magnitude of the effect is small. There is also a difference between the effects of marital status on the chances of earning higher wages: for men, evidence suggests that being married increases their chances of falling into the high-wage category, but the opposite is true for women, whether they leave the workforce or work part time to assume childcare responsibilities. This holds for the general population as well as for the non-college and college graduate subgroups. Divorced and never-married women may choose to or be compelled to devote more time and energy toward earning higher incomes, compared to married women. Finally, the year-fixed effects differ between women and men, suggesting that women made real wage gains over the twenty-year period compared to men and compared to the overall average. However, these real wage gains are relative to what women earned in the past; women remain less likely to fall into the high-wage category than men are (recall Figure 3.1). For estimates including all observations, coefficients on the year indicator variables are negative, but not all are statistically different from zero. Results are the same using estimates that include men only. Estimates including women only result in positive and statistically significant coefficients on all year-fixed effects, which are robust to changes in the model. This is consistent with other research concluding that women have made real wage gains since the 1970s, particularly college-educated women.

The NTO variable is the key variable of interest in this model. A positive and significant coefficient on this variable indicates that NTOs are also higher-paying occupations. Estimating this model demonstrates that to train for NTOs *is* to train for high-paying, highly skilled occupations. For non-college women, these findings are especially important because policy interventions seeking to increase women's participation in NTOs have received sporadic attention over the years.

The NTO as Locus of Employment and Training Policy

Several government programs have targeted NTOs for women to increase women's economic efficacy. In the early 1980s, the Women in Nontraditional Careers program focused on secondary education curricula and emphasized the increased participation of adolescent girls in vocational programs and math and science classes. In 1981, the Women's Bureau of the U.S. Department of Labor launched the Women in Apprenticeship Training Initiative to increase women's participation in high-wage apprenticeable jobs because "opening apprenticeship opportunities to women has been a major focus in the Women's Bureau for a number of years."[23] This was a one-year program, among other model programs developed by the Bureau, under the Comprehensive Employment and Training Act (CETA). The Bureau also created a model program for employer-sponsored childcare systems, for employers interested in offering childcare.[24] To raise awareness of the effects on women of the change from CETA to the Job Training Partnership Act (JTPA), the Bureau conducted nearly two-dozen workshops entitled "JTPA: Its Implementation and Impact on Women." Within the context of JTPA, the Bureau continued creating model programs, as it had done using the CETA structure. CETA decentralized the provision of employment services from the federal level to state and local governments. JTPA continued this decentralization, but placed a far greater emphasis on private sector involvement in providing training and employment services than did earlier programs. In 1988, the secretary of labor created the Task Force on Women in Nontraditional Jobs in the Aerospace and Construction Industries. That same year, Women's Bureau of the U.S. Department of Labor awarded a grant to an organization in the state of Washington to fund a conference for tradeswomen in Chicago[25] and launched programs with the Employment and Training Administration (ETA) to increase women's employment in highway construction occupations.[26] According to Sharon Harlan, the change to JTPA made women slightly worse off by placing greater importance on the private sector than CETA had; in addition, there were no provisions for targeting women in recruitment, job counseling, individualized needs assessment, or daycare under JTPA.[27] In 1991 and 1992, respectively, two Women's Bureau programs were launched: Nontraditional Employment for Women and Women in Apprenticeships and NTOs. WANTO continues to award grants to non-profit, community-based organizations (CBOs) to assist employers and unions to integrate more women into their ranks. Brigid O'Farrell refers to current NTO employment and training programs as "the third time the government sought to encourage women into nontraditional fields" after World War I and World War II.[28] NTOs have been a focus of employment and training policy for many years.

Given the earlier findings that a focus on NTO training and employment provides opportunities for high-wage, high-skilled occupations and that the majority of the population does not graduate with a college degree, it stands to reason that it would be important to understand the best practices of policy and job counseling interventions. The next section highlights techniques that effectively develop women's senses of empowerment and confidence regarding their career-related decisions and activities.

Women in Apprenticeships and NTOs and Nontraditional Employment for Women as Alternative Paths to Career Preparation

The above statistical analysis demonstrates the link between NTOs and earning higher-than-average wages. NTOs for women also tend to be higher-skilled jobs that afford workers opportunities for advancement. Through education and training programs that target NTOs, women have received additional information on nontraditional jobs and specific training and job search and placement services to help them find a job in skilled trades and some manufacturing fields, beyond what they would have received without these programs. Women in Apprenticeships and NTOs and NEW represent precisely the kinds of education alternatives described throughout this chapter: they are targeted toward women and incorporate many of the self-efficacy and retention practices outlined above. Nontraditional Employment for Women was a four-year demonstration program to get states started on their own NTO programs without continued federal money. While over three-fourths of the states received grants, it is important to recall that the National Coalition for Women and Girls in Education (NCWGE) survey showed how so many of these programs have shrunk or have never really taken off in the first place. Even though WANTO has continued over the years, its small annual appropriation is in jeopardy every year as the federal government looks for ways to reduce spending and minimize budget deficits, despite their lack of politically sensitive quotas, timetables, and set-asides. Both have been administered by the Women's Bureau of the U.S. Department of Labor.

Nontraditional Employment for Women

The Nontraditional Employment for Women Act amended the JTPA, and included funds to be awarded to state governments via competitive grants. The NEW Act's grant program was a four-year, $6 million demonstration program for the purpose of encouraging efforts by the federal, state, and local levels of government aimed at providing a wider range of opportunities for women under JTPA; providing incentives to establish programs that will train, place, and retain women in nontraditional fields; and facilitating coordination between JTPA and other programs to maximize the effectiveness of resources available for training and placing women in nontraditional employment.[29]

Nontraditional Employment for Women expanded JTPA employment and training services, created financial incentives for states to establish such training programs for women via its grant program, and sought to streamline the delivery of services to leverage the resources available for women seeking employment in NTOs.

Nontraditional Employment for Women awarded roughly $6 million over four years to about six grant recipients per year, making the average grant to a state approximately $260,000.[30] Compared to other employment and training programs, NEW awards were fairly modest. Nontrational Employment for Women grants gave states the *incentives* to establish programs but were *not* intended to provide the total amount necessary to operate employment and training programs for women seeking NTOs. Because NEW was intended only as a capacity-building program and limited to four years of funding, the role of *leverage* was key to a successful state's implementation and execution of its own NTO program. Successful state programs leveraged both their modest NEW funds as well as information on demonstration programs.

The NEW program encouraged states to leverage resources by facilitating coordination between JTPA and vocational education initiatives funded by the Perkins Act. Relatively modest NEW grants could benefit women seeking nontraditional employment by drawing on Perkins funds. NEW also promoted leveraging *information* by favoring grantees that offered to produce and distribute materials about their projects so other states might replicate them, and those who showed a high level of private sector involvement in their JTPA activities. The overall goals of NEW were somewhat general, no quotas were set and no specific actions were dictated to grant recipients for meeting these broad objectives, specifically:

> [O]utreach, to develop awareness of, and encourage participation in, education, training services, and work experience programs to assist women in obtaining nontraditional employment, and to facilitate the retention of women in nontraditional employment, including services at the site of training or employment.[31]

The Act did not indicate how many women should be trained, how they should be trained, or the occupations they were to receive training in, other than to state that *women* were to be trained and placed in *NTOs* for women.

The NEW four-year demonstration grant program awarded funds between 1992 and 1996 to twenty-two states. Grant-funded projects covered many employment fields and offered a range of services. For example, the state of Texas's *Project TExAS* included an intense, fourteen-week training program, sexual harassment awareness workshops and job search assistance. The State of Washington provided a nontraditional skills training program with two area military bases and one community college. The state of Ohio used its grant to build a state-level training system, linking the Bureau of Employment Service and the Vocational and Adult Education Division of the State Department of Education. The state of Wisconsin focused on urban areas and increasing women's exposure to potential nontraditional careers. Many grant recipients also published training manuals and handbooks, and some produced training videos.[32]

NEW grants allowed states to build and institutionalize state-level nontraditional training systems for low-income women, who are heads of households in about half of all low-income families. Women are a part of dual-income households in the vast majority of families, as the single-earner male head-of-household structure is increasingly rare. Increasing women's economic efficacy through state training programs will allow them to better provide for their families and transcend barriers to employment in higher-wage, higher-skilled occupations. Without the federal seed monies, low-income women probably would not have received any additional assistance in training for or being placed in an NTO.

Women in Apprenticeships and NTOs Act

Women in Apprenticeships and NTOs awards grants to nonprofit CBOs, not states, and focuses on the needs of employers and unions rather than low-income women. One million dollars per year has been awarded to several grantees per year since 1994 for the purpose of informing employers and labor unions of the availability of technical assistance to help them employ women in NTOs and apprenticeships; providing grants to CBOs to deliver technical assistance to employers and labor unions to help them recruit, train, and retain women in their workplaces; authorizing the Women's Bureau of the Department of Labor to serve as liaison among employers, labor, and CBOs through its national office and regional administrators; conducting a comprehensive study to examine the barriers women experience to their employment in NTOs and apprenticeships, with recommendations to remove these barriers.[33]

Women in Apprenticeships and NTOs helps employers and union organizations that want to recruit, train, and retain women in NTOs in their workplaces.[34] Unlike NEW, which awarded grant monies to states, WANTO funds projects for technical assistance to employers and labor unions, rather than direct skills training to women interested in nontraditional employment. Projects under WANTO have the capacity to reach more women than did the projects under NEW: women targeted for employment in WANTO need not meet any income threshold, monies are actually leveraged by providing the technical assistance to employers and labor unions, which in turn, recruit and hire women, and the grant program has not been limited to a set number of years. Although the methods differ, the objectives of WANTO and NEW are the same: to increase the numbers of women in NTOs.

Through the end of 2001, the WANTO technical assistance grants have awarded over 70 grants, or nearly $8.0 million to nonprofit community-based and union organizations. These grant-funded projects have involved a range of services to employers and labor unions. Wider Opportunities for Women (WOW) in Washington, DC, created and maintains the "Workplace Solutions" Web site, allowing grantees to share information about their projects. Women in Nontraditional Employment Roles in Long Beach, California, provided tradeswomen group support meetings, coordinated a speakers' series, published a monthly newsletter and maintained a job hotline. Century Housing Corporation in Los Angeles provided on-site technical assistance to fifteen employers, five labor unions and more than a dozen apprenticeship programs around the Los Angeles Empowerment Zone project. Northern New England Tradeswomen in Barre, Vermont, developed a one-on-one mentoring program for women hired by participating employers to provide personal support in their first year of employment.

WANTO may represent a greater commitment to increasing the numbers of women hired and retained in nontraditional employment because employers and unions are targeted rather than individual women; it attempts to change the employment structure women face by operating on the labor demand side; WANTO is not scheduled to end, even though it is in constant jeopardy; and the women who benefit from the assistance given to employers and labor unions need not meet any income threshold.

The programmatic differences between WANTO and NEW allow one to examine them from a couple of different theoretical perspectives. On the one hand, as a result of these grant programs women will become new candidates to certain occupations through direct skills training. On the other hand, the grant programs spur employer demand for women in nontraditional employment by providing technical assistance to employers emphasizing the importance of hiring women and reducing levels of sex segregation. Although NEW and WANTO were intended to increase and retain women in NTOs, the Women's Bureau has no enforcement power over unions or employers, and these acts do not include sanctions. Officials on both the national and regional levels believe that encouraging or *spurring demand* for women's labor by firms in target industries engenders better relationships and longer lasting results than an enforcement-and-sanctions environment would; by encouraging certain activities rather than sanctioning undesirable actions, these programs are more "carrot" than "stick." However, as carrots go, these are fairly bland: employers are not given subsidies or tax credits to hire and retain women, either.

These grant programs are explicitly operating on the demand side when they provide technical assistance to employers, while not reducing the costs of hiring via subsidies or tax credits. Indeed, costs to a firm *can* increase. What this also means is that there is a bit of bias in the "sampling" of firms receiving direct technical assistance. Without the mandatory compliance stick or the subsidy carrot, only firms *agreeing* to receive the services of a grantee will actually receive them. Likewise on the supply side, without the stick of mandatory participation, only those women already interested in receiving skills training actually participate. Women are not assigned randomly to NTO training and employment programs, nor are employers and unions required to comply with set hiring and promotion quotas. On one hand, this can result in underserving women seeking NTO employment and in achieving goals too slowly. On the other hand, the lack of quotas and enforcement also helps leverage resources because participants self-select into the program reducing costs of implementation, and it has allowed WANTO and NEW to survive politically hostile times, when affirmative action programs are being eliminated or reduced drastically on both the state and federal levels.

Conclusions and Implications

The statistical analysis in this chapter determined that to train for nontraditional employment is to train women for higher-wage, higher-skilled occupations that provide opportunities for advancement. This chapter also surveyed the career counseling literature, which describes the types of activities needed to engender a sense of workplace self-efficacy, and also introduced WANTO and NEW, which have employed several of these activities.

The next chapter is devoted to measuring the effects of WANTO- and NEW-funded projects on women's participation in NTOs, to determine whether the predictions of the career counseling literature, as well as other best practices, are correct and effective in increasing women's participation in high-wage, high-skilled occupations. The statistical analysis in Chapter 5 uses an innovative econometric model and external data that do not rely strictly on participation data provided by grant recipients. Despite the career counseling literature and evidence of best practices, there are plenty of reasons why these programs should *not* have worked: they are small, involve little funding, and must address the sex-role socialization patterns of training and employment processes: a tall order. However, the surprising result is that these modest grants *did* have an impact on increasing women's employment in NTOs, compared to employment of individuals who did not have access to these programs, including men.

Chapter 5

A Little Goes a Long Way

Statistical Evidence of Small Program Effectiveness

The previous chapter established that employment and training initiatives targeting nontraditional employment are appropriate and relevant foci of analysis, insofar as they train women for high-skilled, high-wage occupations that provide opportunities for advancement. Women in Apprenticeships and Nontraditional Occupations (WANTO) and Nontraditional Employment for Women (NEW), represent the most enduring programs targeting women in nontraditional occupations (NTOs) to date, and they provide the greatest promise for actually altering patterns of occupational segregation by gender. Do they work? This chapter features an innovative statistical technique to gauge the effects of these modest programs, and reveals that, indeed, they have had a positive and significant impact on women's participation in NTOs.

Nontraditional Employment for Women and Women in Apprenticeships and NTO Work

Extremely modest amounts of federal government dollars allowed many women to find their pathway out of the pink-collar ghetto. This very positive note must be tempered with reminders that many issues discussed here were policy priorities several decades ago. The rhetoric and enthusiasm in support of many of these principles are not new at all. These programs involved miniscule amounts of federal funds, yet their outcomes were significant both statistically and in practical terms for the women benefiting from them and for their families. The shame is that the appropriations have *always* been very small, and are in jeopardy every fiscal year. There is one great success story to tell here, and that is the focus of this book, but it is somewhat lessened by the knowledge that if any one of the earlier programs targeting women in NTOs had been sustained and supported over the years, non-college women today would experience even greater economic efficacy and the idea of women in skilled trades would not seem extraordinary at all.

Again, while these results were rather unexpected and remarkable, the government funds involved have been shamefully small and the principles underpinning these policies are not new at all. This book should have been written decades ago, but *it could not have been* because none of the earlier initiatives to increase the numbers of women in NTOs were allowed to stick around long enough to make an impact. The earliest systematic initiatives not involving war emergencies were implemented in the late 1970s.[1] The Reagan Administration zeroed out or cut deeply most if not all of whatever was left, and nothing new was funded on the federal level throughout the 1980s.[2] As Robert Glover observes, "Just as the campaign to place women into apprenticeships was beginning to show results, it was wiped out."[3] The emphasis during the 1980s was largely on women business owners, who clearly are not among the population of interest here. Nontraditional Employment for Women and WANTO, developed and financed in the early 1990s, involved *tiny* amounts of money, less than one percent of the Bureau's budget, and they were nevertheless in constant jeopardy of being cut or zeroed out. That they lasted as long as they have—NEW completed its four-year run as planned, and WANTO hobbles along yet today—could have been less a deliberate act and more a function of the growing economy during the mid- and late 1990s. Whether the federal government chooses to sustain this initiative remains to be seen. It is not clear whether prevailing public sentiment perceives sex-segregated employment patterns as a responsibility of government or just an outcome of market forces.

The previous chapter provided the framework for determining what ought to be in any policy designed to address sex-role socialization in employment and training institutions. Before examining the features of WANTO and NEW in detail, it is necessary to determine whether these programs were successful: did they increase the numbers of women in NTOs, or not? Based on a before-and-after comparison of the populations targeted by these programs compared to the populations that were not, this chapter illustrates that these programs have a positive and significant impact on women's employment in NTOs. Women who had access to the projects funded by WANTO and NEW were *from 5 to 15 percent more likely* to get a job in a nontraditional field, compared to women who did not have access to these training programs. Granted, the likelihood of a woman holding a nontraditional job has always been fairly low to begin with, but the statistically significant impact attributed to the presence of these employment and training programs is remarkable as well, especially given the size of the programs. How can this statement be made?

Measuring the Effects of Policy Intervention: Difference-in-Differences Methodology

Given the evidence that women are restricted from certain occupations, given this study's objective to evaluate programs that seek to redress the issue of women's limited participation in certain occupations, and given the lack of longitudinal data on participants, how can the effects of these policies be measured? Several analyses of this type have demonstrated the effectiveness of a before-and-after model as a very simple and elegant statistical method to assess policy effectiveness. Economists have frequently employed the technique called the "difference-in-differences" estimator to determine the impact of policies in several fields, including employment policy,[4] health care,[5] tax policy,[6] and the effects of policy by gender and race.[7]

This model is similar to simple before-and-after evaluation techniques, similar to Cook and Campbell's "Untreated Control Group Design with Pretest and Posttest."[8] Information is gathered before and after an intervention, and by controlling for relevant external factors, the difference between the before and after data can be attributed to the intervention: whether this is a policy or an unanticipated exogenous shock such as that illustrated by the Mariel boatlift, which is what David Card analyzed when he introduced the technique in 1990.[9]

The key to conducting this type of analysis is to isolate a very specific treatment, an *exogenous* policy intervention executed at a *discrete* period of time targeted to an *identifiable* population. This chapter estimates the effects of policy intervention on the employment of women in NTOs. Daniel S. Hamermesh describes three conditions for employing difference estimators to measure the impacts of policy interventions:

> Time 1 must be sufficiently before Time 2 that group T did not adjust to the treatment before Time 1, otherwise (the difference) will not reflect the effect of the treatment. Time 2 must be sufficiently after Time P to allow the treatment's effects to be fully felt.
>
> We must be sure that the same difference . . . would have been observed at Time 2 if the treatment had not been imposed, that is, C must be such a good control that there is no need to adjust the differences for factors other than the treatment that might have caused them to change.[10]

Hamermesh emphasizes the first condition when analyzing policy changes, that the "before" period must truly be prior to a change and prior to any anticipatory behavior changes by the target populations. He notes that "laws do not just happen . . . they are discussed at great length prior to their enactment, and they are often preprogrammed years in advance of their effective dates."[11] For example, welfare reform, the Personal Responsibilities and Work Opportunities Act (PRWOA) of 1996 was debated for months and received a great deal of public attention, and it is easy to imagine that the target population, people on welfare rolls, could have changed their behaviors in anticipation of the actual law change by taking jobs, moving in with relatives to reduce expenses, or making any other change in anticipation of losing their benefits. In this example, if PRWOA was enacted in the middle of 1996, taking a snapshot of welfare recipients in May of that year would not produce a true picture of the "before" state because this policy was very publicly debated for many months leading up to its enactment. Continuing with the example, if a snapshot of welfare recipients were then taken in August of 1996, it probably would not be a true picture of the "after" state because many PRWOA provisions were phased in over time. The difference between the before and after states, if any, could not be attributed to welfare reform. Moreover, the control group must indeed be a control, none of the differences experienced between time one and time two would be the result of the treatment.

Three Features of the Women in Apprenticeships and NTO and Nontraditional Employment for Women Grant Programs for "Differences" Estimation

Projects funded by WANTO and NEW are exogenous, they target an identifiable population and are implemented at an observable point in time, and the data exist to allow one to properly define all three. This makes the difference-in-differences approach viable to estimate the effects of WANTO and NEW.

One feature of NEW- and WANTO-funded projects is that the training and education provided lasts generally anywhere from several days to a couple of months. Therefore, once the program is operating in an area, clients can receive training and job placement fairly quickly, particularly in a strong economy. The impact of projects funded by these grants would be almost immediate; it is felt in the short term, not several years hence. If the grants make a difference, then the effect should be felt sooner rather than later. Moreover, WANTO and NEW grants are one-year awards. Grant monies must be spent within the year of award, and final reports must be submitted to the Women's Bureau offices in Washington, DC; therefore, equating the year of grant award with the year of project implementation is quite appropriate. Because grant-funded projects were very small and very narrowly focused on delivering services to women and employers and unions, the policy interventions represented by WANTO and NEW funds were small and narrow enough to be considered discrete policy interventions targeting a specific population.

A second feature of these programs is the flexibility they allow in implementing grant-funded projects. Grantees can provide direct technical assistance to employers, or direct hands-on training to female job candidates, or take other approaches to achieving the stated goals of WANTO and NEW. However, this flexibility confounds a priori expectations when effects on wages are estimated, the influx of women into certain occupations could cause the supply curve, the supply of workers to that occupation, to shift out and exert downward pressure on wages, or training programs could increase the number of women interested in an occupation and cause the demand curve to shift out, exerting upward pressure on wages. Or, a combination of both forces could result in ambiguous net effects on wages, insofar as several projects operating at once could have offsetting effects on demand and supply factors influencing wages in these NTOs.

Third, although WANTO and NEW were the result of legislation, and "laws do not just happen" they can be considered exogenous for several reasons. The programs, always very small, did not receive the high-profile public attention that PRWOA did. It is not reasonable to expect that significant numbers of women became interested in NTOs before the projects were implemented. Moreover, it is unreasonable to argue that, in anticipation of the passage of these two programs, employers and unions began recruiting, training, and hiring women. Sanctions were not parts of WANTO or NEW, so employers and unions had no incentive to comply with these laws before they were passed, which would not be the case with welfare recipients anticipating the elimination of their benefits. Without anticipatory behavior changes, however, it is acceptable to interpret enactment of the NEW and WANTO grant programs as exogenous events, albeit not natural experiments.[12] However, Hamermesh suggests that the analysis of policy is actually more interesting and useful than the study of purely natural phenomena, as there is a greater degree of "human control" over policy.[13] A greater understanding of the things we choose to do is more beneficial than a greater understanding of past random events, which by definition, cannot be anticipated again. Finally, this analysis employs difference-in-differences estimation using lots of little interventions or treatments instead of one big intervention, which is unlike the applications of this technique to date. Successfully employing the technique in this way could make it available for examining the implementation of numerous, block-granted, and small projects, which is often more realistic in policy analysis.

For these three reasons, use of the differences estimator is appropriate to addressing the questions at hand. The model had to define three key variables: the two grant programs are exogenous in the practical sense, the implementation period is discrete, and the target population is identifiable. The question that this estimation answers is, "What is the effect of WANTO and NEW grant projects on women in the areas where they were implemented, compared to those same women before these services became available, to women in areas who did not have access to them, and compared to men overall?"[14]

The Model and the Data

"Double" difference-in-differences estimation measures the impact of an intervention, or a treatment, using two factors, before/after, control/treatment. In this case, the before-and-after comparison would be between a control group and an experimental group.

In the present analysis, employment of women in NTOs is gauged before and after the implementation of a grant-funded project, which is a discrete intervention applied to a well-defined area; and differences between women's levels of employment before and after are compared, holding constant the effects of the economy overall by using never-treated areas and male worker as controls. The basic model is as follows:

$$Y_{iat} = \alpha (X_{iat}) + \gamma 1(T_{iat}) + \gamma 2(A_{iat}) + \gamma 3(F_{iat}) + \gamma 4(T_{iat} A_{iat}) +$$
$$\gamma 5(T_{iat} F_{iat)} + \gamma 6(A_{iat} F_{iat}) + \gamma 7(T_{iat} A_{iat} F_{iat}) + \varepsilon. \qquad [1]$$

Where i is an individual, a is an area, and t is time: before and after treatment (T). Y equals one if the individual observation represents the intended effect of the policy intervention, and zero if not. A vector of demographic data on individuals in both treatment and nontreatment areas is also included and is depicted by X. Like Y, the variables A F and T are dummy variables: Treatment (T) denotes whether the observation is in the treatment area. After (A) denotes whether the observation is after the treatment in time, and Female (F) indicates whether the observation is an individual targeted by the policy intervention, in the case women.

To examine WANTO and NEW, a modified version of the basic model was used because, unlike in the above example, there was not one year when these programs became effective in an area, and treatment areas were located throughout the country. The treatments, or policy interventions, took place at different points in time as WANTO and NEW grants were awarded and grantees implemented their projects. The grant-funded projects were specific enough, however, to permit use of the difference estimator: the implementation of a $50,000 project in Augusta, Maine would not have influenced women's NTO employment in, say, Washington, DC. The modified version of the model is as follows:

$$Y_{iat} = \alpha (X_{iat}) + \gamma 1(T_{iat}) + \gamma 2(A_{iat}) + \gamma 3(F_{iat}) + \gamma 4(T_{iat} A_{iat}) +$$
$$\gamma 5(T_{iat} F_{iat}) + \varepsilon \qquad [2]$$

Where X is a vector of demographic variables, Y is equal to one if the individual is in a job defined as an NTO for women, and zero if not. T equals one if the observation is located in a geographic area where a grant-funded project was implemented and zero if not; A equals one if the observation is located in one of the treatment areas, after treatment, and zero otherwise. Therefore, A always equals zero for observations in never-treated areas. The interaction of A and T causes this variable to equal zero for all observations except those in treatment areas, after treatment, allowing one to focus on individuals in treatment areas after the implementation of a WANTO or NEW project. Female (F) denotes whether the observation is female, the population of interest. F equals one if the observation is female and zero if male. Because A implies T (all observations for which A equals one already has T equal to one) the variables $(A_{iat}\ T_{iat})$ and $(A_{iat}\ T_{iat}\ F_{iat})$ are unnecessary and in fact undesirable, as they would introduce redundancy into the model. Therefore, $(A_{iat}\ F_{iat})$ is the key variable of interest, as this interaction term equals zero for all observations except those for women in treatment areas, after treatment. Gamma 5 (γ_5) is therefore the coefficient of interest in Equation 2, and captures the effect of a WANTO or NEW project on the probability of holding an NTO for women in treatment areas, after treatment. A positive sign on γ_5 would indicate that, after implementation of a NEW or WANTO project, women were more likely to hold an NTO. A statistically significant and positive sign on γ_5 would indicate that the increase in employment was not due to chance alone.

Both "double" and "triple" differences estimators can be used to gauge the effect of a treatment. Equations 1 and 2 are triple-differences estimators: Three "things" are interacted to capture the effects of an event. In the present study, a double-differences estimator was also used with a sample of women only and so did not include the Female variable (the "third thing"). Equation 3 below is the basic double-differences model, and because the sample is comprised of women only, γ_3 captures the effect of holding an NTO in treatment areas after treatment:

$$Y_{iat} = \alpha\,(X_{iat}) + \gamma 1(T_{iat}) + \gamma 2(A_{iat}) + \gamma 3(A_{iat}T_{iat}) + \varepsilon \qquad [3]$$

This would be fine, except if a positive impact of policy were found (a positive and statistically significant γ_3); could one be certain that it was the effect of policy, or something else that happened to expand employment opportunities of all women, or all treatment areas? Including men in the sample allows one to control for local labor market dynamics in the treatment areas. The triple-differences estimator is used with a sample of women and men and, by doing so, captures the effect of policy on employment outcomes for women in treatment areas after treatment compared to men and women in never-treated areas, men and women in treated areas before treatment, *and* men in treated areas after treatment.

Finally, several other variables were defined and included in the model. Appendix 5A describes all the variables in detail. Like most difference-in-differences analyses, this study uses Current Population Survey-merged outgoing rotation group (CPS-MORG) data.[15] As in previous chapters, to ensure against double counting, estimations using even and odd years were conducted.[16]

Treatment areas are located throughout the United States, in heavily unionized states and industrialized urban areas like Chicago, Philadelphia, Los Angeles, and Boston, in so-called "right to work" states like Texas, and in rural areas in West Virginia, Montana, and Vermont (variable means in Table 5.1 for treatment and nontreatment areas indicate that the two do not differ, except for the implementation of a grant-funded project). WANTO and NEW funded projects have operated in urban and rural settings across the United States.

The means in Table 5.1 reveal noteworthy comparisons. Over the entire period, the sample is roughly divided evenly between women (49.04 percent) and men (50.96 percent). Mean weekly earnings over the period for men were $635.27, or about $33,000 per fifty-two-week year, while women's earnings were $432.50, or roughly $22,500 per year. The earnings differences between women and men were consistent across subpopulations, as well. An earnings gap was found among women and men in treatment versus nontreatment areas and among women and men in NTOs versus occupations not defined as NTOs. This consistency allows one to be more confident that the treatment and nontreatment areas do not differ in significant ways other than in receiving a WANTO or NEW grant. A difference-of-means test confirms this; therefore, policy impacts cannot be explained by differences in the economic and social contexts in which the grant-funded projects were implemented. Similarly, although the gap between male and female earnings was narrower in NTOs compared to occupations not defined as NTOs, there was still a gap.

Therefore, the group of occupations defined as nontraditional for women does not substantially differ from those not defined as NTOs, other than being higher paying across the board. For women over the entire period, NTOs are 21.5 percent higher paying than occupations not defined as NTOs, while for men, NTOs pay about 9.7 percent less on average over the entire ten-year period. Similarly, the mean number of weekly hours is consistent across occupation types: NTOs tend to be in the construction and manufacturing industries, while occupations not defined as NTOs tend to be in services.

Another comparison worth noting is the difference between the overall percentages of divorced women versus divorced men. The survey question

Table 5.1

Means for Selected Variables Using Weighted Current Population Survey Merged Outgoing Rotation Group Data, 1990–1999

	N	Weekly earnings ($)	Usual weekly hours	High school diploma (%)	Four-year degree (%)	Hispanic (%)	Black (%)	Married (%)	Divorced (%)
Entire sample	1,132,173	538.36	38.7	32.21	18.23	2.78	12.45	56.61	14.66
Men	576,984	635.27	41.1	31.41	18.25	2.87	11.17	60.22	10.06
Women	555,189	432.50	36.2	33.09	18.21	2.67	13.85	52.67	19.68
Treatment areas	382,330	551.27	38.6	31.20	18.82	3.17	8.42	56.33	14.42
Men	197,159	647.18	40.7	30.27	18.83	3.29	7.64	59.69	10.03
Women	185,171	444.47	36.0	32.24	18.80	3.04	9.29	52.60	19.31
Nontreatment areas	749,843	531.46	38.8	32.75	17.92	2.57	14.60	56.76	14.79
Men	379,825	628.82	41.2	32.03	17.94	2.65	13.08	60.51	10.07
Women	370,018	426.18	36.3	33.54	17.90	2.48	16.25	52.70	19.88
Nontraditional occupations (NTOs)	241,918	593.00	41.7	40.29	10.59	3.20	10.95	62.88	12.23
Men	220,759	599.52	41.9	40.78	10.23	3.23	10.69	64.12	11.28
Women	21,159	520.72	39.7	34.86	14.45	2.86	13.80	49.22	22.67
Treatment areas	7,046	553.36	39.6	32.48	15.59	3.35	8.72	49.80	22.42
Before treatment	4,310	509.25	39.4	35.14	14.17	3.92	8.05	49.59	22.58
After treatment	2,736	609.84	39.9	29.07	17.41	2.62	9.57	50.06	22.21
Nontreatment areas	14,113	503.41	39.8	36.13	13.84	2.60	16.49	48.91	22.80
Non-NTOs	890,255	522.94	37.9	29.93	20.39	2.66	12.87	54.84	15.34
Men	356,225	657.81	40.6	25.50	23.31	2.65	11.47	57.77	9.28
Women	534,030	428.96	36.0	33.02	18.36	2.67	13.85	52.80	19.57
Treatment areas	178,125	440.09	35.8	32.23	18.93	3.02	9.32	52.71	19.19
Before treatment	112,304	410.83	35.7	33.96	17.76	3.56	8.40	52.81	19.07
After treatment	65,821	482.22	36.0	29.73	20.60	2.26	10.64	52.57	19.35
Never-treated areas	55,905	423.10	36.1	33.43	18.06	2.48	16.24	52.85	19.76

Source: Author's tabulations of Current Population Survey annualized data, 1990–99.

asks whether the respondent or other household member is currently divorced, never divorced, or married (including if a person remarries). Divorced women comprise 19.68 percent of all working women, a percentage nearly twice that for working men (10.06 percent). This difference is consistent in all the subgroups shown in the table: women and men in treatment areas versus nontreatment areas and in NTOs versus occupations not defined as NTOs, which may indicate that more women may be heads of households with dependents—primary economic providers—because women are more likely to gain custody of children in a divorce than was anticipated originally.

Finally, these averages demonstrate the differences between women in NTOs in treatment areas, before and after treatment, and women in NTOs in never-treated areas. Weekly earnings for NTO women in treatment areas over the entire period are, on average, $553.36, or about $28,800 per 52-week year. This is, on average, nearly 10 percent higher than weekly earnings for women in the same occupations, yet in never-treated areas over the period. But, this simple comparison is not enough to state that the difference is because of the presence of WANTO and NEW projects. This is where the statistical technique comes in.

Basic Results

Employment Effects

First, the effects on employment are analyzed. Again, the double-differences model estimates the likelihood of being in an NTO, given that one is female and in a treatment area, after treatment, compared to the probability of holding an NTO before policy intervention or where no policy intervention takes place. The triple-differences model estimates the probability of a woman in a treatment area after treatment holding an NTO, compared to that of women and men in treatment areas before treatment, of women and men in never-treated areas, and men in treated areas after treatment.

Table 5.2 shows results for both the double- and triple-differences models, as well as two definitions of "after treatment"; t-statistics appear italicized and in parentheses below each coefficient. The double-differences estimator is simply the model run with women only. Results from the triple-differences model are of greatest interest to control for economic changes during the period that may have affected men and women differently. All regression equations are found in Appendix 5B.

From the baseline probability of having a job that is an NTO ($p/Y^*/=1$) at the means or modes of all the independent variables, the increased probability

due to being in a treatment area after treatment represents from a 5–15 percent increase in a woman's chances of holding an NTO, all other things being equal and depending upon the model specification. Column (1) shows
the results from estimating the probability of being in an NTO for three groups:
women in areas where NEW and WANTO programs were implemented, after they had been implemented; women in areas where programs were implemented, but before they were implemented; and women in areas with no
such programs available. Calculating from the baseline probability at the
means, this 0.00219 percentage point change represents about a 5 percent
increase in the likelihood of holding an NTO. The positive sign on the coefficient for γ_3 indicates that women with access to NEW or WANTO programs were more likely to hold better-paying nontraditional jobs after these
programs were implemented compared to women who did not have access
to these programs. The coefficient is statistically significant at the 90 percent level, so this effect cannot be attributed to chance alone. Column (2)
shows the results when demographic characteristics like educational attainment, age, and marital status are included in the model, and the findings of
an increase in the likelihood of a woman holding an NTO are not changed by
the inclusion of these demographic variables: the direction of the sign and
the statistical significance do not change.

The triple-differences model does a better job of explaining the likelihood
of a woman holding an NTO than does the double-differences model.[17] Columns (5) and (6) show that the magnitude of the policy impact is greater
when men are included, because the values of the coefficients are much larger
in the triple-differences model. Again, calculating from the baseline probability of holding an NTO at the means of the independent variables, the
0.018228 point change (Column 6) represents about a 15 percent increase in
the likelihood that a woman holds an NTO after program implementation.
Impacts using the triple-differences estimator are three times the impacts
found from the double-differences model.

Interestingly, when men were included in the sample, the effect on women's
increased employment in these occupations is more pronounced than when
employment outcomes for women were compared to those of other women
only. A clue into the potential source of this dramatic difference may be found
in the T and A coefficients (in Equation 2, γ_1 and γ_2, respectively—not reported
here). Although the probability estimates of After are not statistically significant, those of Treatment are statistically significant and *negative*. That is, the
probability of all workers holding an NTO in treatment areas is less than that of
nontreatment areas. Men were apparently less likely to obtain employment in
these jobs between 1990 and 1999. One could speculate that total employment, in some NTOs at least, was on the decline during the period.

Table 5.2

Effects of Women in Apprenticeships and Nontraditional Occupations and Nontraditional Employment for Women Grants on Employment in Nontraditional Occupations, using Weighted Data, 1990–1999 (t-statistics)

	Women workers only				Working women and men			
	(1)	(2)	(3)	(4)	(5)	(6)	(7)	(8)
Women after treatment vs. other women	.0022[a] (2.18)	.0025[b] (2.55)						
Women after treatment vs. all men and all other women					.0165[b] (5.41)	.0182[b] (6.09)		
Women after treatment vs. women in never-treated areas or before treatment (by number of years after treatment):								
1			-.0006 (-0.29)	-.0005 (-0.25)				
2			-.0001 (-0.05)	.0002 (0.11)				
3			.0003 (0.12)	.0006 (0.30)				
4			.0023 (0.98)	.0027 (1.19)				
5			.0059 (2.25)	.0065 (2.50)				
6			.0077 (2.55)	.0087 (2.92)				
7			.0028 (0.68)	.0035 (0.86)				

	1	2	3	4	5	6	7	8
Testing the null hypothesis of no effect:		(13.85)		(16.72)				
Testing whether parsing out matters:		(13.70)		(16.41)				
Women after treatment vs. men after treatment, men and women in never-treated areas or men and women before treatment (by number of years after treatment):								
1							.0031 (0.47)	.0043 (0.65)
2							.0049 (0.69)	.0046 (0.66)
3							.0088 (1.24)	.0094 (1.35)
4							.0158 (2.06)	.0156 (2.11)
5							.0253 (2.94)	.0266 (3.14)
6							.0284 (2.93)	.0330 (3.44)
7							.0064 (0.48)	.0103 (0.79)
Testing the null hypothesis of no effect:							(13.16)	(15.93)
Testing whether parsing-out matters:							(13.16)	(15.90)
Demographic characteristics	no	yes	no	yes	no	yes	no	yes
Indicators for years 1991–99	yes	yes	yes	yes	yes	yes	yes	yes
Number of observations	555,189	555,189	555,189	555,189	1,132,173	1,132,173	1,132,173	1,132,173

Note: $P |NTO| = f$ [Treatment Area, After Treatment, Demographic Characteristics (Female, Black, Hispanic, Married, Divorced, High School Diploma, Some College, College Degree, Grad. Degree, Age), 91–99].

[a]Significant at the 0.05 percent level.
[b]Significant at the 0.01 percent level.

From these basic results using the simple definition of the post-treatment period, one can conclude that the WANTO and NEW grant programs had statistically significant effects of considerable size on raising the numbers of women in NTOs. More important, these results are economically significant: women participating in WANTO and NEW programs were trained for and placed in NTOs, which we know from Chapter 4 provide higher wages and more opportunities for career advancement. Children and families rely on women's earnings and their careers over the long term. WANTO and NEW made real changes to the lives of non-college working women and their families.

Parsing out the Post-Treatment Period

Columns (3) and (7) contain results from using a more detailed definition of the post-treatment period where the effects of policy intervention are measured each year for the seven years after treatment. Column (3) shows that, after slightly negative effects in the first two years after treatment, there are positive effects on women's employment in NTOs and annual increases in magnitude; years five and six show the largest positive impacts, and these results are statistically significant. Each year after the policy intervention, women in post-treatment areas are more and more likely to hold NTOs than are other women.

The first value below the seven coefficients, 13.85, is the F-test result of jointly testing whether or not these seven coefficients are actually equal to zero, although their respective t-statistics betray its findings. The p-value associated with the F-test result is 0.0540, indicating that the null hypothesis can be rejected at the 10 percent level of significance. Therefore, the overall increase in the probability that a woman holds an NTO after treatment is statistically different from zero at least a 90 percent level of confidence. The second value below the seven coefficients, 13.70, is the F-test result of jointly testing whether the coefficients are in the statistical sense equal to one another. That is, this tests whether anything is gained by parsing out the post-treatment period and estimating effects for each of seven years. The p-value associated with this F-test result is 0.0331. With at least 95 percent confidence, one can conclude that the seven coefficients are statistically different, and we therefore improve the analysis by separating the post-treatment period by the number of years after treatment. Both F-test results are always displayed in parentheses but not italics, to differentiate them from the t-statistics shown below the individual coefficients.

Column (7) contains results from estimating triple differences and shows that, when men are included as control groups against which the women are compared, the effect of these grant-funded projects is to increase the chances that a woman will hold a job defined as an NTO. These estimates remain positive for every year after implementation of a grant-funded project, with statistically significant estimates in years four, five, and six. The F-test of the null hypothesis indicates whether these seven estimates are, jointly, no different from zero. The result of testing the null hypothesis of no effect is 13.16, with a p-value of 0.0682. Therefore, the null hypothesis can be rejected at least at the 10 percent level of significance. Estimates from both equations (3) and (7) in Appendix 5B suggest that the effects of these grant-funded projects are not temporary. Finally, Columns (2), (4), (6), and (8) contain results similar to those in columns (1), (3), (5), and (7), except that the former include controls for demographic characteristics, while the latter do not.

Effects on Earnings and Hours

Second, the effects of policy intervention on earnings are estimated, compared to cases when no such policy intervention takes place or before it has taken place. The regression results on earnings were not robust to changes in the model: signs on coefficients changed with minor changes to the model, and none of the results approached even generous levels of statistical significance. Similarly, the regression results on hours were neither robust nor statistically different from zero. The estimates for effects on hours would reveal any tradeoffs between employment and hours in NTOs , that is, the grant-funded projects may have achieved the expressed goal of increasing the *numbers* of women hired and retained in nontraditional employment, yet they may also have reduced the number of hours worked by incumbent women workers. The results do not indicate an effect one way or another, because these results are all statistically insignificant. By increasing employment of women in NTOs, the objectives of WANTO and NEW would be met, but finding evidence of reduced hours would undermine these objectives.

It is important to determine whether such tradeoffs occurred. The Department of Labor's Office of Federal Contract Compliance Programs (OFCCP) requires federal contractors, as a condition of having a federal contract, to engage in a self-analysis for the purpose of discovering any barriers to equal employment opportunity. OFCCP has established the standard that women must work at least 6.9 percent of the total hours worked on construction mega-projects, which have figured prominently in WANTO-funded projects. Although estimating the effects of grant-funded projects on usual weekly hours would provide important insight into the real effects of these grant programs on new and incumbent workers, it appears that this model does not allow one to measure these effects, the lack of a significant result might mean there were no effects on hours, but model identification problems are more likely the cause.

Threats to the Validity of These Findings

Do participants in these grant-funded projects differ from nonparticipants in a systematic way, that is, are the differences more than just whether they participated or not? If so, then there is a problem of self-selection, which may confound the conclusions of this analysis. In a working paper that is important here, Heckman, Ichimura, Smith, and Todd address self-selection bias in applications of the difference estimator.[18] They also detail explicit criteria for effectively utilizing this model. For nonmandatory programs, there are some who elect to participate and some who do not. Estimates will be biased if the difference between the two groups is systematic and not captured by use of a control group. If outcomes from nonparticipants systematically differ from participant outcomes in ways not attributable to the program, results will be biased. Isolating self-selection bias is essential to evaluation research because randomized experiments are rare, often due to cost considerations.

The authors use nonexperimental Job Training Partnership Act (JTPA) data with experimental data from the National JTPA Study (NJS), a randomized, controlled experiment involving individuals eligible for this program. Their objective was to determine which of three model specifications best controlled for self-selection bias by comparing estimates from the three models using experimental and nonexperimental data. The first type of estimator was the "index-sufficient" model, which was weighted by one's probability of being selected to participate. The second type was a matching model, where pairs of nonparticipants and participants were matched according to their probability of being selected into the sample. Differences between matched pairs represented the effect of the program. The third type of model was the difference-in-differences estimator. Both a nonweighted and a weighted model were run, as weighted by the probability of selection. For all three specifications, the authors assume that the probability of participation remained constant over time. That is, the distribution of bias did not change over time. The results that were closest to those using experimental data were considered more effective in controlling self-selection bias.

The authors find that the best estimator for mitigating self-selection bias was the difference-in-differences model weighted by the probability of program participation. Concerning the calculation of probability itself, the authors observe the importance of labor force transitions as a variable because it appeared that many participants used such programs as job search vehicles. In addition, adding these transition variables as covariates also captured selection bias. One major finding of this paper is the observation that labor force transition variables are important for determining the probability of program participation. Finally, the authors describe three criteria for arriving at the most efficient estimates when using nonexperimental data in which self-selection bias is an issue. First, nonparticipants must be located in the same labor markets as participants. Second, the same questionnaire must be administered to both groups; and third, information on recent labor force histories must be comparable for both groups. The authors refer to the third criteria as "common supports," the control and treatment groups must possess comparable characteristics. Adhering to these three criteria and using the difference-in-differences model weighted by the probability of participation or controlling for covariates that explain the probability of participation mitigates self-selection bias. This is especially important to education and job training programs, as these programs are rarely experimental, and the authors focused on JTPA, to which NEW and WANTO are amendments. The authors conclude, "Since the JTPA program we consider is typical of a variety of training programs in place around the world, the lessons from our study apply more generally."[19]

Heckman and Smith also tackle selection bias in the difference-in-differences model.[20] The authors extended their findings and employed a difference-in-differences model to estimate the effects of participating in JTPA on different demographic groups. Again, they use nonexperimental data from JTPA participants and experimental data from the NJS to determine the probability that participation will decrease self-selection bias.

Heckman, Ichimura, Smith, and Todd recognize the importance of weighting the difference estimator by the probability of participating in the JTPA program. They also acknowledge that in weighting the model, earnings were not critical, but rather, labor force history was because participation in these programs often served as a job search. Similarly, these authors compare estimates using NJS experimental data with those using JTPA nonexperimental data, and control for covariates such as age, schooling, marital status, and family income. They discover that an important factor in calculating the probability of participation for adult men is labor force dynamics, including unemployment. The key factor for adult women is family status dynamics: "The effect is especially strong for adult women for whom training programs often provide a bridge back into the labor force following divorce."[21] These studies are consistent with analyses discussed in the previous chapter, which underscore the importance of labor market institutions such as unemployment and the minimum wage, and reproductive factors such as childcare and childrearing. However, in Heckman and Smith, the results are statistically significant only for adult men, and not for adult women or youths. In sum, it remains unclear after this study whether controlling for covariates or weighting the model by probability of participation matters when exploring effects for groups other than adult men.

Although the self-selection bias these authors seek to offset is that among individuals and not treatment areas, their findings provide good information for this analysis insofar as women are not forced to participate in these training programs, nor are the data experimental. Including controls for demographic characteristics may help control self-selection bias among women voluntarily participating in grant-funded projects and communities voluntarily competing for grant monies, as well.

Including the control variables supplies information about labor force history and may help to mitigate problems of selection bias. In addition to conducting the extensive sensitivity test described above, likelihood ratio tests were conducted on the models to determine whether the control variables "mattered" or not. The likelihood ratio test compares a pared-down version of the model to a saturated one and generates chi-squared statistics on the difference. If the control variables do not matter, then including them only makes the model less efficient, but the control variables were found to be significant.

Spurring Demand and Expanding Supply

These findings demonstrate that the WANTO and NEW programs were successful in spurring employer demand for, and, through skills training, expanding the supply of, women workers in NTOs, although there is evidence of tradeoffs between hours and workers. The better question, "does the program raise overall welfare by improving trainee outcomes without too much loss for nontrainees or incumbents?" has not been conclusively answered. Although there was no conclusive evidence of tradeoffs between workers and hours, it remains an important area for investigation. If there were such tradeoffs, it would suggest that the overall goals of WANTO and NEW were undermined.

These Grant Programs Should Not Work

How can these small grants, awarded to fairly small community-based organizations, have the impact found here? How were these one-time grantees with modest grant awards able to make the impact that they have?[22] The case study analyses of the next two chapters shall provide further evidence about the best practices of selected grantees, revealing what these organizations did right. In addition, case study analysis shall help illustrate a firm's response to the grantees' appeal to hire women. The next chapter focuses on selected grantees to make sense of the rather surprising results of this statistical analysis. Children and families rely on women's economic efficacy, WANTO and NEW made real changes to the lives of non-college working women and their families, and the following case studies demonstrate how.

Chapter 6

Nuts and Bolts I

How States' Programs Worked

A former dislocated worker now operates a front-end loader
and a rubber-tire roller for a living. When she applied to the
NEW program, she was a 23-year-old single parent with two
young children. As part of her three-month training, she studied
blueprint reading, workplace mathematics, industrial measure-
ments, heath and safety, an introduction to the trades, first aid,
and CPR. She also worked out three times a week to develop
her upper body strength. A month after graduating from the
program, she began to work as an apprentice operating
engineer earning $8.50 an hour plus excellent benefits. Her
pay will increase to $10 per hour after 1,500 hours of
training, with the potential to earn $20 an hour when
she becomes a journey-level worker in three years.
—*Profile of a Maryland NEW Participant,
as reported by Brigid O'Farrell, 2000.*[1]

We are at an all-time high in terms of the services offered at the
Women's Resource Center, we're becoming more and more
accepted, people know what we're all about and women
students have more awareness of the benefits of technical
education. . . . [under Project TExAS, we had] full-time
staff, faculty with academic training, personal
counselors, and JTPA workplace counselors.
—*Frances Worthey, Texas State Technical College, 2001*[2]

The Nontraditional Employment for Women (NEW) programs in Texas and
Wisconsin demonstrate how initiatives are institutionalized where a high
degree of coordination exists between the public and private sectors. These
states were selected for their differences: organized labor plays a significant
role in training, placement, and the working experiences of tradeswomen,
while organized labor is much less influential in Texas, which is a so-called

"right to work" state. Moreover, undocumented labor plays a much more influential role in Texas, particularly in construction trades, than it does in Wisconsin. Finally, the state of Wisconsin has a reputation for pursuing progressive social policy, both statewide and locally, and coordination efforts between state and local entities is facilitated by a high degree of communication as well as geographical proximity of major metropolitan entities: Madison and Milwaukee are much closer than are Austin and Dallas. In Texas, an absence of geographical proximity also leads to more local administration and control and less statewide coordination, which is as much an administrative necessity as it is a preference. Studying the implementation of similar programs in these two contexts should lead to interesting lessons that could inform other states' efforts. Both *Project TExAS* and Wisconsin's *NTO Tool Kit* trained and placed non-college women in desirable skilled trades, and provided employers with well-trained workers. In this chapter, case study analysis reveals how two very different contexts helped to determine whether these training programs were institutionalized, or not. Among O'Farrell's grantee best practices, which are discussed in detail below, two emerged as most predictive of long-term success for state programs: leadership buy-in and networking. Long-term institutionalization occurred where grant-funded projects were part of interactive networks of employers, unions, and public sector partners. Coordination with employers and unions helped training providers meet the needs of their female clients and their local labor markets, as was the case in Wisconsin. Institutionalization failed to occur where such networks did not exist, and in fact, where a negative perception of government involvement prevailed, which was the case in Texas, where local successes remained local.[3]

These two cases show how government involvement via policy intervention remains necessary to unite segments of the labor market that fail to communicate in the absence of sustained networks. These grantees implemented successful training programs when they effectively leveraged their human and financial resources within networks, demonstrated program effectiveness to union and employer stakeholders, and demonstrated effectiveness in their political environments. Where effective leveraging did not take place, support for nontraditional occupation (NTO) programs did not endure. Stakeholder networks successfully institutionalize initiatives because they are able to alter the structures of local labor markets in ways that diffuse, loosely connected entities cannot. Non-college women reap the benefits.

In the last chapter, rather surprising results from statistical analysis were found: that in the locations where grant-funded projects were implemented, there was a statistically significant increase in women's participation in NTOs. This prompted an inquiry into *how* these small grants could have had the impact that they did on women's participation in NTOs because the statistical analysis in Chapter 5 indicated only *that* there was a positive impact, but not *how* that could have happened. Therefore, the focus of this chapter is on examining selected grant recipients more closely using case study methodology to reveal some reasons why grantees were successful in meeting the objectives of the NEW program. The analysis uses Brigid O'Farrell's "best practices" of successful project implementers[4] as well as information on other grantees. Because the statistical analyses of Chapters 4 and 5 established that, on average, these grant programs were successful in increasing the participation of women in NTOs, case study analysis is used here to determine whether the grantee possessed the characteristics identified as best practices or not. The unit of analysis is the grantee that implemented a NEW-funded project, which differs from previous excellent anthropological analyses that have focused on tradeswomen such as *Hammering It Out* by Vivian Price,[5] *Pink Collar Workers* by Louise Kapp Howe,[6] *We'll Call You If We Need You* by Susan Eisenberg,[7] *Hard Hatted Women* by Molly Martin,[8] and *Nickel and Dimed* by Barbara Ehrenreich,[9] among others. Selecting NEW-funded projects as the units of analysis is supported by previous research on "women's policy machinery" by Dorothy McBride Stetson and Amy Mazur. Stetson and Mazur focused on the activities of public-sector entities involved in policy formulation and implementation, rather than feminist activities of entities outside the state: "Social movements provoke official action, especially by democratic governments. Whereas movement activists seek real change and permanent access to arenas of power, government actions may be symbolic or even cosmetic, a way of damping the fires of reform . . . [on the other hand] the state could, through its institutions, become an actor in promoting equality between men and women."[10]

If the "women's policy machinery" fails to follow its mandate adequately, women's movement activists intervene. The point is not whether movement activists actually influence the state, but rather, that they have access to an entity upon which to focus their efforts. If a state supports and maintains an agency or office devoted to providing women access to higher-paying, high-skilled jobs, women will have greater access to NTOs, compared to a state where these issues are not addressed within the "policy machinery," but rather, left to private- and third-sector entities.

Criteria Defining "Success"

The definition of "success" when evaluating these grantees is twofold based on near-term and long-term goals. First, NEW sought to increase the numbers of women recruited, trained, and retained in NTOs. To the extent grantees increased women's participation in NTOs at all, they were successful, and as the statistical analyses of previous chapters established, these programs met this near-term goal. Another goal of NEW was to assist states in establishing their own programs for women in nontraditional jobs. An exemplar might be the state of Ohio's Orientation to Nontraditional Occupations for Women (ONOW) program, which has continued to date with the assistance of Perkins funds. Recently, ONOW received an excellent rating by the Gender Equity Expert Panel, "Exemplary & Promising Gender Equity Programs, 2000" and uses marketing materials such as those shown in Figure 6.1.

> A five-year longitudinal study by Ohio State University tracked the earnings of women who had completed the ONOW program. The data showed higher wages for those who entered nontraditional employment and confirmed that 70 percent of the respondents continued to be employed; however, because the study measured a limited population, it is not sufficiently conclusive to be entered as a claim of success. . . . A 1996 study of ONOW participants who had been on public assistance when accepted for the program found that 76 percent were working full time, completely off of public assistance, and earning an average of $9.38 per hour. . . . The holistic nature of the program sets it apart from others. Inter- and intra-agency cooperation (for example, receiving funding for tools or childcare from partner agencies) aided in the program's overall success.[11]

For the present case study analysis, using a long-term definition of success establishes whether or not the grant-funded project became an institutionalized part of the training and employment approach of the state, as it has in Ohio; expanding the scope of the project by defining success as having a positive impact on women's participation in NTOs as an institutionalized part of a state's economic development strategies over time. Brigid O'Farrell established several best practices, as listed in Table 6.1.

Labor market analyses, staff training, recruitment, training, retention, and prevention tend to be the order in which training programs proceeded: grantees conducted local labor market analyses to determine which occupations were most promising in their areas; staff training was provided to ensure that job center intake specialists did not channel women into traditional areas and did provide them with important NTO information; interested women were recruited into appropriate training programs, trained, and placed in growing high-skilled occupations, and given support after placement to retain them in zero-tolerance workplaces. Accountability is important throughout to gauge impact and demonstrate effectiveness to public- and private-sector partners, as is leadership buy-in.

Figure 6.1 **The State of Ohio's Orientation to Nontraditional Occupations for Women (ONOW) Program Course Flyer**

Orientation to Nontraditional Occupations for Women (ONOW)

Women in nontraditional jobs earn 20% to 30% more than women in traditional occupations. And, according to the U.S. Bureau of Labor statistics, 15% of all jobs are unskilled. 20% require a professional degree (bachelor's degree or higher) and more than 65% of all jobs require specific skills demanding specialized education – that is, more than a high school diploma but less than a four-year college degree.

Orientation to Nontraditional Occupations for Women is a FREE 6-week course outlining all areas of nontraditional trades to offer women options in earning high wages.

ONOW offers training in:

Carpentry	Auto Technology
Machine Trades	Computer Basics
Electricity	CPR Certification
Welding	Forklift Training & Safety
Test Taking Skills	Thermo & Fluid Dynamics
Self-Esteem	OSHA Safety & Certification
Sexual Harassment	Spatial & Mechanical Reasoning

More than eight hands-on labs are offered as well as assistance in Career Guidance, Resume and Cover Letter Writing, Job Placement, Job Training, Apprenticeship Training and Continuing Education. Call ext. 241 for more information.

Jan 15 - Feb 27	M-F	9:00am-2:00pm
Apr 9 - May 21	M-F	9:00am-2:00pm
150 Hours	Tuition FREE	Registration Fee $15

The Ohio Department of Education's Gender Equity Panel recently rated the Ohio ONOW Program an "Exemplary Program" and noted that 84% of ONOW participants were placed in nontraditional training programs, employment apprenticeships, or GED classes and in 2000-2001, the ONOW Program at EHOVE was rated the "Best in Ohio".

Table 6.1

Best Practices of Nontraditional Employment for Women State-Level Grant Recipients

Best practice	Characteristics
Leadership buy-in	Support to "set the example for everyone in the company [including] subcontractors" and "establish a team of stake-holders from all levels of the companies [and unions] involved"
Accountability	Setting goals that are measurable and hold management responsible for the progress made on achieving those goals, by "measur[ing] not only the number of women recruited and trained, but the hours they work, by trade, during the life of the project"
Recruitment and staff training	Engaging in proactive recruitment of women and including tradeswomen in activities like job fairs and high school visits, providing specific training to recruiters on how to attract potential women employees, and ensuring marketing materials feature tradeswomen
Training	Offering skills training to women who are interested or who may need it, ensuring that the training requirements are job-related and skill-based
Retention	Establishing policies against sexual harassment in advance, ensuring against isolation of women on job sites, clarifying pro-motion, transfer and layoff, and discharge policies in advance
Prevention	Creating a "zero tolerance" workplace by advising both men and women about their legal rights and grievance procedures
Networking	Leveraging human resources, financial resources, and human capital, and coordinating efforts by distributing lessons learned among interested parties, to make the most of limited funds
Labor market analyses	Conducting labor market analyses to find high-growth industries and occupations in which to train women; labor market analyses help grant recipients to train women for occupations in growing areas that benefit the community

Source: Brigid O'Farrell, "The WANTO Technical Assistance Program"; "The New Demonstration Program."

In a political context, leadership buy-in is perhaps the most influential best practice, in that it gauges specifically whether grantees actively maintained NTO issues on their states' agendas. To successfully institutionalize NTO training for women, state agencies had to maintain and support networks of stakeholders, including unions and employers, and provide documentation to support their activities during budget negotiations, and actively maintained their issues on decision makers' agendas. For a state agency, leadership buy-in has two audiences: unions and employers who must be convinced that such programs are worthwhile to them, and political actors who make budgetary decisions. The case study analysis proceeded with these best practices in mind, and consisted of site visits, interviews, and archival analyses to capture the ways grantees implemented and ran their grant-funded projects. Twenty-three grant-funded projects reached 2,600 women over a four-year period, with the goal of systematically changing federal job training programs to train and place more women in NTOs.

If exemplary cases share some characteristic that would provide an alternative explanation to the results found from the statistical analysis, the case study analysis should reveal this.

Case Study Methodology

These cases are not strictly analytical in the same way Yin described, because a general result has been found already: Chapter 5 established the positive impact of these grant-funded projects. In addition to providing more insight into how grantees implemented their projects and potential reasons why they had an effect, examining Women in Apprenticeships and Nontraditional Occupations (WANTO) and NEW grantees is appropriate because case study methodology "is preferred in examining contemporary events, but when the relevant behaviors cannot be manipulated."[12] Case study analysis cannot affect the outcomes of interest of NEW and WANTO grantees. The NEW program stopped awarding grants in 1996, and WANTO-funded projects are not current projects, so the act of analyzing them would not "manipulate" the grantees' implementation and operation activities.

Pattern-Matching Using Multiple Cases

The present analysis is of the type described by Yin as "pattern-matching," where the investigator "compares an empirically based pattern with a predicted one . . . if the patterns coincide, the results can help a case study to strengthen its *internal validity*."[13] The empirically based pattern is comprised of the practices of grantee organizations in implementing and operating their grant-funded projects, which was observed through site visits, documentation, archives, and interviews. The predicted pattern is comprised of the practices of successful government grantees as determined by theory. The present analysis can be characterized as matching *simple patterns* across multiple cases, which Yin defines as those "having a minimal variety of either dependent or independent variables."[14] The dependent variables were whether the project was successful in increasing the participation of women in NTOs or not. The independent variables were whether the grantee possessed the characteristics identified as "best practices" or not.

Determining the use of best practices involved some subjective judgment, and a successful implementer need not have possessed *every* characteristic identified in the literature nor did the project have to include every aspect considered desirable. Some characteristics tended to be more influential than others, and this is discussed throughout the findings. In *Feminist Methods in Social Research*, Shulamit Reinharz describes feminist case studies as "research that focuses on a single case or single issue, in contrast with studies that seek generalizations through comparative analysis or compilation of a large number of instances . . . feminist theory is impoverished without case studies."[15] In Reinharz's view, women's experiences have been ignored or have presumed a subset of men's experiences for so long in social science research that the case study is integral to illustrating a separate theoretical path centered on the different effects of social phenomena involving women.

The unit of analysis is the *grantee* that implemented a grant-funded project. Selecting this unit of analysis is supported by the previous research on "women's policy machinery" that examined public-sector entities involved in policy formulation and implementation, which was carried out by Stetson and Mazur, who focus on the activities of public-sector entities. The cases are the organizations implementing grant-funded projects, and *not* individual women who went through the training courses. Focusing on the implementation of the projects and using best practices as criteria emphasizes the manner in which services were delivered as factors in the success or failure of the project. Yin identified six sources of evidence in case study analysis: documents, archival records, interviews, direct observation, participant-observation, and physical artifacts.[16] Because the units of analysis were the grantee organizations themselves, this case study analysis lent itself to the use of interviews, documents of the organization, and its archival records more than did the other three sources of data. If individual women in training programs were the units of analysis, participant-observation would have played a greater role.

Nontraditional Employment for Women Demonstration Grants

Although information from each NEW-funded project informed this analysis, two cases are exemplary in their differing approaches, and provide interesting contrasts in effective project implementation: the state of Wisconsin's *NTO Tool Kit* and the State of Texas' *Project TExAS*.

State of Wisconsin: The NTO Tool Kit

The state of Wisconsin received its NEW grant in 1995. The Job Employment and Training Services Division within the Wisconsin Department of Workforce Development, Division of Workforce Excellence (DWE) rolled out a statewide implementation of a model nontraditional training program designed for Wisconsin job centers to use as the basis for statewide technical assistance and training strategies. This model was written by staff from the Nontraditional Employment Training Programs of the YWCA of Greater Milwaukee, based on Project NEW Start, which was tested in the Milwaukee service delivery area (SDA). The YWCA of Greater Milwaukee is a member of the Wisconsin Regional Training Partnership (WRTP), which is a consortium of over 100 employers and unions and was founded in 1992. The WRTP has been lauded as a fine example of a network to "provide collective solutions to problems that single firms cannot afford or are unable to devise on their own, with the price tag of solid wages, job security, and career ladders for workers."[17] The AFL-CIO Working for America Institute highlighted WRTP as an example of an effective partnership promoting high-road economic development strategies in their *High Road Partnerships Report.*[18]

The DWE subcontracted with the Milwaukee YWCA and the SDA to distribute the model statewide using the Nontraditional Tool Kit, which includes the *NTO Resource Guide* and the *Mentor Handbook.* As a result of the project, women in NTOs increased from 7 percent in 1994 before the project to 13.4 percent.[19] Wisconsin's *NTO Tool Kit* sought to provide exposure to nontraditional training and occupations to 100 percent of the women who use Job Center services; increase the placement of women into nontraditional jobs to 16 percent in the Milwaukee SDA; attain an average wage at placement for women entering NTOs of $8.25 per hour; ensure retention of at least 85 percent of women placed in nontraditional jobs through support activities; integrate nontraditional exposure, training, and preparation into each participant-related function of the Job Center; provide a specific focus on nontraditional elements in the inter-agency planning; create and disseminate a technical assistance tool kit that is designed to function as a guide to SDAs; and utilize the experiences in the Job Center program model development and implementation and the resources in the *NTO Tool Kit* to build the strategies that will systematize an effective statewide system of technical assistance and training.[20]

The *NTO Tool Kit* was written based on the experience of implementing the Milwaukee SDA 12 project. The state partnered with Ed Ventures Unlimited, Private Industry Councils, YWCAs, technical colleges, and community-based nonprofit organizations to test the model and implement it statewide. To assist statewide replication, a steering committee was created to oversee and direct NTO efforts. This committee, the Wisconsin Leadership Team on Nontraditional Employment for Women, included men and women from DWE and other state agencies, the Governor's Glass Ceiling

Commission, nonprofit service delivery organizations, area community and technical colleges, and the Office of Federal Contract Compliance Programs (OFCCP).

Unlike *Project TExAS* and other NEW-funded projects, the state of Wisconsin did *not* apply its NEW grant funds to individualized skills training for non-college women in NTOs, but rather, worked to create a program for Job Centers across the state that would help *them* advise women on their options in nontraditional fields. In fact, their approach coupled technical assistance to Job Center staff with technical assistance to employers for the purpose of changing labor market structures themselves. The Tool Kit addressed three populations: Job Center staff, female clientele, and employers. First, the project sought to change the way Job Center staff operated in both their interactions with female clients and their performance evaluations, and to have them include referring women to nontraditional jobs. Second, the grant-funded project provided job descriptions and earnings information to women who were unaware of their NTO options. Third, the project sought to advise employers who made gender-stereotyped requests about the benefits of hiring women. As Brigid O'Farrell observed: "In Wisconsin, Job Centers are the focal point for delivering employment and training services to employers and job seekers. The Tool Kit was developed to assist Job Center staff in incorporating nontraditional elements for women into the 'usual' service delivery system."[21]

The issue for the state of Wisconsin's NEW-funded project involved systematic integration of NTO information in its Job Center network to achieve its goal of increasing women's participation in NTOs. Its approach was to provide information to women job seekers, intake staff, and employers, as well as change the service delivery system itself, and increase the numbers of women in NTOs. The approach here was to change the delivery system and steer women toward nontraditional employment options and work with employers and help make them more receptive to employing women in capacities in which they had not been employed.

To meet these goals, the tool kit was distributed to more than seventy Job Centers and public libraries. In addition, DWE incorporated NTO language into the Job Center performance standards to provide incentives for staff to emphasize NTO in counseling and client assessment. Finally, the Leadership Team provided technical assistance to Job Centers and SDAs to modify the model to provide additional materials to help Job Centers achieve their NTO goals. The NEW-funded project identified techniques for exposing female Job Center clients to NTOs, which included placing brochures, flyers, and posters in grocery stores, hair salons, Laundromats, community centers, women's shelters, churches, childcare centers, and so-called stall tactics, or advertising in public restrooms. The model also suggested using, if resources

Figure 6.2   **Machinist Graphic Created for the *NTO Tool Kit* by Keith Ward, September 16, 1996**

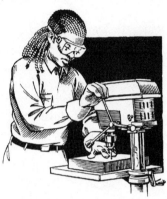

Figure 6.3   **Drafter Graphic Created for the *NTO Tool Kit* by Keith Ward, September 16, 1996**

allowed, newspaper advertisements and radio or television spots. Furthermore, DWE presented information on NTOs at church meetings, job fairs, employer associations, and parent-teacher association meetings. One very important part of increasing exposure to women's options in NTOs was the use of images of women working in these jobs. The state contracted with an artist to create illustrations of women in high-skilled occupations in electronic form so they could be distributed and incorporated into brochures, flyers, and information packets. Figures 6.2 through 6.5 present four of the illustrations created and distributed as part of the grant-funded project.

In addition to providing statewide SDAs with tips on increasing awareness and materials such as these to assist in their exposure efforts, the State also administered an survey at one Job Center near Milwaukee. For one day, women exiting the Center were asked to complete the survey, and a total of forty-four

Figure 6.4 **Mechanic Graphic Created for the *NTO Tool Kit* by Keith Ward, September 16, 1996**

Figure 6.5 **Plumber Graphic Created for the *NTO Tool Kit* by Keith Ward, September 16, 1996**

women responded. Although the DWE did not consider the results statistically significant, they did feel that since the vast majority of women responded that they had been exposed to training programs in nontraditional fields, this was a positive indication that the level of exposure to nontraditional options was at least heading in the right direction. The *NTO Tool Kit* also provided Job Centers with electronic versions of forms for conducting meetings, implementing work plans, career assessment surveys, retention strategies to keep women in NTOs, sample brochure templates and flyer templates, and other information sheets.

The tool kit also included staff training materials, case manager checklists, apprenticeship information, agendas for client orientations, and workshops and evaluations forms, staff training workshops and evaluation forms for workshops, and information sheets on women in high-skilled, male-dominated occupations, also in electronic form for ease of use. Extensive staff training was necessary to inform intake, assessment, and case management staff about the importance of exposing non-college women to alternative training and employment programs. Staff members needed to be educated on the importance of these options to a non-college woman's ability to support her family before they could discuss the role of these occupations with Job Center clients. The *NTO Tool Kit* provided guidelines for ensuring that there would always be an emphasis on alternative employment and training paths for non-college women among staff in intake, assessment, and case management, thus ensuring a high rate of exposure to NTOs for female Job Center clients. The tool kit asserted:

> Inter-Agency planning is the cornerstone of the process for integrating nontraditional occupations into the function of the Job Center. Every agency that participates in providing Job Center services should be included in each step of the development and implementation process. The Local Collaborative Planning Team and the Management Team are responsible for the "Top Down" policies and oversight. The Project Team, Coordination Team, and Job Center staff are responsible for the "Bottom-Up," front-line integration of the NTO elements. Project and Coordination Team members can influence both by bringing an NTO focus to each Job Center and community planning meeting they attend.[22]

Local Collaborative Planning Teams (LCPTs) were local groups that coordinated the planning and administration of Job Centers within each SDA. The idea of Inter-Agency Planning was to diversify the interest in increasing women's participation in training programs for placement into high-skilled occupations across all entities involved in employment and training services delivery. The individuals who participated in the LCPTs and the Management Teams worked to solidify the commitment to this initiative in the state bureaucracy. The individuals who were responsible for the bottom-up, front-line application of NTO-focused activities were important in achieving the Job Center goals, because, again, staff had to be informed about the benefits women can experience through non-college alternative careers before they can discuss these benefits with female Job Center clients. In its final report, the state of Wisconsin indicated that the response to the *NTO Tool Kit* has been positive:

> It has been used in several statewide events including the Governor's Employment and Training Conference, a Follow-up Session to the Governor's Conference, JTPA and Job Center Roundtables, Wisconsin Employment and Training Association Conference, and the Wisconsin Sex Equity Cadre Roundtable.[23]

The tool kit still enjoys wide distribution, and the quarterly meetings of review and advisory teams continue to update it with feedback from Job Centers. Even with the end of the NEW project and initial waning of interest, grassroots support existed to maintain the effort, which was taken up in the state shortly thereafter. The DWE appropriated funds toward a reinterpreted effort, which is the basis of the current initiatives. The initial model was the *NTO Tool Kit*, and the revised version is the *NTO Resource Guide*, which incorporates many of the goals and methods of the tool kit, including the electronic forms and graphics mentioned above.

The *NTO Tool Kit* also provides Job Centers with electronic versions of forms for conducting meetings and implementing work plans, career assessment surveys, retention strategies to keep non-college women in alternative post-secondary employment and training programs, sample brochure templates and flyer templates, and other information sheets.[24] The tool kit also includes staff training materials, case manager checklists, apprenticeship information, agendas for client orientations, and workshops and evaluations forms, staff training workshops and evaluation forms for workshops, and information sheets on non-college women in NTOs, also all in electronic form for ease of access. Extensive staff training informs intake, assessment, and case management staff about the importance of exposing female clients to training and employment options. The *NTO Tool Kit* provides guidelines for ensuring that there will always be an NTO emphasis among staff in intake, assessment, and case management, thus ensuring a high rate of exposure to alternative training programs for female Job Center clients interested in high-skilled employment and training opportunities. Developing a commitment to NTOs throughout the service delivery system is essential.

The Dane County Job Center

The Dane County Job Center (DCJC) in Madison was established in 1993, and the comprehensive *NTO Resource Guide* was first incorporated into the Center's service delivery standards in 1997. DCJC staff were evaluated on their ability and success in exposing women to and placing women in nontraditional training programs and jobs. The second edition of the resource guide was printed and distributed in June 2000. It provides detailed and comprehensive methods for integrating certain services at a Job Center and flowcharts depicting the process of integrating services, as well as basic information on barriers to women's employment in NTOs, employer concerns, and census data on nontraditional jobs and wages. The resource guide distills the relevant state and federal laws into a usable format. DCJC offers a wide range of services that clients used on their own, or as a part of job counseling groups to get job information and assistance. DCJC services include an employment search Web site, industry-specific job fairs, a current opportunities bulletin, medical and financial assistance, veterans' services, group employment searches, state testing services, career planning, and unemployment insurance services. DCJC has an on-site childcare center available for clients.

At the time of this analysis, DCJC had received approximately 500 female clients each month, not including "self-service" Job Center clients, those who obtain information remotely from the DCJC Web site. The software needed to track referrals of women to NTO resources was not on-line at the time of this analysis. According to Nancy Nakkoul's evaluation of the *Building the Tool Kit Initiative*, out of nearly 1,800 women who entered the workforce between July 1999 and May 2000, approximately 6.7 percent obtained an NTO, up from 5.2 percent over the same period during 1998 and 1999.[25] Nakkoul also notes the diversity of nontraditional jobs obtained by the women clients of DCJC from 1999 to 2000, which included plumber apprentices, sheet metal workers, firefighter paramedics, landscapers, and bus drivers. On-site counselors from the Madison Area Technical College (MATC) referred most of the women interested in NTOs to appropriate training programs.

Classrooms hold both computer classes and "life skills" classes for DCJC clients. Pretraining workshops are regular parts of training, particularly for clients receiving welfare who had a difficult time holding down jobs for lack of knowledge about workplace fundamentals. "Earned apparel" is also available to clients, with items ranging from work boots and tool belts to blazers, neckties, and blouses.[26] Post-placement mentoring is available, as well. The *Building the Tool Kit Initiative* partnered with *Tools for Change*, a grassroots organization of tradeswomen that was established in 1979 with about 100 members. A Mentor Handbook was created to organize and guide the mentoring process. The evolution of the State of Wisconsin's project from the NEW-funded demonstration in the Milwaukee SDA to the statewide rollout of the tool kit model to its latest version testifies to the NTO Coordination Team's sensitivity to feedback and willingness to update and change their approach to increasing Wisconsin women's participation in NTOs. Members of *Tools for Change* were surveyed by the NTO Coordinating Team to gauge whether there would be interest in mentoring women entering NTOs, or interest in recruiting and community outreach to employers.[27] The level of interest in all these activities turned out to be very high, and DCJC maintains a database to keep track of contacts, mailings, and member information for this group. A Mentor Handbook was created to organize and guide the mentoring process. A recent project evaluation observes: "Since . . . 1997, most efforts to integrate NTO have focused on increasing staff knowledge of NTO, adding NTO services and tools at the Job Center, and developing job seeker resources. Now that these are underway, it is time to turn the focus to the employer sector."[28]

The evolution of the state of Wisconsin's project from the NEW-funded demonstration in the Milwaukee SDA to the statewide rollout of the tool kit model, to its latest version, testifies to the Team's sensitivity to feedback and willingness to update and change their approach to increasing non-college Wisconsin women's participation in high-wage, high-skilled occupations.

The initial grant-funded project included most of the attributes of a successfully implemented grant-funded project, and the long-term work emphasizes retention, accountability, and leadership buy-in to an even greater degree. Wisconsin's initiatives are continually responsive to stakeholder feedback via client surveys, and the NTO Coordination Team met monthly to improve the resource guide and the services it delivers. The mentoring program with *Tools for Change* provides the ongoing support that many of these women have needed to complete their training and stay in their nontraditional jobs. In short, the state of Wisconsin's NEW-funded project and its continuing efforts may be an exemplar for longer-term institutionalization. In fact, their efforts continue today: a recent story in the *Milwaukee Journal Sentinel* reported that the YWCA of Greater Milwaukee and the WRTP opened a new job-training center. The story also profiled a thirty-six-year-old single mother of two who went from "five part-time jobs as a nursing assistant to stitch together the income and support her family needed" to a union job with a road construction company.[29]

Conclusions and Implications of the Findings from Wisconsin

At the time of the analysis, DWE continued its involvement with NTO efforts. To ensure that NTOs remain a priority for employment and training service delivery, the Leadership Team, nonprofit service delivery organizations, and DWE continue to meet quarterly and monitor Job Center activities: "The goal remains having information about nontraditional training and employment integrated into all components of the Job Center System and systematically presented to 100 percent of the women served."[30]

A significant difference between the state of Wisconsin and the state of Texas projects has been in their continuing efforts. Although the two grant-funded projects demonstrated many of the "success" criteria, the projects were not the same. Their differences help explain the differences in the paths each initiative took after their NEW-funded projects were completed. Mary Cirilli, DWE policy analyst, who was also an NTO Leadership Team member, observes that the DWE continued to appropriate funds for the state's initiative, even as other budget priorities emerged.[31] In 1997, after an extensive study of the existing conditions at DCJC, the NTO Coordination Team, a group of eleven staff and management from nonprofit service delivery units, the MATC and other state agencies, established seven goals for DCJC and nineteen work plans that outline the activities to achieve them. Recent state budget cutbacks jeopardize extensive support for alternative employment and training services, however.

In terms of pattern-matching, Wisconsin's projects, both the initial NEW-funded one and the ongoing efforts, very closely matched the pattern of successful grant-funded project implementation predicted in the nonprofit literature and in O'Farrell's analyses. As mentioned above, the difference between the state of Wisconsin and the state of Texas projects has been in their continuing efforts. While the former kept its efforts within the state, the latter watched its endeavors continue only in the state system of technical schools, and implicitly at that. Although the two grant-funded projects demonstrated many of the attributes of the predicted pattern, they were not the same. The differences in their attributes explained the differences in the paths each initiative took after the NEW-funded project was completed.

The state of Texas was among the first NEW grant recipients in 1992. The grant was awarded to the Texas Department of Commerce, and the Heart of Texas Council of Governments (HOTCOG) in Waco, Texas, in partnership with the Texas State Technical College (TSTC) also in Waco, implemented this project. The HOTCOG was also the Heart of Texas Service Delivery Area under Job Training Partnership Act (JTPA). Under JTPA, SDAs delivered the NTOs services specified under NEW, usually in partnership with community-based nonprofit organizations, or as in this case, with local vocational and technical schools.

The state of Texas focused its project in two areas; first, pretraining to address women's barriers to nontraditional employment, and second, training to place women in high-technology occupations, which was determined to be a high-growth employment area at the time. The Technical Education and Ascending Self-Empowerment project (*Project TExAS*) provided training and placement in high-growth, high-technology occupations where women were underrepresented. According to Gaylen Lange, the project director, the objective of *Project TExAS* was to increase investments in individual women, rather than maximize the numbers of women through the program. The overall objective emphasized long-term impacts on women's lives, rather than short-term impacts on the numbers of JTPA-eligible women put through training.

The HOTCOG provided a full-time, rigorous fourteen-week pretraining program entitled "Transformation Through Technology" (T3) for seventy women, which addressed basic workplace behavior issues such as showing up on time and consistently and resolving conflicts, and also provided instruction in basic reading and math, usually achieving an eighth-grade reading and math level. Participants completing the T3 program could choose either to finish their training and be placed in a high-technology job at the basic level or to continue their education at TSTC and receive a higher placement upon completing a technical degree program. Forty-five of the seventy women who completed the T3 program continued their education at TSTC in their two-year "Tech Specialty" degree program, and half of them finished the degree program and/or were placed in a high-technology job.[32] Overall, *Project TExAS* reported that they trained and placed eighty-five women over the grant period,[33] including women who did not complete the T3 program, but received a high-technology job placement anyway, and were considered "successful."

Gaylen Lange is currently the HOTCOG workforce development director, and within *Project TExAS*, she supervised the team of three instructors and taught the life skills component of the T3 at their offices in Waco, while the other two instructors taught math and reading skills, orientation to alternative employment and training paths, and hands-on training with tools. The overall responsibility for implementing the grant-funded project was Lange's, including recruiting, making arrangements for childcare, transportation, and financial assistance, and pairing individual students with academic and personal counselors at the Women's Resource Center. The math and reading classes, tools training, and job orientation sessions were held on the campus of TSTC in Waco. The project was advertised in regional newspapers, and HOTCOG held information and orientation sessions and screened interested women for eligibility. Recall that, for the NEW demonstration grant projects, participants had to be JTPA-eligible, or low-income, women. Childcare, transportation, and financial assistance services were provided for participants, as well.

Over the grant period, three groups of non-college women went through the T3 program: there were twenty-five participants in the first and second groups and twenty in the third, and participants met in the same classrooms throughout the program. For eight hours a day, five days per week over fourteen weeks, the first group learned basic "life skills" during the first two weeks, including professional behavior and dress, the importance of consistently maintaining a schedule, and dealing with coworker conflicts. Over the remaining twelve weeks, the group received intensive training to improve their basic reading and math proficiency, computer skills, and extensive jobs and skills orientation, which exposed them to the differences in pay and stability of NTOs compared to "traditional" women's jobs. They were also introduced to high-technology employment and the career possibilities therein so they could make an informed decision about whether to enter the NTO skills training program or not, and which trade to enter. Participants received small stipends and some living expenses to keep them enrolled in the program because it took up so much time that they could not realistically hold down a job and participate in the project.

Several changes were made to this project based on the experience of the first group. According to Lange, by the sixth or seventh week of the first T3 session, tensions had built up because of the intensity and rigor of the first round.

Changes to the T3 program included the requirement of interviewing women who were interested in the program to determine motivation levels and attitudes toward commitment to a long training program. Second, the class time was shortened. Two days each week, sessions ended at two o'clock in the afternoon. Women from the first group complained that they had no time to go to the grocery store or run errands with their full-time schedules. Third, the classrooms were rotated regularly and the arrangements in them were changed from desks to seminar tables and chairs, by request of the students. Finally, and perhaps most important, the Women's Resource Center (WRC) at TSTC was institutionalized on the campus, and provided a half-time academic counselor to the women in the second and third groups. In addition, WRC played a role in mentoring women students and providing personal counselors once a week for mandatory sessions with students to discuss issues within and outside the classroom.

In all three groups, the math and reading scores of the participants was initially low, but improved after T3. Lange screened applicants in the second and third groups for their attitude and perceived level of motivation, not for basic math and reading proficiency. The third group benefited from the experiences of the first two. Participants possessed a much clearer understanding of what was expected of them, they were given time to take care of errands such as applying for food stamps and visiting food banks, and interpersonal problems were far less severe among participants in the third group. In addition, Lange discussed the importance of volunteering, or "giving back" to the community in the interviews she conducted prior to the beginning of the second and third T3 sessions. While the first group was hostile to the idea of volunteering their time, the second and third groups were not, because they had discussed the issue in their interviews. Finally, participants in the second and third sessions had more support systems, and more positive attitudes regarding the potential benefits of training and education than did the first group of participants. The barriers they faced to improving their lives through training, both external and internal, were less severe than those experienced by women in the first group. Lange stated that she learned to communicate better with participants by the third round of T3 classes. In her evaluation of *Project TExAS*, Brigid O'Farrell observed:

> A single mother of two was working for the minimum wage and receiving food stamps. In the Texas NEW Project, she first attended a two-week survival skills course to increase her self-esteem and begin behavioral changes while learning job search skills, assertiveness, money manage-ment, legal rights, coping with crisis, health, and nutrition. She followed with a 13-week course called Transformation Through Technology (T3) at Texas State Technical College. The course focused on mathematics, com-munication skills, personal computers, and the basic scientific principles underlying today's technology. This provided the background for her to choose a two-year occupational training program in automotives, drafting, computer maintenance, or electro-optics. In all phases of the project, she was supported by mentors, financial assistance, counseling, and academic guidance (at WRC.) She graduated with a degree in drafting and obtained a job locally for $20,000 a year. She transferred to a new job with a salary of $23,500 a year.[34]

With extensive resources, NEW participants experienced significant career-related achievements. However, measuring success in dollars captures only a part of the story. As the career counseling literature revealed, to increase their career self-efficacy, many women have to overcome emotional as well as physi-cal obstacles. In *Project TExAS*, most of the women participants were in their twenties, *all* of them had dependents, and wanted to train themselves and to move away from the hand-to-mouth existence for their children or spouses, most were unwed mothers, either divorced or never married. Many had men in their lives throughout their participation in *Project TExAS*, and according to Gaylen Lange, the men were a detriment to the success of some women par-ticipants. Some gravitated toward domineering men out of a sense of low self-esteem, and several demonstrated signs of physical and psychological abuse, or indicated that they had suffered such abuse. Lange attributed many of the negative attitudes and tendencies toward violent conflict resolution that she observed in class to unsupportive personal situations. Participants' achieve-ments carried over into other aspects of their lives, and, as many have ob-served, as these women succeeded in their careers, they made healthier and more supportive choices in their personal lives, as well.

The Texas State Technical College at Waco

The TSTC System is comprised of four main campuses and three exten-sion centers, TSTC Waco partnered with HOTCOG on implementing *Project TExAS*. TSTC Waco is the largest TSTC campus in terms of student enrollment, with 3,836 students enrolled in the 2000–2001 academic year, which is approximately 40 percent of total TSTC System enrollment.[35] Like all TSTC campuses, TSTC Waco is a state-funded, coeducational, two-year residential institution of higher education, offering Associate of Applied Science degrees and Certificates of Completion in more than forty technology programs.

Texas State Technical College at Waco is located on a very large tract of land on the site of an air force base that was decommissioned in 1965. At TSTC Waco, there is plenty of room for large-scale technical education classes such as aviation mechanics, as well as thousands of housing units, including dormitories, apartments, and family quarters. For several decades, TSTC teachers were practicing professionals in industry and its students were mostly young white men. A recent change in status from "technical institute" to accredited college has changed the profile of the campus. Teachers are now more likely to have an academic and practitioner background, and the college has prioritized equal opportunity and diversity for its faculty and student body. The director of External Resource Development confirmed that there has been a great deal of growth and change in the organization over the past five to ten years; more women have become head administrators both at TSTC Waco and within the TSTC System.

According to this director, the impact of *Project TExAS* on TSTC has been threefold. First, the WRC became a permanent resource on campus and a focal point of support services for both male and female students. A similar resource center operated on a limited basis for a short time prior to *Project TExAS*. Second, this project raised faculty and staff awareness of the benefits female students receive through training in nontraditional fields. Other students could see more women in every area, and not just in dental assisting and other traditional fields, where virtually all women were before. Third, the director felt *Project TExAS* allowed the faculty and administration of TSTC Waco to better understand that their training and support services tended to be more holistic than were similar post-secondary technical training programs at the time, and their approach was effective, and continues to be. Their students tended to be "at risk" and therefore required more support services to manage the barriers in their personal lives that often impeded their progress in school.

One instructor in the Laser Electro-Optics Department worked with several successful female students and graduates from this technology. He believed women students comprise 20–25 percent of all students in laser electro-optics, which requires strong math and science skills, and prepares students for high-technology careers in medicine, auto manufacturing, and science. TSTC Waco continues to actively recruit female students from high schools and at career fairs for placement in this area. In addition, the instructor noted that employers often extend offers to their students before they have completed their coursework at TSTC, as economic growth throughout the 1990s resulted in a demand for high-technology workers that exceeded supply. According to this instructor, employers have exhibited no hesitation in hiring women, and he has also witnessed this in technologies like welding.[36]

The administrators and instructors this researcher interviewed believed that on the TSTC Waco campus outright sexual harassment of students was undermined by an emphasis on what one can do. The campus-wide emphasis on one's skills and abilities forced them to judge their fellow students on their talents in the trade, which eclipsed any gender stereotyping. Female students who are talented welders were treated as talented welders and not as interlopers in a trade where women do not belong. Perhaps their positions as administrators and instructors colored their view of student's experiences.

On the whole, TSTC Waco *has* diversified its administration, faculty, and student body, but while the old stereotypes may be overlooked in times of labor shortage, there will always be those with very rigid, gender-specific ideas about women and work, and these individuals do not wholly change their minds even though their academic and economic realities have changed. The WRC at TSTC Waco verified this suspicion insofar as female students still seek a significant amount of counseling and support from WRC. Overall, however, the atmosphere and practices at TSTC Waco were very supportive of diversity and intolerant of discrimination, and a very high premium was placed on students' abilities. However, there still appeared to be a high demand for WRC services, including the support services for women in technology and trades. The WRC existed for a short time prior to *Project TExAS*, but the NEW-funded grant established the Center and helped it broadly advertise its services in ways that had not been done previously. From the WRC director's perspective, the Center is heavily involved on the TSTC Waco campus. Male students, commonly male single parents, have taken advantage of the counseling, mentoring, and support services available at WRC, but the Center's director emphasized the importance of maintaining the focus on women. According to her, female students must remain the focus of WRC, because women-focused services are still very necessary, and "mainstreaming" their needs would eventually shortchange both the support services they offer and the female students they target.

Services of WRC include counseling, support groups, financial aid, information and referrals to social service agencies, assistance with daycare, parenting skills seminars, networking and mentoring, transportation information and assistance, and job placement services. Many students at TSTC Waco have small children, attend classes, and work full time, and the WRC has provided support services to help them balance school, work, and family.

During *Project TExAS*, additional academic and personal counselors were housed at the WRC offices, and T3 participants could take advantage of all the services available there, too. *Project TExAS* had full-time staff, faculty with academic training, and JTPA workplace counselors available to its participants. According to the WRC director, Gaylen Lange, the NEW-funded project was highly successful, and she and a handful of project participants traveled to Washington, DC to testify on the project's success. The project targeted a specific population of women with barriers to employment and training, and the counseling and supervision they received was intense. But targeting particular students has not been the WRC goal; they provide services to all students at TSTC Waco. So, when *Project TExAS* ended and the needs of its participants were assimilated into the overall needs of all students at the school, effectively "mainstreaming" them, some women who needed the extra supervision dropped out of school. The support services offered through *Project TExAS* were no longer available for particularly at-risk female students, above and beyond the regular services of WRC.

Findings from the Evidence

Project TExAS included several activities that helped them achieve impressive near-term successes, but not institutionalized in the long run. Among the key short-run attributes were the pretraining services, ongoing mentoring and support to ensure a high rate of retention, and the initial labor market analysis. As a pretraining service, the T3 program was designed to address the significant barriers to employment and training that most of the female participants had. T3 was also responsive to participants' feedback, and made improvements to subsequent sessions. The WRC provided the ongoing support that many of these women needed to complete their degree or certificate programs. It appears as though the significant contribution of *Project TExAS* was not in the technical training itself, which was really only the tuition to TSTC, but rather, in the support services that prepared these women for their training programs: investments in the women themselves.

In her research at the University of North Texas, Gaylen Lange conducted a returns-to-investment analysis of *Project TExAS* and found that, in about two years, projects such as these had produced a positive and significant benefit to the local economy.[37] She found that the value of the pretraining outweighed the value of the directly job-related technical training. Regardless of the amount of money allocated to a project beyond these basics, Director Lange found that the positive economic impacts to the local community had eclipsed the initial investment into *Project TExAS* in a little less than two years. The money for pretraining, stipends, and tuition at TSTC would be paid back in terms of economic benefit to the community if the women graduates stayed in the Waco area to work and shop.

However, the lack of leadership buy-in appears to have hindered the project's long-term success within the state of Texas. *Project TExAS* did not continue past the life of the NEW grant. By all accounts, the hiring, recruiting, and promoting practices at all TSTC campuses have changed toward greater gender diversity in technical degree programs once dominated by men, and greater diversity among administrative staff and faculty. However, as a special population, the emphasis on increasing women's participation in nontraditional employment fields is no longer the priority it was. First, increasing women's participation in NTOs is no longer a major project at either TSTC or HOTCOG. Second, without a state-led initiative to increase women's participation in NTOs, it is unclear what is being done systematically in the state of Texas. While in operation, *Project TExAS* was effective in increasing the numbers of at-risk women in high-wage, stable, high technology jobs. As a NEW grantee, the state of Texas developed and implemented a successful project that had a positive impact on women's participation in NTOs. Unfortunately, the seed monies did not appear to spur longer-term action within the state.

Conclusions and Implications of the Findings from Texas

This grant-funded project was successful in the short term, but not in the long term. Because there has been no continuing state effort to increase women's participation in NTO training and employment since the NEW-funded project expired, the issue failed to become institutionalized and largely vanished from the political landscape. In contrast, the perspective of one TSTC administrator was that the lack of a state-run initiative for women in NTOs meant that the issue was, in fact, deeply institutionalized; the lack of a state-run initiative would indicate that the commitment to gender diversity in technical education existed because of the lack of state money to promote gender diversity. From this point-of-view, continued government involvement signaled a need for support that, if a change were truly institutionalized, would not be necessary. But, without the presence of a specific initiative, where might a woman who is unaware of NTO career paths find out about them? Without an explicit initiative, no single institution or group of institutions existed to spearhead an effort or provide a central location to sustain it, especially when economic fortunes change. Without state involvement, any appeal for change must take place among the diffuse service delivery units. The assessment of *Project TExAS* remains: it was a remarkable short-term success, yet it did not influence the system of delivering training and employment services in the state of Texas over the long term. The case of the state of Wisconsin provides a contrast in terms of its approach to institutionalizing change with respect to increasing women's participation and retention in NTOs.

Conclusions and Evidence from States and the Nontraditional Employment for Women Program Overall

This chapter demonstrated the best practices of state agencies in providing alternative employment and training services to non-college women. The evaluation criteria existed in both *Project TExAS* and the NTO Tool Kit in varying degrees. First, in terms of leadership, Wisconsin's Tool Kit was a priority of state government, and a state budget line item provided a continued funding stream to support it. While the activities and goals of *Project TExAS* obtained leadership buy-in at TSTC Waco, the state government showed little interest in continuing the project or adopting its activities and goals into its employment and training service delivery system. These differences manifested themselves in the long-term outcomes of the individual projects. Second, in terms of accountability, the Wisconsin NTO Leadership Team continued to hone its database and review its progress in published documents such as DCJC's "Building the Tool Kit Initiative: 2000 Annual Report and Evaluation." *Project TExAS* set very modest goals, emphasizing investments in individual women over total numbers. Both projects actively recruited women, as well. Third, concerning pretraining options, *Project TExAS* really highlighted the importance of pretraining by devoting most of its resources toward it. The pretraining regimen provided through T3 could be considered a model pretraining program, as it targeted the barriers to employment faced by its participants. Both projects developed strategies for retaining women in NTOs and preventing sexual harassment in the workplace, but the retention and prevention actions in *Project TExAS* were primarily those of TSTC. Finally, both *Project TExAS* and the *NTO Tool Kit* channeled their efforts toward growth industries based on local labor market analyses.

The ideal NEW project would incorporate aspects of both *Project TExAS* and the *NTO Tool Kit*: both provide up-front investments in women workers and alter the structures of local labor markets to integrate them into high-skilled, well-paying fields. Texas emphasized the importance of up-front investments in women to improve their economic welfare over the long term, but lacked the leadership buy-in to incorporate the project into the state's service delivery system. Wisconsin consolidated a vast and diverse network of individuals working toward increasing women's participation in high-skilled jobs, but its emphasis on placement could undermine the overall goal of increasing women's economic welfare in the long run. Rather than making a special effort to expose non-college women to alternative training and employment paths, eventually, all job seekers will receive information on all types of jobs, to simply guarantee an informed career choice.

The difference in long-range outcomes for *Project TExAS* and the NTO Tool Kit showed the important role of networking and leadership buy-in. Moreover, the difference between long- and short-run successes of training and placing women in NTOs in these two programs showed two different approaches to employment and training projects. The Texas project emphasized pretraining and relatively costlier, front-end investments in the education of a small number of at-risk women, although Gaylen Lange's return on investment analysis revealed the fairly quick payback of the state dollars invested. The Wisconsin project sought to change the structure of local labor markets; thereby operating on the labor demand side, while Texas emphasized the labor supply side. Human resources were leveraged through expansive and deep networks of women who have been involved with alternative post-secondary employment and training projects for years. Information was highly leveraged through research and publications on best practices, through conferences, networking with other organizations, and via electronic means, where information was shared between tradeswomen, nonprofits, and researchers.

It is not clear what the effects of the current economic slump have been on initiatives for non-college women in high-skilled, high-paying jobs. State budgets have been hit hard, and Texas and Wisconsin are no exception. While economic downturns sometimes spur activity in employment and training policy, it is not clear whether or not this has occurred or will occur. Regardless, this case study analysis demonstrates the importance of government involvement via policy intervention necessary to unite segments of the labor market that fail to communicate in the absence of sustained networks. When grantees effectively leveraged human, information, and financial resources within networks, demonstrated program effectiveness to union and employer stakeholders, and obtained political buy-in, NTO became best practices. Initiatives lacking policy involvement cannot alter the structures of local labor markets and bring about institutionalized change where change is needed. The next chapter analyzes nonprofit, community-based organizations and their best practices in grant-funded employment and training service delivery, and combines those findings with the findings from state-level programs in this chapter.

Chapter 7
Nuts and Bolts II

How Nonprofits' Programs Worked

> I wanted a union job because I am not just supporting myself,
> I have two children to think of . . . it's awesome because
> when people ask my kids someday, "What does your
> mommy do?" they can say, "She's a brick mason." I
> have to work harder for them.
> —*Tonya, brick mason*[1]

Tonya recognizes not only the value of nontraditional employment for herself and her family, but also the importance of her succeeding in a nontraditional occupation (NTO) for other women who want to follow in her footsteps, "next time a woman comes looking for a job, I can hire her."[2] Just as mentoring and retention are key factors in the success of state Nontraditional Employment for Women (NEW) funded projects, so they are key for nonprofits' Women in Apprenticeships and Nontraditional Occupations (WANTO) funded projects, as well. Criteria for evaluating nonprofit grantees are the same as those used to evaluate state agency grantees in the previous chapter: Brigid O'Farrell's WANTO and NEW grantee best practices outlined in Table 6.1.[3] The WANTO grantees help employers and unions to recruit, train, and retain women in NTOs. Employers receive assistance reaching out to the largely untapped female workforce with guidance from, for instance, the Home Builders Institute's (HBI) *Opening New Doors in Residential Construction: A Manual for Employers Seeking to Hire Women for Nontraditional Occupations*, which contains templates for help-wanted advertisements, a selection of these are shown in Box 7.1.

In addition to assistance with recruitment, HBI's *Manual* provides in-depth information and step-by-step guidance on placement, mentoring, and retention, and on preventing sexual harassment on jobsites. Similarly, Tradeswomen of Purpose/Women in Non-Traditional Work, Inc. (TOP/WIN) in Philadelphia, another WANTO grantee, created *Workplace Diversity: Achieving a Unified Workforce Trainer's Manual* with the International Union of Operating Engineers (IUOE) National Training Program. The TOP/WIN, IUOE

Box 7.1

Help-Wanted Ad Templates: "Successfully Recruiting Women for Nontraditional Jobs: Step Three, Effective Classified Ads, Fliers, Mailing Lists, PSAs and Media" by the Home Builders Institute, 1997

WOMEN—Tired of the same old work routine with the same low pay? Do you like a job that requires being physically active, where at the end of the day you see something besides a pile of papers? A job in home building could be the answer. The building market is hot—call xxx–xxx–xxxx about jobs/training that use your hands, your energy, your brains. Reliable transportation a must. Call now: xxx–xxx–xxxx.

BIRDS DO IT, BEES DO IT . . . WE ARE TALKING BUILDING, AND YOU CAN DO IT TOO!
Women and men wanted to grow with our company—positions as [insert trade] available today. You will earn; we will train; together we will build the future. Call xxx–xxx–xxxx today.

CAN YOU FOLLOW A PATTERN? DOUBLE OR HALF A RECIPE? WORK WITH YOUR HANDS? DO YOU ENJOY KEEPING BUSY?
Use the skills you know and like to use to get a job, and a career, in the residential construction industry. XYZ Company needs carpenters (plumbers, drafters, whatever). Call today to see how your skills fit our jobs. Call xxx–xxx–xxxx now.

Source: Home Builders Institute (HBI), *Opening New Doors in Residential Construction: A Manual for Employers Seeking to Hire Women for Nontraditional Occupations* (Washington, DC: HBI, 1997).

Manual provides a list of "Tips for Successful Diversity Training," a selection of which is listed in Box 7.2.

While recruitment, placement, retention, and prevention are key to program success—indeed, they are the very definitions of success according to the language in the WANTO Act—networking and leadership buy-in were critical factors in nonprofits' long-term success. Leveraging human resources, financial resources, and information allowed nonprofit organizations to work together toward common goals and have a greater impact on women's participation in NTOs than any of their individual resources would have allowed. Recall from Chapter 6 that the successfully

---

Box 7.2

Sexual Harassment Prevention: "Tips for Successful Diversity Training" by Tradeswomen of Purpose/Women in Nontraditional Work, Inc. and the International Union of Operating Engineers, 1995

DO:

ENCOURAGE PARTICIPANTS TO TALK—Try to draw out the quieter participants.

HANDLE DISAGREEMENTS—Effective diversity training includes some volatile issues. Disagreements may occur so you may have to "referee." Try to work through disagreements to find common ground. There are no perfect answers when dealing with attitudes, stereotypes, and prejudices.

DON'T:

LET A FEW PARTICIPANTS MONOPOLIZE THE CONVERSATION—Use phrases like, "What does someone else think about this?" or "Let's make sure everyone has a chance to contribute before someone speaks twice."

BE AFRAID OF SILENCE—There may be moments when no one speaks. It's not uncommon in diversity training.

BE JUDGMENTAL—This is the quickest way to stifle a conversation, and, after all, this whole workshop focuses on being less judgmental.

Source: Tradeswomen of Purpose/Women in Nontraditional Work, Inc. (TOP/WIN) and the International Union of Operating Engineers (IUOE) National Training Program, *Workplace Diversity: Achieving a Unified Workforce Trainer's Manual* (Philadelphia, PA: TOP/WIN and IUOE, 1995).

---

networked state agency created those networks with nonprofit and advocacy organizations, including tradeswomen's advocacy and mentoring groups. A key difference between state agency NEW grantees and nonprofit WANTO grantees is in the manner in which leadership buy-in is secured. For nonprofit organizations, leadership buy-in takes the form of political advocacy. Although state agency grantees secure the buy-in of political decision makers, employers, and unions, they cannot overtly lobby on behalf of their issues to policymakers. While nonprofits must also secure buy-in from employers and unions, securing leadership buy-in from policymakers often takes the form of political advocacy, an activity that is very important to nonprofit effectiveness.[4]

Political Advocacy and Government Grant Programs

The Strengthening Nonprofit Advocacy Project (SNAP) is a collaboration between the Office of Management and Budget (OMB) Watch, Tufts University, and charity lobbying in the public interest "to investigate factors that motivate nonprofit organizations to engage in public policy matters."[5] A report of the initial research phase of SNAP, an ongoing project, was released in the fall of 2002. Through a nationwide survey, telephone interviews, and focus groups that reached over 1,700 nonprofit organizations, SNAP researchers found that roughly three-fourths of their nonprofit respondents engaged in key policy activities, including: "direct or grassroots lobbying or testifying at a legislative or administrative hearing . . . they have encouraged their members to write, call, fax or email policymakers . . . they have lobbied on behalf of or against a proposed bill of other policy pronouncement, and . . . have testified at legislative or administrative hearings."[6]

Despite the high rate of political advocacy among nonprofits, SNAP researchers also find that nonprofits' levels of public policy participation were low and inconsistent; however, executive directors and nonprofits consistently reported that advocacy and participation in the policymaking process "is essential to carrying out their mission . . . [and] . . . being a policy advocate is a key responsibility of running an organization."[7] Advocacy activities were emphasized as well by Curtis W. Meadows, Jr., former president, chief executive officer, and director of the Meadows Foundation in Dallas, Texas, and a professor of Public Affairs specializing in nonprofit management and philanthropic organizations. He underscores the importance of a nonprofit organization's involvement in its political context, particularly its role in lobbying public decision makers on behalf of its interests.[8]

The present analysis, which focuses on nonprofits in contracting regimes and those receiving government funds through grants or contracts, finds further evidence of the importance of advocacy to an organization. This population is very important because the earliest antilobbying provisions limited the advocacy activities of entities receiving public monies. Although the contracting regime is characterized by an asymmetric balance-of-power between the public funder and the nonprofit grant recipient, particularly as more restrictions are placed on the use of government funds, contract relationships have been found to be largely mutually beneficial and voluntary. Two studies by Sharon Harlan and Judith Saidel examined the role of boards of directors in nonprofit–government relationships, focusing on board functions that "encourage or maintain the contracting relationship between government and voluntary organizations" including acting as facilitators, political advocates, buffers, and "values guardians."[9] As facilitators, boards of directors can foster positive and mutually beneficial interdependence between their nonprofits and government funders by meeting with government grant officers during the application, review, and renewal periods. Boards can also mitigate the imbalance of power in the contracting regime by reviewing and negotiating contract terms. These actions are also part of a board's political advocacy role, but, board members can and do directly lobby legislators on behalf of their nonprofits, as well. The roles of "buffer" and "values guardian" are also related. The board can protect its nonprofit organization from vendorism: "the potential of government-set objectives to undermine nonprofit autonomy through mission distortion or priority reordering." Boards can mitigate vendorism by "monitoring the potential divergence between government and nonprofit interests."[10]

When the risk of vendorism is high, board members can reconsider its relationship with the government funder, and as a values guardian, the board of directors is in the position to appeal to its community clientele and gain buy-in on its mission and autonomy. By raising its profile in the community and expanding its range of potential stakeholders, a nonprofit organization protects itself from being relegated to the role of conduit or vendor of government services. Harlan and Saidel conclude, "executives and boards pull together to strike a balance of power that may strengthen the nonprofit in getting from government what it needs and resisting unwanted encroachments on autonomy."[11] Herman and Renz[12] emphasize the role of stakeholders and practitioners in properly measuring the effectiveness of nonprofit organizations. In contracting regimes, government is a key stakeholder. Some authors note the risk of "vendorism": when a government funder dictates its needs to such an extent that the nonprofit organization becomes just a conduit of government services, jeopardizing its mission, autonomy, and character.[13] While this risk exists, most government–nonprofit unions are mutually beneficial ones in which both parties *elect* to engage. The power imbalance of these unions benefits the public sector entity, however. Persistent political advocacy allows nonprofits to preserve their missions and goals, and avoid falling prey to vendorism. Recent Federal Election Commission rule changes could outlaw some political advocacy activities, making the sometimes-asymmetrical contracting regime even more lopsided.[14]

In their survey of 215 nonprofit agencies in New York, Saidel and Harlan found that most of the government-funded nonprofits in their sample used their boards to act as buffers between themselves and their government grantors. The authors also observed the following:

Over one-third of the nonprofits with government revenues in our sample were *bystanders in political advocacy.* Neither executive staff nor members of the board were involved in influencing public policies that may have had immediate or longer-range impacts. This finding may indicate that a high proportion of individual nonprofit organizations engaged in contracting with government *are on the public policy sideline.*[15]

Why would this be, if the findings of both this study and SNAP are correct, and nonprofits acknowledge the importance of advocacy? Furthermore, SNAP researchers also found that nonprofits, especially those receiving government funds, overestimate the antilobbying limits imposed on them.[16] Saidel and Harlan stated that nonprofits are capable of playing a much greater role in policymaking than they currently are. Misunderstanding the complex and increasingly politicized legal environment curbs important advocacy work. This is consistent with SNAP's findings that, although nonprofits know advocacy is important, participation is inconsistent.

The nonprofit community-based organizations (CBOs) studied here receive funds from the WANTO program to provide technical assistance to employers and unions for the purpose of increasing women's participation in NTOs. Would female-headed nonprofits be expected to behave differently with respect to lobbying and advocacy? Although the literature is not unanimous, evidence suggests women in nonprofits play significant and effective roles in lobbying and advocacy, and that nonprofits resembling their constituencies are especially effective in achieving their missions.[17] Such findings are particularly relevant, in that women have run the majority of nonprofit grantees under WANTO.

Women in Apprenticeships and Nontraditional Occupations Technical Assistance Grants

According to O'Farrell's overview of the WANTO technical assistance grant program, since 1994, the twenty-seven CBOs that have received grants have assisted over 2,500 employers and unions in training, placing, and retaining more women into nontraditional occupations.[18] The two organizations that have received more WANTO grants than any other grantee were chosen for the current case study analysis, as exemplary cases.

Wider Opportunities for Women

The literature on nonprofit organizations in contracting regimes reveals the characteristics or practices of nonprofits with government contracts that successfully deliver services and achieve their objectives. Many of these best practices are already covered by Brigid O'Farrell's criteria for judging successful grantees implementing projects for women in NTOs. This case study analysis consisted of site visits, interviews, and archival analyses, to capture the ways in which the organization implemented and ran grant-funded projects. Just as in the previous chapter, it is important to note that the cases are the organizations that implemented WANTO-funded projects, and not individual women who went through the training courses. Focusing on the implementation of the projects assumes that the manner in which services were delivered was a factor in the success or failure of the project. In addition, focusing on the nonprofit organizations themselves follows other analyses that study institutions.[19]

Wider Opportunities for Women (WOW) was created in 1964 as a local Washington, DC, effort to help women gain economic self-sufficiency, and has since become a multifaceted women's employment organization with national recognition of its training models, technical assistance, and advocacy for women workers. With roughly ten employees plus some volunteers, WOW has never been much larger. It received WANTO in 1994, 1996, and 1997, and partnered with the HBI in 1995, Urban Family Institute in 1998, and the *Centro del Obrero Fronterizo* for *La Mujer Obrera* in 1999 on joint WANTO projects.

Wider Opportunities for Women operates several local and national women's employment projects. Nationally, WOW runs the State Organizing Project for Family Economic Self-Sufficiency, Workplace Solutions, and Work4Women. Workplace Solutions is a Web-based, technical assistance network to help employers and unions increase women's access to, and support and retention in, apprenticeships and nontraditional employment. Work4Women is a technical assistance project to help women, girls, and educators, and workforce development professionals increase women's access to and advancement in NTOs.

In the Washington, DC, area, WOW has operated several projects targeting women who are on welfare and those transitioning from welfare to work. These projects included the Blueprint for the Capital Region, a training program to help welfare recipients to understand and overcome barriers to employment; the Constructing Avenues Project, a skills training program to prepare welfare recipients and noncustodial parents for employment in residential and commercial construction; the Work Skills program for local women making the transition from welfare to work through basic skills training and an orientation toward high-wage, nontraditional jobs for women. Job Connections 2000 links employers, unions, and apprenticeship programs in the information technology and telecommunications industries with qualified low-income women.

To date, WOW's major WANTO-funded projects have involved the development and expansion of on-line resources to provide technical assistance to employers and unions to improve the workplace for women entering and working in NTOs. They have created a standard curriculum addressing a range of technical assistance needs of employers and unions, including in-service training for managers, line staff, union members, and bargaining personnel on strategies for making the workplace more responsive to women in nontraditional jobs. Through on-site consultations, WOW technical assistants have created model employer policies and procedures, as well as a checklist to evaluate current policies for women in NTOs.

Wider Opportunities for Women has played a key role in both NEW and WANTO. As a member of a larger network of women's advocacy organizations in the Washington area, WOW mobilizes its sister organizations to preserve WANTO on an annual basis, and has helped to create the NEW and WANTO programs in the first place. Wider Opportunities for Women worked with Congresswoman Connie Moriella, Republican representative of Maryland's Eighth District, and Representative Patricia Schroeder of Colorado to draft the enabling legislation of WANTO and NEW. Not only has WOW shaped these programs in the legislation, but they have also shaped NEW and WANTO program implementation, as Sandra Kerka observes:

> WOW's (1993) Nontraditional Employment Training (NET) Project has become a model for implementing the Nontraditional Employment for Women [NEW] Act. In the District of Columbia, for example, 80 percent of NEW participants are placed in nontraditional jobs averaging $8.50 per hour. . . . Goodwill Industries' NEW Choices for Women places 89 percent of its graduates in construction jobs.[20]

Although WOW no longer operates its own training centers, it works with an extensive network of other service delivery organizations to provide women training and placement in high-wage jobs, to help women manage their money through financial workshops, and to provide micro-enterprise training and business skills workshops for women interested in operating their own businesses. One of their more widely used products is the "Myths and Realities about Women in Nontraditional Jobs" quiz and fact sheet, which appears in the technical assistance materials for employers, unions, and job center intake workers, and was assembled by several other WANTO grantees. The wide distribution of the "Myths" quiz and fact sheet is an excellent example of leveraging resources and networking by WOW. There are fourteen Myths in all, with extensive information about Realities accompanying each. Box 7.3 contains a selection of WOW's "Myths and Realities."

Box 7.3
**"Myths and Realities About Women in Nontraditional Jobs"
by Wider Opportunities for Women**

Myth 5.
Blue-collar work or heavy, physical labor is nontraditional for women.
FACT
Many jobs now thought to be nontraditional for women have been performed by women in the past. Throughout history, women have done heavy labor on the farm and in the fields alongside men. During World War II, over 6 million women entered the labor force to build ships and airplanes and make factory goods. These jobs are currently considered nontraditional only because women are underrepresented in them at the present time.

Myth 6.
Women are not strong enough to do heavy labor.
FACT
The strength requirements for nontraditional jobs are often exaggerated. Many nontraditional jobs are less physically demanding than housework, and many traditional women's jobs, such as nursing and waitressing, are just as physically demanding as some nontraditional jobs. Moreover, the Occupational Safety and Health Administration (OSHA) requires that special equipment be provided for every heavy job regardless of whether it is being performed by a man or a woman. In addition, mechanization continues to decrease the level of physical strength demanded by many jobs. Finally, while the average man is stronger than the average woman, some women are stronger than some men. In addition, women can develop both upper-body and lower-body strength with training.

Myth 10.
Women will leave a job to get married and have children; therefore, the job should go to a man who will stay.
FACT
A survey conducted in March 1992 found that the average woman worked 30 years over the course of her lifetime, regardless of whether or not she was married. More than half of the women who do leave

Box 7.3 *(continued)*

work to have children return to the labor force when the child is one year old or younger. By the time their youngest child is three years old, at least 6 out of every 10 mothers have entered or returned to the labor force.

Myth 12.

Women on a job site make it difficult for men to concentrate; the women are too distracting.

FACT

It is different, at first, to have a woman on a work site if an employer has never hired a female worker before. Employers can ensure the productivity of all the workers by telling employees that a qualified woman has been hired and that harassment will not be tolerated. While sexual harassment can happen in any work environment, it can be particularly harsh for women working in nontraditional occupations. The problem that must be stopped is the harassing behavior, not women's entrance into the workplace.

Source: Wider Opportunities for Women (WOW), "Myths and Realities about Women in Nontraditional Jobs," www.wowonline.org/workplace%20solutions/about/myths.cfm. Wider Opportunities for Women information was collected via several sources: Camille C. Inez, project and Web site manager, WOW interview by author, Washington, DC, March 14, 2001; Wider Opportunities for Women, *Respect That Woman*, 30 min. video, prod. and dir. WOW, 1995; Wider Opportunities for Women, site visits by author, Washington, DC, March 14, 2001.

In its political advocacy activities, WOW channels its resources into networking with other CBOs on projects that help them achieve their goal of assisting women to become self-supporting. Each year during budget negotiations on Capitol Hill, WOW has mobilized its networking partners to preserve the WANTO line item. Moreover, WOW played a significant role in mobilizing the opposition to the Bush administration's 2001 proposal to eliminate the Women's Bureau's regional offices and drastically cut the budget and personnel of the Washington office. The president's proposal would have eliminated the eighty-year-old Women's Bureau and all of its programs, including WANTO.[21] WOW and a nationwide network of women's advocacy organizations alerted policymakers and supporters, culminating in a letter to the White House signed by nearly seventy members of Congress.[22]

Workplace Solutions

Wider Opportunities for Women's major WANTO-funded projects to date have involved the development and expansion of the Workplace Solutions project. For their first WANTO grant in 1994, WOW established Workplace Solutions, a program providing technical assistance to employers and unions to improve the workplace for women entering and working in NTOs. This project developed, piloted, and adapted technical assistance for different settings (large urban, multistate metro areas, large state with urban and rural communities, and largely rural areas), and created a standard curriculum addressing a range of technical assistance needs of employers and unions, including in-service training for managers, line staff, union members, and bargaining personnel on strategies for making the workplace more responsive to women in nontraditional jobs. Through on-site consultations, WOW technical assistants created model employer policies and procedures, as well as a checklist to evaluate current policies for women in NTOs. In addition, WOW developed recruitment, screening, and employment testing strategies, created employee orientation and pretraining program models, organized on-site and off-site support groups, and developed techniques for addressing different facilities and equipment needs for women workers, and sexual harassment issues.

The Workplace Solutions project provided direct technical assistance to more than fifty employers and nine unions, and produced three manuals for use by unions and employers: *Workplace Solutions Manual for Unions*, *Workplace Solutions Manual for Employers*, and *Making the Workplace More Receptive to Women in Nontraditional Jobs*, which was based on a "train the trainer" conference, "What Trainers Need to Know." They also created a training video and guide entitled *Respect That Woman*,[23] on sexual harassment in the workplace.

Their second WANTO grant was awarded in 1996, for the purpose of developing a Web site and an on-line technical assistance network, based on the original Workplace Solutions project. These materials are still available today, the Web site, on-line resources, and e-mail lists. In this grant project, WOW provided technical assistance to develop and pilot Workplace Solutions, a national computer-based technical assistance network and Web site (www.WorkplaceSolutions.org). The Web site continues to offer free resources, including assessment tools, publications, and videos, and services, and referrals to expert technical assistance providers, to assist employers and unions to increase the access and success rates of women in nontraditional apprenticeships, training programs, and occupations. Unfortunately, WANTO funds have not been sufficient to support the ongoing maintenance of this Web site. Through Workplace Solutions, WOW also operates an information clearinghouse to assist employers and unions in their preparation to increase the participation of women in apprenticeship and NTOs in their workplaces and job sites.

Work4Women

Wider Opportunities for Women's 1997 WANTO grant was awarded to extend the original Workplace Solutions project to populations of women other than those targeted in the first phases of the project. Building upon the work of Workplace Solutions on-line, WOW created the Work4Women Web site to serve women, girls, and workforce development professionals. This site, www.Work4Women.org, continues to provide tools, strategies, and a virtual community to help increase the integration and retention of women in high-wage NTOs and increase the number of girls involved in nontraditional "Tech Prep" programs or in math and science courses in secondary school.

Partnership Projects of Women in Apprenticeships and Nontraditional Occupations

Wider Opportunities for Women and the HBI received a WANTO grant in 1995 to work with employers and unions in residential and light commercial construction. In 1998 and 1999, WANTO grants were awarded to WOW in partnership with the Urban Family Institute and the *Centro del Obrero de la Mujer Obrera*. For each, WOW implemented their Jobs Connection 2000 project, which was mentioned earlier as one of WOW's DC-area initiatives.

Under their 1999 WANTO grant, WOW and *La Mujer Obrera* worked with the El Paso Hispanic Chamber of Commerce and provided technical assistance to ten employers and labor unions in the local construction industry, targeting displaced homemakers and low-income women workers in El Paso County, particularly those living or studying in the El Paso Empowerment Zone. Wider Opportunities for Women and *La Mujer Obrera* focused on employee attitudes toward promoting female workers in apprenticeship and other nontraditional jobs to make systematic changes in employers' recruitment and training of women in construction, and to increase the numbers of women in construction apprenticeships. *La Mujer Obrera* has provided services to low-income Spanish-speaking women workers in the El Paso area for several years, most recently to those affected by the growth in low-wage border-area manufacturing jobs. *La Mujer Obrera* has developed strong working relationships with employers, unions, and government entities, and has helped to establish the Fashion Development Center to provide training and technical assistance to employers and workers in the garment industry.

Based on the Workplace Solutions products, the manuals, the video, and on-line resources, WOW has made a significant impact on women's participation in NTOs *by filling the information gaps* held by both workers and employers. Filling information gaps in this way helped to mitigate the effects of stereotypes held by employers, which kept them from recruiting women. Filling these gaps also helped to mitigate the effects of stereotypes held by women who might be interested in these jobs but had not considered them because they were unaware of the potential of such jobs or because they believed that women were not suited for them.

However, it would not be appropriate to depict the contribution of WOW's technical assistance to mere information. Many women require weight training to become strong enough to do the work in some NTOs, particularly construction and the trowel trades, including masonry and tile setting. WANTO grantees like WOW refer many women to weight training programs to build strength. Many women also require smaller-sized tool belts, work boots, work gloves, and hard hats, than those usually available. In addition to referring women to special retailers, WOW receives in-kind donations of shop equipment, fitness equipment, and apparel, and provides it to women at no charge.

Employers and unions require more than just information. According to WOW and other WANTO grant recipients, many NTO employers were aware of their labor shortages, but did not know where to begin recruiting and training women. Wider Opportunities for Women's *Workplace Solutions: The Employer Manual*[24] and *Workplace Solutions: The Union Manual*[25] provide strategies developed by employers and unions across the country to increase the numbers of women employed in nontraditional areas. Wider Opportunities for Women created these and other manuals and videos to inform employers and unions about sexual harassment laws, definitions of sexual harassment, and what NTO women tend to face in the workplace. Employers and unions have required not only this information, but also on-site assistance to implement change.

As grant recipients, WOW maintains good records to track progress of their projects. This addresses the accountability issue that Brigid O'Farrell found to be so important. With respect to the delivery of training and employment services, WOW recognized that their moderate human and financial resources would be put to use more effectively by working with other CBOs that offer recruitment, training, and placement services, rather than operating a training center themselves.

Wider Opportunities for Women specializes in networking and partnering with other organizations, mainly in the Washington area. Clearly, their ability to network successfully is because there are many organizations in the area with which WOW can network and partner. More geographically isolated grantees may not be able to leverage their resources so effectively. Wider Opportunities for Women is a small organization that has worked in the same issue areas for many years. It was apparent that it successfully implemented its projects, whether WANTO-funded or not, because it filled a niche in the issue area and targeted its efforts in a very specific way. The organization also appears to be very effective in its political environments, advocating on behalf of its issues, no doubt due to its longtime presence in Washington, DC. It has been a player in drafting and implementing legislation on issues of women and work since 1964, and has made the most of its location in the nation's capital.

Chicago Women in Trades

Similar to WOW's focus on bringing employment and training service delivery organizations together and leveraging their networks in the beltway, Chicago Women in Trades (CWIT) has focused on projects and organizations in the Midwest. A grassroots organization, CWIT has worked to increase the numbers of women in construction trades since 1981. In recent years, it has expanded its focus beyond construction and has worked with employers in the manufacturing industry. In six of the eight years of the WANTO program, CWIT received grants. Like WOW, CWIT has devoted a significant amount of resources to gathering information and assimilating it into manuals and handbooks so that future efforts may capitalize on their work. Its grant-funded projects have focused on regional collaborations and large-scale construction projects, on building relationships and securing support from the highest decision makers among their employer and union clients, and on maintaining close ties over time with tradeswomen who have been in these occupations.

In 1994, CWIT received its first WANTO grant in collaboration with four other Midwestern organizations: Minnesota Women in the Trades (MWIT), YWCA of Milwaukee Nontraditional Employment Training, Employment Options, Inc. (EOI) of Madison, Wisconsin, and Hard Hatted Women of Cleveland, Ohio. This collaboration occurred in part due to CWIT's realization of a lack of support services and employment strategies for women in trades, resulting from its in-depth study of over 450 tradeswomen in construction. Its findings were reported in *Breaking New Ground: Worksite 2000*, published in 1992.

Worksite 2000 revealed that women in construction either learned to cope with hostile work environments, or they left. No workplace strategy existed, and the individual, ad hoc, case-by-case approach common in the industry created a hostile work environment. This violated a woman's right to try to make a living in a job she was trained to do, in a nonviolent workplace. *Worksite 2000* was created as a replicable model that could be implemented at other worksites, and it represented a strategic approach to integrating women into construction trades:

> *Worksite 2000* shifted the focus away from the individual woman to the institutions that held legal responsibility for Equal Employment Opportunity (EEO) and Affirmative Action. That shift required an institutional approach to increasing the numbers of women working under equitable conditions in construction. Only partnerships of industry, labor, government, and the community would achieve both concrete change and better outcomes.[26]

Its recommendations, which included educating employees on the definitions and the laws about sexual harassment, providing separate bathroom and changing facilities, avoiding isolating women on worksites, and imposing a zero-tolerance policy on the job, were based on the experiences of tradeswomen, and were intended for use by contractors, unions, training programs, and public agencies "to prepare for a workforce in which two-thirds of all new entrants will be women and minorities."[27] These findings should sound familiar because many people interested in women in NTOs have discussed them. This report spurred the creation of the Great Lakes Tradeswoman Alliance, spearheaded by CWIT, and helped develop several WANTO-funded projects.

Drafting the Blueprint

The Great Lakes Tradeswoman Alliance consists of six tradeswomen's advocacy organizations in five midwestern states, plus Tools for Tomorrow, a training organization housed at the Madison Area Technical College. Recall that Madison Area Technical College was involved with the *Tool Kit* initiative for the state of Wisconsin, and they continued to participate there, too. The Great Lakes Tradeswoman Alliance received a WANTO grant in 1996 to implement the *Worksite 2000* recommendations[28] at several "mega-project" construction sites, including projects for the Chicago Public Schools, a new football stadium for the Cleveland Browns, a new federal courthouse in Cleveland, a St. Paul, Minnesota hockey arena, the Hennepin County jail, the Minneapolis convention center, the Miller Park baseball stadium in Milwaukee, and a Milwaukee-area economic redevelopment project. Participants worked with thirteen construction mega-projects in four states, comprised of twenty-nine general contractors and twenty-four subcontractors, and conducted more than ninety technical assistance and strategic planning meetings and thirty-eight training sessions to industry, labor, government, and CBOs throughout the project period.

To build on the *Worksite 2000* model, the experiences of each of the Alliance members were incorporated into a how-to manual, entitled *Drafting the Blueprint: A Planning Guide for Achieving Workforce Diversity and Equity in Construction*.[29] Completing this manual was a major contribution of the WANTO-funded project, and, as the project evaluation found, the "Midwest regional partners wanted to add something different to the small library of nationwide materials that concentrate on women in nontraditional occupations."[30] Moreover, the Alliance "Focused its efforts on influencing the baseline systems, goals, and procedures used on site-based workforce equity projects for the construction industry. Because of this emphasis, the effects were widespread and will endure well beyond the grant activity timeframe."[31]

Women's "workforce utilization" increased on all the mega-project sites. It is important that the measures of success were "utilization," because that took into account not just the numbers of women on the site, but also the numbers of hours they worked.

Drafting the Blueprint described the process for working with contractors on mega-project sites. The *Blueprint* emphasized the principles mentioned before: collaborate and network with other organizations, focus on large-scale construction sites, build relationships and secure support from the highest decision makers involved, and maintain close ties with tradeswomen. Most important, the *Blueprint* hoped to improve the technical assistance provided to construction contractors by emphasizing planning and relationship building in the overall process, to a far greater degree than had *Worksite 2000*.

Although CWIT's political activities have been less pronounced than WOW's have been, it would be a mistake to presume that their interests are regional and exclude political influence. The founding conference of CWIT's Tradeswomen Now and Tomorrow was held in March 2002. Tradeswomen Now and Tomorrow (TNT) is a "national coalition of tradeswomen's advocates and organizations combining regional efforts to create a national voice . . . to promote policies and actions that achieve women's economic equity by increasing the number of women in trade and technical jobs and by improving their working conditions." It seeks "to influence national policies relating to women in the trades and technical fields [and] promote the enforcement and expansion of federal policies to increase women's access to trades and technical jobs."[32]

Moreover, CWIT has testified before the Illinois Legislature in Springfield to support a bill that would make information about state-funded job opportunities available on the jobsite and require state contractors to submit monthly reports detailing their hires by race and gender. Hard-Hatted Women found "politics can play a significant role in determining whether or not tradeswomen have increased access to construction jobs" and that "building future partnerships with employers, labor and government" is essential to their long-term success. Likewise, MWIT asserted that the "people in positions of authority over the project—who truly support women in construction, are an essential key to project success." Change came most readily when "those with power supported the change, whether it was a prime contractor, project owner, or government entity with jurisdiction over the site."[33] In addition to TNT's activities, marshaling support for projects has required CWIT to provide information to political decision makers.

Manufacturing Opportunities for Women

In partnership with the Tooling Manufacturing Association, CWIT received WANTO grants in 1998 and 1999 to provide technical assistance to manufacturing employers and unions and the training programs that serve them. The goal of CWIT was to create the *Guide for Manufacturing Intern Programs* as a model for manufacturing, akin to *Worksite 2000* for construction, and to place fifteen women in manufacturing internships.[34] This project was designed to expand the pool of well-trained women for jobs in higher-end manufacturing occupations including tool and die, machining, and metal fabrication.

Initially, CWIT sought to build relationships with five manufacturing training programs and several employers and to provide the same types of technical assistance that it had provided for the construction industry. However, it soon discovered that manufacturing employers were interested in receiving only well-trained job candidates to address their current labor shortages, and were not receptive to engaging in longer-term technical assistance projects.[35]

Chicago Women in Trades has expanded its manufacturing program to a third year because the process of building relationships with industry had proved to be a longer-term activity than they had anticipated. The *Manufacturing Opportunities for Women* project was evaluated by the Center for Research on Women and Gender (CRWG) of the University of Illinois at Chicago (UIC) in 2000.[36] So far, CWIT's manufacturing industry efforts have allowed them to contact more than ninety firms, work directly with thirty of them, and engage in technical assistance projects with ten firms. CWIT worked with seven training programs in woodworking, tool and die making, and metalworking. One training program was the Greater West Town Training Partnership, in which thirty-two women had been placed at the time of the evaluation, and eight internship positions had been created. The UIC evaluation of this project emphasized the importance of realistic project goals and record-keeping procedures, and recommended that CWIT continue to build relationships with key manufacturing organizations and further develop this project. CWIT's 2002 WANTO grant project replicates the initial *Worksite 2000* model to test its generalizability in changing economic conditions.

Five of the six grant-funded projects of the Great Lakes Tradeswoman Alliance were successful because they increased women's participation, in both their numbers and hours worked, in construction trades. Employment Options, Ínc. initially worked with contractors on a University of Wisconsin capital improvement project, but the project was abandoned after key EOI staff resigned and the organization permanently disbanded in 1998. Other members of the Alliance were not able to provide the staff to take on that project, and, therefore, the technical assistance promised in the WANTO grant application was never delivered. This was a unique circumstance "due to significant, ongoing, internal staffing and leadership issues at the organiza-tion,"[37] which has not reflected poorly on the Tradeswomen Alliance.

Summary of Findings from Nonprofit Grantees and Women in Apprenticeships and Nontraditional Occupations Overall

Networking: Leveraging Human, Financial, and Information Resources

The Great Lakes Alliance's WANTO grant evaluation observed:

> An economy of scale exists on large construction sites where the limited resources of community, government, and industry can be utilized where they will have the most effect. Modifications of systems to support workforce equity can be accomplished all at once—rather than small site by small site, contractor by contractor, union by union—thus having more widespread results and reducing duplication of effort.[38]

The small grant amounts forced all grantees to leverage resources, but the mega-project site allowed Alliance members to make the most of their staff and grant monies. The Great Lakes Tradeswoman Alliance also lever-aged information by working in collaboration, and by building on the *Worksite 2000* model, then publishing and distributing their best practices. Finally, several Alliance members leveraged their limited funds. Hard Hat-ted Women provided WANTO technical assistance services through a project that received Intermodal Surface Transportation Efficiency Act (ISTEA) funds; YWCA/NET provided technical assistance on a project that was part of an Enterprise Zone redevelopment project. Chicago Women in Trades fully capitalized on its WANTO grant by obtaining a fee-for-service contract from its technical assistance client; receiving pay for services allowed CWIT to use remaining WANTO funds in other ways to support its workforce equity project. Hard Hatted Women and MWIT proposed similar arrangements to their industry partners, as well.

Leadership Buy-In/Political Advocacy

Every organization in the Tradeswoman Alliance found that the support of leaders in industry, government, and the community was crucial to their success. Recently, CWIT testified before the Illinois Legislature in Springfield to support a bill that would make information about state-funded job opportunities available on the job site and require state contractors to submit monthly reports detailing their hires by race and gender.[39] Chicago Women in Trades also focused on obtaining the buy-in of the communities and clients it served, particularly public- and private-sector decision makers who could impact their efforts. CWIT had enough to do and too little money and time to do it, to try to work in hostile environments where employers and union leaders were not interested in complying with EEO on their job sites: "CWIT learned that technical assistance is only as good as—and often limited by—the existing framework of EEO compliance . . . and that, essential to meeting *their* goals as a tradeswomen's advocacy organization, they need to combine external advocacy with internal technical assistance on a project to achieve desired outcomes."[40]

Similarly, in Cleveland, Hard Hatted Women found "politics can play a significant role in determining whether or not tradeswomen have increased access to construction jobs" and that "building future partnerships with employers, labor, and government" would be essential to their long-term success.[41] Likewise, MWIT asserted that the "people in positions of authority over the project, who truly support women in construction, are an essential key to project success." Change came most readily when "those with power supported the change, whether it was a prime contractor, project owner, or government entity with jurisdiction over the site."[42] Advocacy benefits nonprofits' missions, as is demonstrated by WOW and CWIT, and evidence from other studies. Informal networking and advocacy are important to nonprofits' roles in policy development.

The Great Lakes Tradeswoman Alliance applied the *Worksite 2000* model to several mega-projects and reinforced earlier findings about the importance of leadership buy-in, and of leveraging information, financial, and human resources. It also demonstrated the fundamental importance of building and sustaining relationships with industry partners, government, and their communities, and the critical role of planning in the success of their projects.

Wider Opportunities for Women went further, not only creating regional collaborations with its counterparts in the Washington, DC area, but also specializing in information gathering and distribution, networking, and political advocacy. Successful nonprofits are involved in their political environments, they creatively make the most of the scant resources they have, and they network and collaborate with other organizations to meet their objectives. These WANTO grant recipients exhibited the practices and behaviors predicted in Brigid O'Farrell's analyses, and their outcomes largely corresponded to predictions of theory: they implemented successful grant-funded projects and institutionalized themselves into the employment and training service delivery community.

The ideal WANTO-funded project might possess the shrewd lobbying and networking of WOW, while maintaining closer links with tradeswomen, as CWIT has done. Both WOW and CWIT have created regional collaborations and have made the best use of their financial and human resources. Both recognize the importance of political advocacy. The grants themselves were just too small to have had the necessary impact on increasing women's participation in NTOs without networking, leveraging, and securing leadership buy-in through political advocacy, which could not have been captured by statistical analysis alone.

These cases highlight creative and effective efforts to increase the numbers of well-trained tradeswomen into the high-skilled, higher-wage occupations for which they have been trained. Julie Nyland's analysis of public sector and third sector actors in Australia's housing authority illustrated "the way in which policy activists affect the policy process through informal interaction."[43] She shows how nonprofits play a significant role in policy development through issue networks, demonstrated by "a chance meeting" between a lobbyist and a policymaker, or "a working relationship developed and maintained between certain members of a branch of the governing political party, policy advisors, and nonprofit housing workers."[44] Both the literature and these cases underscore the importance of informal networks and political advocacy to nonprofit effectiveness.

Long-Term Success: Institutionalization

The critical role of building and maintaining relationships with industry partners, the community, and government also had a bearing on the degree to which these organizations have insinuated themselves into the larger processes surrounding construction projects. All the members of the Tradeswomen Alliance, even EOI, had long track records in their fields and had credibility with their industry partners and other important groups, prior to collaborating in the Great Lakes Alliance: "All six organizations are well-established, nonprofit community organizations with long histories of work with women in nontraditional occupations and involvement of tradeswomen as staff and as Board members."[45]

Another important factor in institutionalization was earning credibility and acceptance with women currently in NTOs. There existed a subtle schism between training and employment professionals and tradeswomen, who believed service delivery organizations invest too much in training and placement and too little in retention and ongoing support services for women on the job. Chicago Women in Trades maintains closer ties to tradeswomen through TNT and Tools for Change, than WOW does.

Case Study Implications for Policy

Leadership buy-in takes different forms for WANTO and NEW grantees. Buy-in had to be secured from the political hierarchy and agency officials whose decisions affected grant recipients, and from the clients with whom grantee organizations provided technical assistance or training. For both WANTO and NEW grantees, support from the top of the political decision-making hierarchy was critical to the long-range prospects of grant-funded projects. Of the four cases under study here, three secured leadership buy-in. Not coincidentally, three continue in their work, and one does not. The difference in long-range outcomes for *Project TExAS* and Wisconsin's *NTO Tool Kit* showed the important role of political buy-in. Moreover, the difference between long- and short-run successes of training and placing women in NTOs in these two programs showed two different approaches to employment and training projects. The Texas project emphasized pretraining and relatively costlier, front-end investments in the education of a small number of at-risk women. Although Gaylen Lange's return on investment analysis revealed the fairly quick payback of the state dollars invested, high placement numbers in the Wisconsin project could have played a role in the securing of leadership buy-in by the latter, but not by the former.

Both WOW and CWIT aggressively worked toward increasing non-college women's participation in high-skilled, well-paying employment and training programs years before WANTO and NEW were enacted. WOW helped draft the legislation for both programs, and rallies its networks to ensure that WANTO funds remain in the federal budget every year. WOW has been successful in securing political support, and this has benefited all WANTO grant recipients. Within the state of Illinois and the city of Chicago, CWIT has been politically active as well.

Increases in non-college women's participation in NTOs cannot be attributed to the grant monies alone, because all grantees, especially the community-based nonprofit organizations, leveraged their Women's Bureau grants with other resources to achieve their ends. Leveraging financial, human, and information resources helped grantees achieve their objectives. Human resources were leveraged through expansive and deep networks of women who have been involved with NTO projects for years, and through building regional coalitions to multiply the influence of individual organizations seeking to increase the numbers of women in nontraditional jobs and focusing on mega-project construction sites. In addition, WANTO's technical assistance approach made the most of human resources by awarding grants to organizations to work with employers and unions, who, in turn, worked with women employees and union members. Under NEW, individual women were trained and placed in NTOs. Finally, information was also highly leveraged through research and publications on best practices for increasing women's participation in these jobs, through networking with other organizations, and via electronic means through the Internet, where information is shared among tradeswomen, nonprofits, and researchers. The final chapter evaluates all the findings, both quantitative and qualitative, in terms of their implications for non-college employment and training programs and policies, and the future research these findings suggest.

Chapter 8
A Call for Action

> Few women enter the trades through conventional or
> institutional paths; most need the support of a program,
> targeted initiative or special policy.
> —*Lauren Sugerman, president of Chicago Women in Trades*[1]

Consistent with Lauren Sugerman's assertion that women need policy interventions to gain access to and succeed in the trades, Vivian Price analyzes the Century Freeway project in southern California and finds that targeted interventions are necessary and "stronger institutional commitment leads to better results for women's employment in the building trades."[2] Some kind of alternative to college is necessary to meet the needs of a non-college population that still seeks high-paying, rewarding, and high-skilled careers, and occupations exist that offer these things, occupations that do not require a four-year degree. Because the market fails to provide the variety of educational opportunities demanded, public policy intervention is necessary to meet the need. The experiences of *Project TExAS* and the state of Wisconsin also demonstrate the importance of government leadership. Without policy intervention, non-college women tend to hold the same low-paying, low-opportunity jobs year after year. The preceding chapters have demonstrated not only that occupational segregation by gender is intransigent, but also that the training and education options are few and vanishing for the majority who will not graduate with a four-year degree or those who will never attend college.

Both men and women demand post-secondary education and training, and that demand has increased over time. Whether job duties require it or not, employers demand a higher-educated workforce, resulting in an effective requirement for more education and training, if not an actual requirement. Moreover, not only does a "college for all" policy presumption hurt non-college workers by causing alternative education and employment options to be overlooked, but the contributions of non-college workers to the economy, of which they represent the majority, are devalued by presuming college for all. In addition, non-college women fare worse than non-college men do; therefore, cutbacks in post-secondary options end up limiting women's labor market opportunities more so than men's. Presuming college for all results in fewer non-college options, which relegates many non-college women to careers comprised of a series of low-wage, low-mobility, low-skilled jobs.

Programs *do* exist that have allowed some non-college women to break that cycle and follow a pathway out of the pink-collar ghetto. Through statistical analyses, this study demonstrated the link between high pay and nontraditional occupations (NTOs) for women. To train for NTOs *is* to train women for better-paying, higher-opportunity career ladders. Nontraditional occupations represent an extremely relevant and important locus for analysis and policy development. Two recent Department of Labor programs have sought to increase women's participation in NTOs, and separate statistical analyses determine that these programs have been effective in doing so. Finally, case study analysis determines how grant recipients have been able to increase women's participation in NTOs with these modest grant monies. The roles of leadership buy-in/political advocacy and networking/leverage were found to be very important to grantees' successes.

Implications and Contributions of Results

Women have made advances in many fields as a result of affirmative action policies, and some advances have been such that an affirmative action approach has been rendered obsolete. If this project has shown nothing else, it has shown that the NTOs addressed here are *not* among those fields where affirmative action is obsolete.

This analysis also finds that occupational segregation by gender results, at least in part, from sticky flows of information. Potentially interested women were unaware of the jobs available, either of the skills necessary or the type of work. Both grant programs emphasized aggressive recruitment. Potential employers were not aware of where to begin getting more women into their firms, nor were they aware of the problems that might occur when their workplaces became more integrated. Both grant programs emphasized placement and retention, and Women in Apprenticeships and Nontraditional Occupations (WANTO) explicitly provided technical assistance to employers and unions. Filling information gaps on both sides, tradeswomen and employers and unions, took the form of pretraining and skills training for the tradeswomen-to-be, and technical assistance for the employers and unions.

Information gaps are less expensive to surmount than are more entrenched market failures. If women were unable to enter these occupations because women are just fundamentally, physiologically, or psychologically incapable of doing the work, then that market failure would be much costlier to surmount than simply by providing timelier, more accurate information to all parties involved. These two grant programs gave many community-based nonprofit organizations the opportunity to expand the services they were already providing. Because this expansion of services had more to do with collecting and distributing information than more labor-intensive or costlier efforts, these nonprofits were able to increase or change the type of information they gathered and researched, or increase or change the audience to whom they distributed that information, without incurring a great amount of new expenses. In addition, the modest grant amounts were more suited to supporting expanded information services than to supporting costlier, more resource-intensive expanded services, as well.

Policymaking by Women, for Women

Policymaking by and for women takes a different shape than it would if women were not involved. There must be something at stake, and it makes a difference to the development and implementation of women's policy issues and programs if women are involved. Gender-focused agencies with gender-specific mandates or "women's policy machinery" are important to achieving gender-specific outcomes. And, gender-specific outcomes remain necessary because market failures still exist that result in the inequitable distribution of resources to women, compared to men. Several million families still live in poverty and over half of them are single-parent households headed by women. Women can still improve their economic security and independence through employment training. Nontraditional occupations for women still tend to bring higher wages, better job security, and longer-range opportunities than do pink-collar jobs. It is still the case that two in every three new entrants to the workforce are women, so industry still must employ women in all occupational areas. Women still face significant barriers to their full and effective participation in NTOs in industries such as construction and manufacturing. These Nontraditional Employment for Women (NEW)-funded and WANTO-funded projects have had an impact, but the fundamental labor market distribution disparities are far too entrenched for two small grant programs to alter on a nationwide scale. Many of the NTOs addressed by the nonprofit service delivery organizations in this research remain very male oriented. Successes in some parts of the labor markets do not crossover into others.

Crucial Role of Government

The results of this research suggest that the involvement of the government is important to the institutionalization of a project or initiative. Related to the justification for continued affirmative action, while gains have been made in many parts of the labor markets, this is not one of them. A role still exists for the state. While some have argued that true institutionalization is the absence of state or policy intervention, this analysis sides with Stetson's interpretation of institutionalism with respect to the integration of women's issues in government and society.[3] She examined the governmental agencies responsible for promoting women's position and rights, rather than individual policymakers or nongovernmental activists. The same approach was taken here by examining the programs and the organizations that implemented them. In democratic governments where the state takes a positive role in social policy matters and not a laissez-faire position, it is very appropriate to interpret issue-oriented agencies as evidence of genuine institutionalization of that issue. Moreover, political buy-in was found to be important to the success of a project and its ability to integrate itself into its larger political and social context. Therefore, "true" institutionalization is the entrenchment of an issue into the policy machinery of the state. The crucial role for the state, then, is to be an active player, not missing in action.

Future Directions

Examining Individual Industries

Perhaps the most important direction for future research based on these findings would be to focus on individual industries. The current study produced baseline results, and included all occupations defined as nontraditional for women, from tool and die maker to funeral director, as long as women comprised less than 25 percent of total employment. Obviously, many of the occupations included in the statistical analysis are not targeted by policy. By excluding white-collar occupations that happen to be nontraditional for women, future analyses could pinpoint the effects of policy interventions on specific industries. However, which industries? In *Created Unequal*, James K. Galbraith proposes an organizing framework to analyze industries along important dimensions, not according to the usual groupings of industries commonly used.

Overcrowding and occupational segregation coinciding with low-wages and few opportunities for advancement contradicts Galbraith's finding that it is *not* the race or gender makeup of an occupation that determines its wage structure, but rather, the overall performance of the *industry* it is in.[4] However, is it possible that the more profitable, or better performing, industries tend to be male dominated anyway? Is it possible that women are left to accept low-wage service-sector jobs in unprofitable industries or industries with very small profit margins like service-sector ones because employers in those industries cannot employ male workers who might have better opportunities? While the current study does not dismiss the issue of whether an occupation's gender composition affects its wage structure, or vice versa, this study does operate from the assumption that gender composition is worth altering. Is this assumption correct? Further study is recommended to dissect the important questions surrounding the fundamental relationship between an industry's wage structure and its gender composition. Again, this relationship is not dissected in the present study; occupational segregation by gender—the "femaleness" or "maleness" of a stereotyped job—is considered a key labor market failure, worthy of policy intervention to therefore increase non-college women's labor market outcomes. An important direction for further research would be to examine women's labor market experiences in the same occupations in different industries to help determine whether altering patterns of *occupational* segregation would have long-term effects. Galbraith suggests that it would not: examining gendered outcomes by industry is more useful and important to policy than examining outcomes by occupation, for wage structures are determined by industry type more than they are by occupation.

Examining the Effects of a Growing Economy

The real proof of program effectiveness in retention will come after an economic downturn is sustained. After such a downturn, the participation of women in NTOs should be measured again and compared to the analytical results presented here, which are based on findings from a period of economic expansion, although appropriate controls were used to ensure that the results cannot be *explained* by the growing economy. The concern is retention: have women been affected disproportionately by the economic downturn, relative to men? As the economy slows and labor markets tighten, women may be the first to be released from NTOs and the last to be rehired. But this would only be revealed by analyzing a period where grant programs like these were in place in the context of an economic slowdown: a repetition of this study is in order, one that captures economic recession to determine whether women have been affected disproportionately.

Examining Tradeswomen's Experiences

Another direction for fruitful research based on these findings would be to conduct extensive follow-up analyses with women who actually participated in WANTO- and NEW-funded projects. In part, this would help reveal the long-run effects of emphasizing placement over education, and vice versa, and is akin to Shirley Dex's excellent research on women's occupational and industrial mobility over time.[5] Such an analysis could synthesize Galbraith's emphasis on analyzing industries rather than occupations and Dex's emphasis on workforce experience and mobility over time by examining an individual woman's career trajectory by industry longitudinally.

These projects exhibited the significant amount of resources that is generally channeled into training and placement, which seems to be done to a greater degree than into retention and prevention. NTO women's groups have criticized policy interventions like these for doing just that, emphasizing training and placement, to the detriment of retention and prevention of sexual harassment. Some organizations of NTO women have faulted training programs for effectively leaving NTO women on their own shortly after they are placed in a position. Unfortunately, the case study analyses demonstrated this, too, emphases on training and placement more so than on retention and prevention. Further research could focus on NTO women's experiences after placement to help determine whether more resources should be placed in retention activities.

Examining Participation by Race and Gender

A further area for continued analysis, based on these results, would be to examine the differential impact of policy interventions on white women compared to women and men of color. Many of the NTOs targeted by these policy interventions have been dominated by white males, so one might assume that an intervention could have an effect on the gender and racial make up of these occupations, and set out to discover whether that was, in fact, the case.

A Call for Action

If nothing else, this study should convince the reader that alternatives to the four-year college degree path are necessary, and that such programs can succeed. The prevailing rhetoric surrounding career preparation is dangerously flawed and perpetuates the pioneering myth on several levels: despite increasing educational attainment in the United States, the majority of workers never obtain a four-year college degree. To assume so not only overlooks the important career aspirations of significant numbers of young women and men, but also understates the important contributions of high-skilled technical work to the nation's economy. One might go so far as to say that the U.S. economy was built on, and continues to be supported by, the backs of the skilled laborer. College-for-all rhetoric ignores this fundamental truth to the peril of the U.S. economy. What is more, this rhetoric is not expressed in a vacuum, but has influenced U.S. culture and policy, which has resulted in severe cutbacks to vocational employment and training programs. Moreover, anti-affirmative action forces have diminished sex set-asides in vocational employment and training programs, and this study has shown that non-college women are worse off than non-college men in terms of the labor market opportunities each faces. Non-college women face limited opportunities to support their families, and the fact remains that women head the majority of single-headed households and play significant roles in dual-earner households. Women no longer work for "pin money," if indeed they ever did.

Deteriorating labor market institutions such as unionization, collective bargaining, the minimum wage, and long-term employment stability, have eroded opportunities for non-college workers even further. Employment and training pathways for the non-college population, particularly non-college women, are essential. Yet, not only have alternative pathways been overshadowed by college-for-all presumptions, they have also been undercut by an increasingly popular free market philosophy that depends on the "bottom tail of the distribution" to preserve the spoils for the rest of the distribution. This thinking is dangerously flawed, as well: patterns of occupational sex segregation do not work themselves out in time. This analysis demonstrates that even modest employment and training programs provide non-college women with opportunities to earn higher-than-average earnings and opportunities for advancement. This analysis also provides a foundation for further work: to determine whether the vigorous economic growth of the 1990s merely allowed otherwise-discriminating employers to set aside their biases to fill labor shortages, or to determine whether industrial performance would provide a better framework for analyzing the experiences of non-college women.

The findings of the preceding pages warrant a call for action. Question college-for-all presumptions in the current culture and their ultimate manifestations in policy. Acknowledge the important contributions of non-college workers and examine the assumption that they hold their jobs only because they are either on their way to, in, or failed to finish, a four-year college degree. Witness the enduring trends in occupational segregation by gender: who are the waitresses, cashiers, nursing aides, housekeepers, and secretaries, and how much do they earn relative to their economic contribution? Demand restorations to training and education programs that prepare workers for high-skilled, high-paying occupations that provide opportunities for advancement; and finally, understand that, without policy intervention, pathways out of low-paying, low-skilled occupational ghettos would not exist.

Appendices

Appendix 1

Table A.1

White-Collar, Blue-Collar, and Service Occupations as Defined in the Employment Cost Index Survey

White-collar occupations
        Professional specialty and technical occupations
        Professional specialty occupations
        Health-related occupations
        Teachers
        Social, recreation, and religious workers
        Lawyers and judges
        Technical occupations
        Executive, administrative, and managerial occupations
        Executives, administrators, and managers
        Sales occupations
        Administrative support occupations, including clerical
Blue-collar occupations
        Precision production, craft, and repair occupations
        Machine operators, assemblers, and inspectors
        Transportation and material moving occupations
        Handlers, equipment cleaners, helpers, and laborers
Service occupations
        Protective service occupations
        Food service occupations
        Health service occupations
        Cleaning and building service occupations
        Personal service occupations

Appendix 2

Table A.2

Bureau of Labor Statistics' Occupations with the Largest Projected Job Growth, 2000 to 2010

Occupation	Employment (in thousands)		Change		Quartile rank by 2000 median hourly earnings[a]	Education and training category
	2000	2010	No. (1,000)	%		
Combined food preparation and serving workers, including fast food	2,206	2,879	673	30	4	Short-term on-the-job training
Customer service representatives	1,946	2,577	631	32	3	Moderate-term on-the-job training
Registered nurses	2,194	2,755	561	26	1	Associate degree
Retail salespersons	4,109	4,619	510	12	4	Short-term on-the-job training
Computer support specialists	506	996	490	97	2	Associate degree
Cashiers, except gaming	3,325	3,799	474	14	4	Short-term on-the-job training
Office clerks, general	2,705	3,135	430	16	3	Short-term on-the-job training
Security guards	1,106	1,497	391	35	4	Short-term on-the-job training
Computer software engineers, applications	380	760	380	100	1	Bachelor's degree
Waiters and waitresses	1,983	2,347	364	18	4	Short-term on-the-job training
General and operations managers	2,398	2,761	363	15	1	Bachelor's or higher degree, plus work experience
Truck drivers, heavy and tractor-trailer	1,749	2,095	346	20	2	Moderate-term on-the-job training
Nursing aides, orderlies, and attendants	1,373	1,697	323	24	3	Short-term on-the-job training
Janitors and cleaners, except maids and housekeeping cleaners	2,348	2,665	317	13	4	Short-term on-the-job training
Post-secondary teachers	1,344	1,659	315	23	1	Doctoral degree
Teacher assistants	1,262	1,562	301	24	4	Short-term on-the-job training
Home health aides	615	907	291	47	4	Short-term on-the-job training
Laborers and freight, stock, and material movers, hand	2,084	2,373	289	14	3	Short-term on-the-job training

Computer software engineers, systems software	317	601	284	90	1	Bachelor's degree
Landscaping and groundskeeping workers	894	1,154	260	29	4	Short-term on-the-job training
Personal and home care aides	414	672	258	62	4	Short-term on-the-job training
Computer systems analysts	431	689	258	60	1	Bachelor's degree
Receptionists and information clerks	1,078	1,334	256	24	3	Short-term on-the-job training
Truck drivers, light or delivery services	1,117	1,331	215	19	3	Short-term on-the-job training
Packers and packagers, hand	1,091	1,300	210	19	4	Short-term on-the-job training
Elementary school teachers, except special education	1,532	1,734	202	13	1	Bachelor's degree
Medical assistants	329	516	187	57	3	Moderate-term on-the-job training
Network and computer systems administrators	229	416	187	82	1	Bachelor's degree
Secondary school teachers, except special and vocational education	1,004	1,190	187	19	1	Bachelor's degree
Accountants and auditors	976	1,157	181	19	1	Bachelor's degree

[a]The quartile rankings of Occupational Employment Statistics annual earnings data are presented in the following categories: 1 = very high ($39,700 and over), 2 = high ($25,760 to $39,660), 3 = low ($18,500 to $25,760), and 4 = very low (up to $18,490). The rankings were based on quartiles using one-fourth of total employment to define each quartile. Earnings are for wage and salary workers.

Appendix 3

Table A.3a

Top Ten Occupations for Non-College Women and Men by Numbers Employed, 1979 and 1999

Women		Men	
1979	1999	1979	1999
Secretaries, nec	Cashiers	Truck drivers	Truck drivers
Sales clerks, retail	Secretaries	Miscellaneous machine operatives	Janitors and cleaners
Cashiers	Nursing aides	Janitors and sextons	Cooks
Waiters and waitresses	Waiters and waitresses	Mechanics, heavy equipment	Laborers, not construction
Nursing aides and attendants	Receptionists	Carpenters	Carpenters
Bookkeepers	Cooks	Stock handlers and baggers	Stock handlers and baggers
Registered nurses	Bookkeepers	Construction laborers	Construction laborers
Cooks	Registered nurses	Foreman, nec	Miscellaneous machine operatives
Assemblers	Sales supervisors	Welders and flame cutters	Assemblers
Sewers and stitchers	Retail sales	Freight and material handlers	Cashiers

Source: CPS-MORG (weighted).
Notes: nec = not elsewhere classified; non-college includes individuals with high school diplomas, high school dropouts, and those with some college education.

Table A.3b

Top Occupations by Numbers Employed, by Educational Attainment for Women and Men, 1979 to 1999

Top Ten Occupations by Percent of Total Employment for Women with a Twelfth Grade Education, 1979 to 1999

1979		1984		1989		1994		1999	
Occupation	% of total	Occupation	% of total	Occupation	% of total	Occupation	% of total	Occupation	% of total
Secretaries	7.87	Secretaries	8.72	Secretaries	8.02	Cashiers	6.93	Cashiers	6.39
Retail sales	6.28	Cashiers	7.05	Cashiers	6.36	Secretaries	6.63	Nursing aides	5.30
Cashiers	5.46	Nursing aides	4.14	Nursing aides	4.18	Nursing aides	4.54	Secretaries	5.27
Bookkeepers	4.55	Waiters and waitresses	4.11	Waiters and waitresses	3.39	Waiters and waitresses	3.04	Waiters and waitresses	2.85
Waiters and waitresses	4.12	Bookkeepers	3.74	Bookkeepers	3.25	Bookkeepers	2.86	Receptionists	2.79
Assemblers	3.35	Retail sales	3.48	Retail sales	3.01	Cooks	2.79	Bookkeepers	2.76
Nursing aides	3.35	Cooks	2.41	Cooks	2.37	Retail sales supervisors	2.53	Sales	2.75
Typists	3.03	Typists	2.17	Managers and administrators	2.23	Receptionists	2.42	Cooks	2.73
Miscellaneous clerical	2.71	Sewing machine operators	2.13	Receptionists	2.09	Sales supervisors	2.19	Retail sales	2.36
Sewers and stitchers	2.31	Assemblers	1.94	Assemblers	1.97	Assemblers	1.94	Assemblers	1.97

(continued)

Table A.3b (continued)

Top Ten Occupations by Percent of Total Employment for Women with Some College Education, Including Two-Year Degrees, 1979 to 1999

1979		1984		1989		1994		1999	
Occupation	% of total	Occupation	% of total	Occupation	% of total	Occupation	% of total	Occupation	% of total
Secretaries	9.59	Secretaries	10.40	Secretaries	9.81	Secretaries	7.71	Secretaries	6.06
Registered nurses	7.70	Registered nurses	6.77	Registered nurses	5.94	Registered nurses	6.54	Registered nurses	5.66
Retail sales	7.20	Cashiers	6.22	Cashiers	5.24	Cashiers	5.08	Cashiers	4.31
Waiters and waitresses	4.72	Waiters and waitresses	4.50	Bookkeepers	3.78	Nursing aides and attendants	3.52	Nursing aides and attendants	4.10
Cashiers	4.20	Retail sales	4.17	Waiters and waitresses	3.74	Waiters and waitresses	3.330	Bookkeepers	2.98
Bookkeepers	3.99	Bookkeepers	3.96	Retail sales	3.38	Bookkeepers	3.05	Receptionists	2.95
Typists	3.74	Nursing aides and attendants	2.91	Nursing aides and attendants	3.05	Receptionists	2.71	Waiters and waitresses	2.86
Nursing aides and attendants	2.92	Typists	2.71	Managers and administrators	2.58	Retail sales supervisors	2.53	Sales	2.22
Miscellaneous clerical	2.91	Licensed practical nurses	2.44	Receptionists	2.30	Administrative support	2.43	Investigators and adjusters	2.17
Practical nurses	2.76	Receptionists	2.12	Licensed practical nurses	2.28	Licensed practical nurses	2.13	Retail sales	2.11

Top Ten Occupations by Percent of Total Employment for Women with a Four-Year College Degree or More, 1979 to 1999

1979		1984		1989		1994		1999	
Occupation	% of total	Occupation	% of total	Occupation	% of total	Occupation	% of total	Occupation	% of total
Registered nurses	14.58	Registered nurses	17.09	Registered nurses	17.14	Registered nurses	15.40	Registered nurses	14.65
Secretaries	6.25	Secretaries	4.96	Secretaries	4.82	Secretaries	4.04	Social workers	3.01
Retail sales	4.08	Clinical lab technicians	3.02	Managers and administrators	3.16	Social workers	2.59	Accountants and auditors	2.94
Elementary school teachers	3.15	Sales	2.77	Clinical lab technicians	2.43	Elementary school teachers	2.37	Secretaries	2.78
Clinical lab technicians	3.04	Bookkeepers	2.76	Bookkeepers	2.40	Accountants and auditors	2.09	Elementary school teachers	2.52
Bookkeepers	2.92	Accountants and auditors	2.38	Social workers	2.30	Clinical lab technicians	2.08	Sales Supervisors	2.04
Waiters and waitresses	2.76	Managers and administrators	2.23	Sales	2.28	Bookkeepers, accountants and auditors	2.04	Managers and administrators	1.93
Social workers	2.19	Waiters and waitresses	2.13	Elementary school teachers	2.25	Administrative support, nec	1.97	Teachers, nec	1.77
Typists	2.17	Social workers	1.92	Accountants and auditors	2.16	Managers and administrators	1.94	Clinical lab technicians	1.71
Therapists	2.12	Cashiers	1.83	Waiters and waitresses	1.92	Waiters and waitresses	1.71	Retail sales workers	1.71

(continued)

Table A.3b (continued)

Top Ten Occupations by Percent of Total Employment for Men with a Twelfth Grade Education, 1979 to 1999

1979		1984		1989		1994		1999	
Occupation	% of total	Occupation	% of total	Occupation	% of total	Occupation	% of total	Occupation	% of total
Truck drivers	4.28	Truck drivers	4.19	Truck drivers	3.82	Truck drivers	6.18	Truck drivers	6.12
Miscellaneous machine operators	3.97	Janitors and cleaners	3.61	Janitors and cleaners	3.50	Janitors and cleaners	3.25	Janitors and cleaners	3.56
Heavy equipment mechanics	3.33	Carpenters	3.05	Carpenters	3.18	Laborers, not construction	3.13	Laborers, not construction	3.15
Carpenters	3.24	Laborers, not construction	2.98	Laborers, not construction	2.94	Miscellaneous machine operatives	2.76	Miscellaneous machine operatives	2.87
Welders	2.92	Miscellaneous machine operators	2.61	Miscellaneous machine operatives	2.46	Carpenters	2.59	Carpenters	2.81
Auto mechanics operatives	2.69	Welders	2.32	Assemblers	2.24	Assemblers	2.45	Construction laborers	2.34
Truck Drivers	2.32	Cashiers	1.76	Cashiers	1.86	Laborers, not construction	1.88	Cashiers	1.67
Heavy equipment mechanics	2.31	Guards and police (not public service)	1.72	Guards and police (not public service)	1.86	Guards and police (not public service)	1.83	Carpenters	1.64
Janitors and cleaners	1.95	Managers and administrators	1.69	Truck drivers	1.83	Managers and administrators	1.81	Stock handlers	1.55

Top Ten Occupations by Percent of Total Employment for Men with a Four-Year College Degree or more, 1979 to 1999

1979		1984		1989		1994		1999	
Occupation	% of total	Occupation	% of total	Occupation	% of total	Occupation	% of total	Occupation	% of total
Managers and administrators	3.87	Managers and administrators	3.71	Managers and administrators	3.69	Managers and administrators	2.84	Managers and administrators	4.28
Accountants and auditors	2.69	Accountants and auditors	2.23	Accountants and auditors	2.48	Accountants and auditors	2.78	Computer analysts	3.23
Police and detectives	1.89	Carpenters	1.92	Sales supervisors	1.69	Sales supervisors	2.67	Sales supervisors	2.23
Pharmacists	1.78	Sales supervisors	1.86	Guards and police	1.59	Electrical engineers	2.55	Police and detectives	2.15
Retail sales clerks	1.78	Janitors and cleaners	1.86	Computer programmers	1.48	Computer analysts	2.46	Electrical engineers	1.95
Carpenters	1.73	Electrical engineer	1.79	Janitors and cleaners	1.47	Truck drivers	1.62	Accountants and auditors	1.91
Electrical engineer	1.68	Pharmacists	1.78	Civil engineers	1.43	Guards and police	1.59	Registered nurses	1.77
Truck drivers	1.54	Police and detectives	1.73	Police and detectives	1.39	Police and detectives	1.54	Truck drivers	1.57
Officials and administrators	1.53	Guards and police	1.43	Registered nurses	1.32	Registered nurses	1.52	Social workers	1.30
Foreman, nec	1.47	Production supervisors	1.31	Computer operators	1.29	Janitors and cleaners	1.45	Civil engineers	1.29

Source: Author's tabulations of Current Population Survey Merged Outgoing Rotation Group data (weighted).
Note: nec = not elsewhere classified.

Appendix 4

Table A.4

Baseline Probabilities of Falling into the "High Wage" Category: Means of All Variables, 1979 to 1999

	Baseline probability of falling into the high wage category	Coefficient of NTO variable (% point change)
Women and men	36.69	0.3192
Women	22.66	0.1276
Men	50.14	0.1551
Non-college women and men (high school or some college)	38.74	0.3290
Non-college women (high school or some college)	35.45	0.3392
Non-college men (high school or some college)	41.88	0.3265
Non-college women and men (College degree = 0)	34.85	0.2975
Non-college women (College degree = 0)	19.73	0.0960
Non-college men (College degree = 0)	48.89	.01429
Women, college graduates	46.18	0.1170
Women, high school only	19.97	0.1300

Appendix 5A

Detailed Descriptions of All Variables, 1990 to 1999

Nontraditional Occupations

The easiest and most straightforward way to define nontraditional occupations (NTOs) for women is simply to use the definition provided by the Women's Bureau: any occupation where women comprise 25 percent or less of total employment.[1] This list has not changed appreciably over the 1990–99 period, except that, curiously, occupations in the categories "Operators, fabricators, and laborers" and "Precision inspectors, testers, and related workers" barely surpassed the 25 percent threshold in both the 1990 and 1983 Women's Bureau listings of NTOs for women (25.4 percent for each) but both groups of occupations are within the NTO definition later in the period (about 24 percent for each).[2] The Women's Bureau has compiled lists of NTOs for women nearly every year for several years. Table A.5a is the 1999 Women's Bureau list, which is comprised of the 257 occupations defined as "nontraditional" in this analysis. It is important to note that no occupational category changes affected this list over 1990–99.

Nontraditional Occupations for Women as Defined by the Women's Bureau, March 2001

Treatment Areas

A "location" is defined as either the state or metropolitan statistical area (MSA) or consolidated metropolitan statistical area (CMSA), depending on grantees' descriptions of project scopes. Locations where grantees have implemented multiple projects, multiple-award recipients, and locations of 1999 grantees' projects are considered nontreatment areas for purposes of the present analysis according to the following rationale:

1. Multiple-award recipients are excluded from the data set because they have operated grant-funded projects in the same areas over several years.
2. Multiple-project areas are excluded from the data set because they confound the process of distinguishing the effects of one funded project—one intervention—from another.
3. Projects of grantees receiving awards after 1998 are ignored for the purposes of this analysis. It is assumed that the impact of an intervention is felt no sooner than year $(t + 1)$, where the grant is awarded in year (t). Therefore, effects of 1999 projects would be too recent to gauge.

Table A.5a

Nontraditional Occupations for Women as Defined by the Women's Bureau, March 2001

Occupations	Employed both sexes (thousands)	Employed female (thousands)	Percent female
Helpers, surveyor	8	2	25
Post-secondary natural science teachers, nec[a]	4	1	25
Atmospheric and space scientist	12	3	25
Precision inspectors, testers, and related workers	148	36	24.3
Messengers	157	38	24.2
Production helpers	75	18	24
Post-secondary theology teachers	21	5	23.8
Architects	215	51	23.7
Metal and plastic processing machine operators	150	35	23.5
Drafting occupations	219	51	23.4
Supervisors, guards	53	12	22.6
Sales workers, hardware, and building supplies	328	73	22.2
Farm managers, except horticultural	149	33	22.1
Chemical technicians	71	15	21.1
Laborers, except construction	1,307	272	20.8
Upholsterers	64	13	20.3
Guards and police, except public service	745	150	20.1
Elevator operators	5	1	20
Athletes	90	18	20
Supervisors, precision production occupations	1,129	222	19.7
Sheriffs, bailiffs, and other law enforcement officers	156	30	19.2
Funeral directors	58	11	19
Farm workers	768	144	18.7
Dentists	168	31	18.7
Metalworking and plastic-working machine operators	349	64	18.3
Supervisors, motor vehicle operators	77	14	18.2
Printing press operators	292	51	17.5
Electrical and electronic technicians	468	79	16.9
Purchasing agents and buyers, farm products	12	2	16.7
Parking lot attendants	60	10	16.7
Police and detectives	1,060	175	16.5
Hand painting, coating, and decorating occupations	25	4	16
Data processing equipment repairers	342	53	15.4
Grinding, abrading, buffing, and polishing	98	15	15.2
Managers, horticultural specialty farms	27	4	14.8
Metal plating machine operators	27	4	14.8
Woodworking machine operators	137	20	14.6
Hand molders and shapers, excluding jewelers	21	3	14.3
Supervisors, handlers, equipment cleaners, and laborers	14	2	14.3
Clergy	369	51	13.8

Occupations	Employed both sexes (thousands)	Employed female (thousands)	Percent female
Vehicle washers and equipment cleaners	313	43	13.7
Horticultural specialty farmers	69	9	13
Meter readers	46	6	13
Air traffic controllers	23	3	13
Horticultural specialty farmers	69	9	12.8
Geologists and geodesists	47	6	12.8
Painting and paint spraying machine operators	187	23	12.4
Helpers, mechanics, and repairers	33	4	12.1
Physicists and astronomers	25	3	12
Compressing and compacting machine operators	17	2	11.8
Fishers, hunters, and trappers	51	6	11.8
Freight, stock, and material handlers, nec[a]	739	86	11.6
Supervisors, farm workers	45	5	11.1
Announcers	54	6	11.1
Precision woodworking occupations	127	14	11
Sales workers, motor vehicles, and boats	329	36	10.9
Drivers-sales workers	167	18	10.8
Taxicab drivers and chauffeurs	280	30	10.7
Engineers	2,093	207	9.9
Construction inspectors	72	7	9.7
Baggage porters and bellhops	42	4	9.5
Supervisors, related agricultural occupations	174	16	9.3
Motor transportation occupations, nec[a]	11	1	9.1
Supervisors, mechanics and repairers	223	20	9
Extruding and forming machine operators	34	3	8.8
Sales workers, parts	186	16	8.6
Patternmakers, layout workers, and cutters	12	1	8.3
Forestry and logging occupations	109	9	8.3
Mixing and blending machine operators	112	9	8
Garage- and service-station-related occupations	184	14	7.6
Surveying and mapping technicians	79	6	7.6
Precision metalworking occupations	865	65	7.5
Miscellaneous metal and plastic processing machine operators	27	2	7.4
Groundskeepers and gardeners, except farm	870	64	7.4
Industrial truck and tractor equipment operators	569	40	7
Stationary engineers	118	8	6.7
Machinists	488	31	6.3
Sales engineers	32	2	6.2
Broadcast equipment operators	33	2	6.1
Helpers, construction and extractive occupations	120	7	5.9
Mechanical engineering technicians	17	1	5.9

(*continued*)

Table A.5a (*continued*)

Occupations	Employed both sexes (thousands)	Employed female (thousands)	Percent female
Furnace, kiln, and oven operators, except food	53	3	5.7
Pest control occupations	71	4	5.6
Grading, dozer, and scraper operators	52	3	5.5
Material moving equipment operators	1,152	62	5.4
Water and sewage treatment and power plant operators and related occupations	264	14	5.3
Mechanics and repairers, excluding supervisors	4,652	230	4.9
Welders and cutters	594	29	4.9
Truck drivers	3,088	145	4.7
Helpers, construction and extractive occupations trades	111	5	4.5
Industrial machinery repairs	524	22	4.2
Rail transportation occupations	127	5	3.9
Airplane pilots and navigators	129	5	3.9
Miscellaneous precision workers, nec[a]	26	1	3.8
Garbage collectors	54	2	3.7
Construction laborers	1,015	38	3.7
Firefighting and fire prevention occupations	248	9	3.6
Separating, filtering, and clarifying machine operators	62	2	3.2
Supervisors, firefighting and fire prevention	32	1	3.1
Excavating and loading machine operators	98	3	3.1
Tool and die makers	121	3	2.7
Construction trades, excluding supervisors	5,153	138	2.3
Supervisors, construction trades	967	22	2.3
Water transportation occupations	56	1	1.8
Operating engineers	253	4	1.7
Extractive occupations	128	2	1.6
Crane and tower operators	70	1	1.4
Stevedores	14	< 1	< 1.0
Marine life cultivation workers	2	< 1	< 1.0
Motion picture projectionists	7	0	< 1.0
Washing, cleaning, and pickling machine operators	8	0	< 1.0
Heat treating equipment operators	11	0	< 1.0

Notes: Nontraditional occupations are those that women comprise 25 percent of less of the total employed.
[a]nec = not elsewhere classified.

Thirty-nine entities received grants between 1992 and 1998, and thirty-four are included in this analysis. Table A.5b lists these grant recipients.

Excluded grantees are the state of Georgia and District of Columbia in the Nontraditional Employment for Women (NEW) program, and Chicago Women in Trades, Wider Opportunities for Women in (WOW) Washington, DC, and the YWCA of Greater Memphis in the Women in Apprenticeships and Nontraditional Occupations (WANTO) Program. First, with the exception of the District of Columbia, each of the excluded grantees has received multiple WANTO or NEW grants and implemented several grant-funded projects in the same areas. Because it is not possible to distinguish the effects of one project from another, these multiple-award recipients are excluded from the analysis. Second, multiple grant-funded project areas are excluded in addition to multiple-award recipients. The District of Columbia is excluded because WOW and other grantees have operated numerous employment projects targeting women in nontraditional occupations there for several years. Although the District's 1992 NEW grant may have had an impact on its own, including it in the analysis unfairly attributes all the activities of other organizations operating in the area every year since 1992. Even though the District itself did not receive multiple awards, the large number of similar employment programs operating in this fairly small geographic area excludes it from the analysis as the area is a multiple-project site. Seattle, Denver, Boston, Portland, Oregon, and Springfield, Massachusetts, are also excluded because more than one grant-funded project has been implemented in each. Excluding these areas biases against finding an effect of the WANTO and NEW grant programs by defining them as nontreatment areas, where, if these grant programs have an effect, one can assume that the effect is larger in multiple-project areas compared to single-project ones.

Third, fourteen organizations received grants in 1999, and they are excluded from this analysis as well. In every instance, the most accurate and detailed geographical unit was used. The geographical coverage of each project was determined by using grantee information from Workplace Solutions,[3] grantees' proposals and final reports to the Women's Bureau,[4] and, where necessary, data were cross-listed with Job Training Partnership Act (JTPA) Service Delivery Areas (SDAs), using The U.S. Census "American Fact Finder" databases and maps.[5] In addition, although Chicago Women in Trades is excluded, the state of Illinois is not. Chicago Women in Trades has conducted multiple WANTO-funded projects in Chicago, but in implementing its NEW program, the state of Illinois focused on a handful of metropolitan areas, of which Chicago was not one. In states like Minnesota, Montana, and New Mexico, officials reported that their NEW programs were implemented statewide, so the "treatment area" is the entire state. The Women's Resource Center of Greater

Table A.5b

Women in Apprenticeships and Nontraditional Occupations and Nontraditional Employment for Women Grantees, 1992 to 1998

Program and year	Grantee	Amount (approx.)
NEW 1992	Louisiana	$300,000
	Maryland	300,000
	Texas	300,000
	Washington	300,000
	Wyoming	300,000
NEW 1993	California	250,000
	Illinois	250,000
	Iowa	250,000
	Missouri	250,000
	New Jersey	250,000
WANTO 1994	Tradeswomen of Purpose/Women in Non-Traditional Work, Inc. (TOP/WIN)	121,087
	Women's Resource Center (WRC) of Greater Grand Rapids	90,587
	Women Unlimited	153,200
NEW 1995	Massachusetts	250,000
	Montana	300,000
	Ohio	300,000
	Oklahoma	300,000
	Wisconsin	350,000
WANTO 1995	Home Builders Institute	249,516
	International Masonry Institute	204,435
	National Council of La Raza	249,516
NEW 1996	Connecticut	300,000
	Minnesota	300,000
	New Mexico	300,000
	Oregon	300,000
	Utah	300,000
WANTO 1996	Women in Nontraditional Employment Roles (WINTER)	152,217
WANTO 1997	Mi Casa Resource Center	199,776
	NEW, Inc.	155,000
WANTO 1998	Century Housing Corp.	150,000
	Oregon Tradeswomen, Inc.	149,970
	STRIVE/East Harlem Employment Services, Inc.	150,000
	Women in the Building Trades	100,000
	Women Work	147,387

Grand Rapids focused their WANTO-funded efforts on women in the local area—so the "treatment area" is simply Grand Rapids, Michigan. The indicator variable "evrtreat" was created to differentiate treatment areas from nontreatment areas. For observations located in an area covered by NEW or WANTO projects, then, for every year, this variable equals one—regardless of whether the project has been implemented yet or not. The issue here is not whether the project has had an effect yet or not, but rather, whether the area has ever been covered by one of these projects. For example, "evrtreat" equals one for observations located in Grand Rapids for the year 1990, even though the Women's Resource Center of Greater Grand Rapids did not receive their WANTO grant until 1994.

After Treatment

Although some areas are defined "treatment" according to the above ratio-nale, observations located in them are only considered "after treatment" in years $(t + 1)$ and later, where projects are implemented (grants are awarded) in year (t). Part of the definition of the post-treatment period is mentioned above as the reason for excluding 1999 grantees. One advantage of consider-ing a treated area "post-treatment" in years $(t + 1)$ and later is that it allows me to isolate the treatment effects. If several years lay between the treatment and post-treatment periods, random influences of time could obscure the actual effects of treatment. I am assuming that the effects of treatment are not felt during the year of project implementation. This may be an unrealistic limitation, given the relatively quick turnaround of training to employers and potential employees. However, this also may bias against finding a sig-nificant impact where only short-lived effects of grant-funded projects exist. Finding any significant impact of WANTO and NEW projects in an environ-ment where *I intentionally raise the bar* only serves to strengthen the overall results—whether an effect is found or not.

Two definitions of "post-treatment" are used in two different model speci-fications—one being more detailed than the other. The simple definition is explained above, and is represented in the data set by the variable "aftertrt," which equals one if the observation is located in the treatment area and at least $(t + 1)$ years after treatment. Given my assumption that the effects of treatment are not felt during the year of project implementation, and the con-sequent exclusion of 1999 grantees from the data set, the variable "aftertrt" equals one for all 1999 observations located in treatment areas. There are three completely pretreatment years—1990, 1991, and 1992—and one com-pletely post-treatment year—1999. The more detailed definition of "after treatment" divides the post-treatment period by the number of years after treatment to help determine whether the effects of treatment—if any—exhibit patterns, such as whether treatment effects are transitory or not. Seven sepa-rate indicator variables are defined for each number of years after treatment. For example, NEW grants were the earliest to be issued, in 1992. For obser-vations in the state of Texas (a 1992 NEW grantee) in the year 1993, the variable "yrsaft1" equals one, while variables "yrsaft2" through "yrsaft7" are equal to zero. For observations in Texas in 1999, only the variable "yrsaft7" equals one, while the others equal zero, because the number of years after project implementation is seven in 1999, not one, two, three, or four. Only the 1992 grantees have nonzero values for "yrsaft7," because the data set does not contain data later than 1999. Finally, because grantees do not receive their grants in the same years, some observations will be in pretreatment status, while others are post-treatment, and still others are never treated. One-third of the total number of women are in a treatment area.

Other Variables

"Yr91–99" are indicator variables that denote the year an observation was surveyed, with 1990 as the reference category. For example, these "year indicator variables" all equal zero for observations surveyed in 1990. For 1994 respondents, "Yr94" equals one, and zero otherwise.

Demographic characteristics are captured by several variables. "Female" is an indicator variable, which equals one if the observation is a female household member, zero if male. Females comprise about 49.04 percent of all observations in this data set (555,189 of 1,132,173) and males comprise about 50.96 percent (576,984 of 1,132,173). "Black" and "Hispanic" are also dichotomous indicator variables equal to one if the household member is Black or Hispanic, respectively. The excluded reference category here is "White, non-Hispanic." Responses to the Current Population Survey (CPS) concerning "Race" include White, Black, American Indian, Asian, or Pacific Islander through 1995, a category "Other" was included. In 1996 through 1999, the "Other" category is eliminated. The variable "Black" equals one if the respondent identifies herself as black, and zero otherwise. About 11.02 percent of all respondents are Black. Ethnicity responses indicate the respondent's Hispanic region of origin using categories including Mexican-American, Puerto Rican, and Cuban. In this data set, all these categories have been reduced to the dichotomous variable "Hispanic," which equals one if the household member identifies himself as of Hispanic origin, and zero otherwise. Approximately 9.19 percent of the respondents in this data set are Hispanic. In all years, the definition of "White" remains the same, and here, it is the excluded category, and comprises about 79.8 percent of total respondents.

"Never Married" is the reference, or excluded, category for the dichotomous variables Married and Divorced. Again, "Divorced" indicates that a person is currently divorced, not ever divorced; if the household member has remarried, she or he would be categorized as "Married" and that variable would equal one. Approximately 57.1 percent of all respondents in this data set are currently Married, and about 12.8 percent were Divorced at the time of the CPS.

The four education variables—Highsch, Somecoll, Colldeg, Graddeg— are based on CPS variables that have changed during the period covered by this data set. The responses to these CPS questions have been refined to result in these four dichotomous variables indicating the level of educational attainment achieved by the interviewee or other household member. "Highsch" equals one if the respondent has a high school diploma and zero otherwise; and comprises about 32.7 of total respondents in this data set. "Somecoll" indicates that the individual has attended college, but does not have a four-year degree; it equals one if this is the case, zero otherwise, and comprises about 27.3 percent of the total. "Colldeg" indicates that the respondent has a four-year degree, and in that case, equals one, zero otherwise. Approximately 18.3 percent of all the respondents and other household members in this data set have a four-year degree. The variable "Graddeg" equals one if the respondent has more than a four-year degree, zero otherwise; and comprises about 9.51 percent of all observations. Responses indicating a less-than-high-school education comprise the excluded, or reference, category for these education variables.

Age is a continuous variable measuring the age of the respondent or other household member between sixteen and ninety-nine years. For years 1994 and later, this variable is capped at ninety. "Agesq" equals the variable Age, squared (Age $\times$ Age). This is included, as it is suspected that the policy interventions under study here have a different effect on individuals in the middle range of Age, compared to those at either extreme. The effect is not linear, increasing or decreasing along with one's age. That is, these policy interventions affect middle-aged persons differently than they affect very young or very old persons.

The variable measuring the number of hours a person usually works on a weekly basis is included only in the earnings equations. "Uhourse" is a continuous variable that takes values of zero to 99 usual hours per week. Like Age, the square of Uhourse is also included—"Uhourse2" (Uhourse $\times$ Uhourse)—because it is presumed that these policy interventions do not have a linear effect with respect to usual weekly hours; they will affect those at the extreme ends of this range differently than they will affect those in the middle. Earnings are measured with the variable "Earnwke," which indicates earnings per week for the household member and takes values between zero and $2,884. Weekly earnings have been capped at this value for all years covered in this data set.

Finally, several interaction variables are included in the above equations in order to execute the double-and triple-difference estimations described earlier. "Femaft" and "Femyrs 1–7" are the interactions of (Female × Aftertrt) and (Female × Yrsaft1. . . 7), respectively; where the only difference between the two is the different definitions of the post-treatment period described earlier. Equations 3, 4, 7, and 8 illustrate the triple-difference model. Interacting these variables isolates the effect of policy intervention on women in treatment areas, post-treatment. Because each one is a dichotomous variable, these interaction variables drop out for all observations that are not female, nor in treatment areas post-treatment.

For triple-difference results, the coefficients on Femaft and Femyrs 1–7 are actually the results of interest described earlier, ($\gamma 7$ [T iat A iat F iat]). Equations (1), (2), (5), and (6) illustrate the double-difference model (i) described earlier, and because only women are included in that estimation, the variable "Aftertrt" isolates the effect of policy intervention on women in treatment areas after treatment. For double-difference results, the coefficient on Aftertrt is ($\gamma 3$ [T iat A iat]).

Appendix 5B

Difference-in-Differences Equations, 1990 to 1999

Employment Equations

Equations 1 through 8 are used to gauge the effects of policy intervention on the probability of holding a nontraditional occupation. Equations 1 to 4 below use the simple definition of "After Treatment" described earlier. Equations 5 through 8 employ the more complex, parsed-out, definition of "After Treatment" described earlier. Equations 1, 2, 5, and 6 generate double-difference results, where employment outcomes for women after treatment are compared to those of women before treatment or in never-treated areas. Equations 3, 4, 7, and 8 create triple-difference results, where employment outcomes for women after treatment are compared to those of men and women before treatment, men and women in never-treated areas, and men after treatment. Each model specification is run with and without controls for demographic characteristics, producing eight sets of results in total. Equations 1, 3, 5, and 7 do not have controls for demographic characteristics, while equations 2, 4, 6, and 8 do.

Double- and Triple-Differences Equations Using "Aftertrt"

1. Nontrad = f (Aftertrt, Evrtreat, Yr91–99)
2. Nontrad = f (Aftertrt, Evrtreat, Yr91–99, Age, Agesq, Black, Hispanic, Married, Divorced, Highsch, Somecoll, Colldeg, Graddeg)
3. Nontrad = f (Femaft, Femevr, Aftertrt, Evrtreat, Yr91–99)
4. Nontrad = f (Femaft, Femevr, Aftertrt, Evrtreat, Yr91–99, Age, Agesq, Female, Black, Hispanic, Married, Divorced, Highsch, Somecoll, Colldeg, Graddeg)

Double- and Triple-Differences Equations using "Yrsaft1 . . . 7"

5. Nontrad = f (Yrsaft1–7, Evrtreat, Yrsbef1–8, Yr91–99)
6. Nontrad = f (Yrsaft1–7, Evrtreat, Yrsbef1–8, Yr91–99, Age, Agesq, Black, Hispanic, Married, Divorced, Highsch, Somecoll, Colldeg, Graddeg)
7. Nontrad = f (Femaft1–7, Evrtreat, Yrsaft1–7, Fembef1–8, Femaft, Femevr, Fembef, Yrsbef1–8, Yr91–99)
8. Nontrad = f (Femaft1–7, Evrtreat, Yrsaft1–7, Fembef1–8, Femaft, Femevr, Fembef, Yrsbef1–8, Yr91–99, Age, Agesq, Female, Black, Hispanic, Married, Divorced, Highsch, Somecoll, Colldeg, Graddeg)

Equations 1 through 8 state that the probability of holding an occupation defined as a nontraditional occupation for women (Nontrad) is a function of whether one is in a treatment area (Evrtreat), in a treatment area after treatment (Aftertrt/Yrsaft#), the year that the observation is surveyed (Yr91–99), weekly earnings (Earnwke), and several demographic characteristics, including sex (Female), age (Age, Agesq), race and ethnicity (Black, Hispanic), marital status (Married, Divorced), and educational attainment (Highsch, Somecoll, Colldeg, Graddeg).

Earnings Equations

Eight equations are used to gauge the effects of policy intervention on earnings—four equations for earnings of all women and men, and four equations for earnings of women and men in nontraditional occupations. Equations 9 through 12 measure the effects of the policy intervention on earnings. Equations 9 through 12 employ the simple definition of "After Treatment" described earlier. Equations 13 through 16 employ the more complex, parsed-out, definition of "After Treatment" described earlier. Equations 9, 10, 13, and 14 generate double-difference results, where earnings of women after treatment are compared to those of women before treatment or in never-treated areas. Equations 11, 12, 15, and 16 produce triple-difference results, where earnings of women after treatment are compared to those of men and women before treatment, men and women in never-treated areas, and men after treatment. Each model specification is run with and without controls for demographic characteristics, producing eight sets of results.

Double- and Triple-Differences Equations Using "Aftertrt"

9. ln(Earnwke) = f(Aftertrt, Evrtreat, Ntoaft, Ntoevr, Yr91–99, Nontrad, Uhourse, Uhourse2)
10. ln(Earnwke) = f(Aftertrt, Evrtreat, Ntoaft, Ntoevr, Yr91–99, Nontrad, Uhourse, Uhourse2, Age, Agesq, Black, Hispanic, Married, Divorced, Highsch, Somecoll, Colldeg, Graddeg)
11. ln(Earnwke) = f (Femaftnto, Femevnto, Aftertrt, Evrtreat, Ntoaft, Ntoevr, Femevr, Femaft, Femnto, Yr91–99, Nontrad, Female)
12. ln(Earnwke) = f (Femaftnto, Femevnto, Aftertrt, Evrtreat, Ntoaft, Ntoevr, Femevr, Femaft, Femnto, Yr91–99, Nontrad, Female, Uhourse, Uhourse2, Age, Agesq, Black, Hispanic, Married, Divorced, Highsch, Somecoll, Colldeg, Graddeg)

Double- and Triple-Differences Equations Using "Yrsaft1 . . . 7"

13. ln(Earnwke) = f (Yrsaft1–7, Evrtreat, Ntoyrsaft1–7, Yrsbef1–8, Ntoyrsbef1–8, Ntoevr, Yr91–99, Nontrad, Uhourse, Uhourse2)
14. ln(Earnwke) = f (Yrsaft1–7, Evrtreat, Ntoyrsaft1–7, Yrsbef1–8, Ntoyrsbef1–8, Ntoevr, Yr91–99, Nontrad, Uhourse, Uhourse2, Age, Agesq, Black, Hispanic, Married, Divorced, Highsch, Somecoll, Colldeg, Graddeg)
15. ln(Earnwke) = f (Femaft1–7nto, Femevnto, Yrsaft1–7, Evrtreat, Ntoyrsaft1–7, Yrsbef1–8, Ntoyrsbef1–8, Female, Ntoevr, Yr91–99, Nontrad, Uhourse, Uhourse2)
16. ln(Earnwke) = f (Femaft1–7nto, Femevnto, Yrsaft1–7, Evrtreat, Ntoyrsaft1–7, Yrsbef1–8, Ntoyrsbef1–8, Female, Ntoevr, Yr91–99, Nontrad, Uhourse, Uhourse2, Age, Agesq, Black, Hispanic, Married, Divorced, Highsch, Somecoll, Colldeg, Graddeg)

Equations 9 through 16 state that weekly earnings are functions of whether one is in a treatment area (Evrtreat), in a treatment area after treatment (Aftertrt/ Yrsaft#), the survey year (Yr91–99), usual weekly hours worked (Uhourse, Uhourse2), whether one is in an NTO (Nontrad), and several demographic characteristics, including sex (Female), age (Age, Agesq), race and ethnicity (Black, Hispanic), marital status (Married, Divorced), and educational attainment (Highsch, Somecoll, Colldeg, Graddeg).

Earnings Among Nontraditional Occupations Only

Equations 17 through 24 estimate the effects on earnings among women and men in NTOs only. Equations 17 to 20 use the simple definition of "After Treatment" described earlier. Equations 21 to 24 use the more complex, parsed-out, definition of "After Treatment" described earlier. Equations 17, 18, 21, and 22 generate results among women only—earnings estimates of women in NTOs after treatment compared to those of women in NTOs before treatment or in never-treated areas. Equations 19, 20, 23, and 24 produce results among women and men—earnings estimates of women in NTOs after treatment are compared to those of men and women in NTOs before treatment, men and women in NTOs in never-treated areas, and men in NTOs after treatment. Each equation is run with (Equations 18, 20, 22, and 24) and without (Equations 17, 19, 21, and 23) controls for demographic characteristics, producing eight sets of results in total, and all are weighted, using the CPS population weights.

Double- and Triple-Differences Equations Using "Aftertrt"

17. ln(Earnwke) = f (Aftertrt, Evrtreat, Uhourse, Uhourse2, Yr91–99)
18. ln(Earnwke) = f (Aftertrt, Evrtreat, Uhourse, Uhourse2, Yr91–99, Age, Agesq, Black, Hispanic, Married, Divorced, Highshc, Somecoll, Colldeg, Graddeg)
19. ln(Earnwke) = f(Femaft, Aftertrt, Evrtreat, Femevr, Female, Uhourse, Uhourse2, Yr91–99)
20. ln(Earnwke) = f(Femaft, Aftertrt, Evrtreat, Femevr, Female, Uhourse, Uhourse2, Yr91–99, Age, Agesq, Black, Hispanic, Married, Divorced, Highshc, Somecoll, Colldeg, Graddeg)

Double- and Triple-Differences Equations Using "Yrsaft1 . . . 7"

21. ln(Earnwke) = f(Yrsaft1–7, Evrtreat, Yrsbef1–8, Uhourse, Uhourse2, Yr91–99)
22. ln(Earnwke) = f(Yrsaft1–7, Evrtreat, Yrsbef1–8, Uhourse, Uhourse2, Yr91–99, Age, Agesq, Black, Hispanic, Married, Divorced, Highshc, Somecoll, Colldeg, Graddeg)
23. ln(Earnwke) = f (Femyrsaft1–7, Yrsaft1–7, Evrtreat, Yrsbef1–8, Femyrsbef1–8, Femevr, Female, Uhourse, Uhourse2, Yr91–99)
24. ln(Earnwke) = f (Femyrsaft1–7, Yrsaft1–7, Evrtreat, Yrsbef1–8, Femyrsbef1–8, Femevr, Female, Uhourse, Uhourse2, Yr91–99, Age, Agesq, Black, Hispanic, Married, Divorced, Highshc, Somecoll, Colldeg, Graddeg)

Like the earlier earnings functions, equations 17 through 24 state that weekly earnings among individuals in nontraditional occupations is a function of whether one is in a treatment area (Evrtreat), in a treatment area after treatment (Aftertrt/Yrsaft#), the survey year (Yr91–99), usual weekly hours worked (Uhourse, Uhourse2), whether one is in a nontraditional occupation or not (Nontrad), and several demographic characteristics, including sex (Female), age (Age, Agesq), race and ethnicity (Black, Hispanic), marital status (Married, Divorced), and educational attainment (Highsch, Somecoll, Colldeg, Graddeg).

Hours Equations

The last set of eight equations is run to determine whether the policy intervention triggered changes in the number of weekly hours usually worked.

These equations measure whether a change in the employment of women in nontraditional occupations, if any, resulted in tradeoffs between workers and hours. That is, did any increase in the employment of women workers decrease the demand for hours of incumbent women workers? If so, then did these grant-funded projects really increase women's overall economic welfare?

Equations 25 through 28 use the simple definition of the post-treatment period, while equations 29 through 32 use the complex one. Equations 25, 26, 29, and 30 produce double-differences, where the usual weekly hours worked by women in treated areas after treatment are compared to those of women before the policy intervention and where grant-funded projects were never implemented. Equations 27, 28, 31, and 32 produce triple-differences, where the usual weekly hours worked by women are compared to those of all workers in never-treated areas and in treated areas prior to the policy intervention, and of men in treated areas post-treatment. Each type of model is run with and without controls for demographic characteristics. In all equations, the natural log of usual weekly hours is the dependent variable.

Double- and Triple Differences Equations using "Aftertrt"

25. ln(Uhourse) = f (Aftertrt, Evrtreat, Yr91–99, Earnwke)
26. ln(Uhourse) = f (Aftertrt, Evrtreat, Yr91–99, Earnwke, Age, Agesq, Black, Hispanic, Married, Divorced, Highshc, Somecoll, Colldeg, Graddeg)
27. ln(Uhourse) = f (Aftertrt, Evrtreat, Yr91–99, Earnwke, Female)
28. ln(Uhourse) = f (Aftertrt, Evrtreat, Yr91–99, Earnwke, Female, Age, Agesq, Black, Hispanic, Married, Divorced, Highshc, Somecoll, Colldeg, Graddeg)

Double- and Triple-Differences Equations Using "Yrsaft1 . . . 7"

29. ln(Uhourse) = f (Yrsaft1–7, Evrtreat, Yrsbef1–8, Yr91–99, Earnwke)
30. ln(Uhourse) = f (Yrsaft1–7, Evrtreat, Yrsbef1–8, Yr91–99, Earnwke, Age, Agesq, Black, Hispanic, Married, Divorced, Highshc, Somecoll, Colldeg, Graddeg)
31. ln(Uhourse) = f (Yrsaft1–7, Evrtreat, Yrsbef1–8, Yr91–99, Earnwke, Female)
32. ln(Uhourse) = f (Aftertrt, Evrtreat, Yrsbef1–8, Yr91–99, Earnwke, Female, Age, Agesq, Black, Hispanic, Married, Divorced, Highshc, Somecoll, Colldeg, Graddeg)

Equations 25 through 32 state that weekly hours of individuals in nontraditional occupations is a function of whether one is in a treatment area (Evrtreat), in a treatment area after treatment (Aftertrt/Yrsaft#), the survey year (Yr91–99), usual weekly earnings (Earnwke), and several demographic characteristics, including sex (Female), age (Age, Agesq), race and ethnicity (Black, Hispanic), marital status (Married, Divorced), and educational attainment (Highsch, Somecoll, Colldeg, Graddeg).

Notes

Notes to Chapter 1

1. Women's Bureau U.S. Department of Labor, draft of WANTO cover memo to Congress and the press, May 9, 2000.

2. Alexis Herman, quoted in dissemination products for the WANTO technical assistance program, developed by Brigid O'Farrell, 2000.

3. James E. Rosenbaum, *Beyond College for All: Career Paths for the Forgotten Half* (New York: Russell Sage Foundation, 2001).

4. Louise Kapp Howe, *Pink Collar Workers* (New York: G.P. Putnam's Sons, 1977), 19–20.

5. Sharon L. Harlan and Ronnie J. Steinberg, eds., *Job Training for Women: The Promise and Limits of Public Policies* (Philadelphia: Temple University Press, 1989), 6.

6. S. Beyer and A. Finnegan, "The Accuracy of Gender Stereotypes Regarding Occupations." Paper presented at the annual meeting of the American Psychological Association, 1997, Chiaco, IL, as quoted in Sandra Kerka, "Has Nontraditional Training Worked for Women?" *Myths and Realities, No. 1* (Center on Education and Training for Employment, Ohio State University College of Education, 1999).

7. Harlan and Steinberg, 8 (emphasis added).

8. John Tyler, Richard J. Murnane, and Frank Levy, "Are More College Graduates Really Taking 'High School' Jobs?" *Monthly Labor Review* (December 1995): 27.

9. Barbara Bergmann, "Occupational Segregation, Wages, and Profits When Employers Discriminate by Race or Sex," *Eastern Economic Journal* 1, nos. 2/3 (April/July 1974): 103–10.

10. Jeremy I. Bulow and Lawrence H. Summers, "A Theory of Dual Labor Markets with Application to Industrial Policy, Discrimination and Keynesian Unemployment," *Journal of Labor Economics* 4 (1986): 376–413.

11. Harlan and Steinberg, 29; Donald J. Treiman and Heidi I. Hartmann, eds., *Women, Work and Wages: Equal Pay for Jobs of Equal Value* (Washington, DC: National Academy Press, 1981).

12. Chris Tilly and Charles Tilly, "Capitalist Work and Labor Markets," in *The Handbook of Economic Sociology*, ed. N. Smelser and R. Swedberg, 301 (Princeton: Princeton University Press, 1994).

13. From Adam Smith's *Wealth of Nations*; government involvement impedes the free flow of capital and labor, making markets inefficient. Equitable distribution of goods, services, and wages obtains from unfettered markets. This is the usual exposition of Smith, the one most of us receive from "textbook propaganda" (James K. Galbraith, *Created Unequal: The Crisis in American Pay* [New York: Free Press, 1998]). However, see Galbraith's analysis (esp. pp. 38–39) where he points out that Smith "blames *governments* for causing excessive inequality of wages . . . by restricting

the free movements of capital and labor and by distributing privileges to the rich and favored at the expense of the poor" (38–39, emphasis original). In Smith's view then, bad government policy was one that maintained lopsided distributions of wealth, not those seeking to redress them. The end result may be the same to some, but the distinction is interesting to point out, albeit in a footnote.

14. Thorstein Veblen, *The Place of Science in Modern Civilization and Other Essays* (New Brunswick, NJ: Transaction Books, [1919] 1990), 73.

15. Herbert A. Simon, "Theories of Decision-Making in Economic and Behavioral Sciences," *American Economic Review* 49 (1959): 253–83.

16. Ray Marshall, Secretary of the U.S. Department of Labor, 1977–1981. Interviews with author throughout 1999–2001.

17. Daniel S. Hamermesh, *Labor Demand* (Princeton: Princeton University Press, 1993), 199–202.

18. Ray Marshall, "Economics of Racial Discrimination," *Journal of Economic Literature* 12 (1974): 849; see also Ray Marshall, "The Economics of Discrimination as Applied to Business Development," in *Eli Ginzberg: The Economist as a Public Intellectual*, ed. Eli Ginzberg and Irving Louis Horowitz, 61–106 (Princeton, NJ: Transaction, 2002).

19. Galbraith, 6.

20. Gary S. Becker, *The Economics of Discrimination* (Chicago: University of Chicago Press, 1957); see also Gary S. Becker, "Nobel Lecture: The Economic Way of Looking at Behavior," *Journal of Political Economy* 101 (1993): 385–409.

21. Galbraith, 7. Emphasis in original.

22. Ibid.

23. Jamie Peck, *Workplace: The Social Regulation of Labor Markets* (New York: Guilford Press, 1996).

24. Vivian Price, *Hammering It Out: Women in the Construction Zone*, 54 min. video, prod. and dir. Vivian Price, Hardhat Video Productions, 2000.

25. Howe.

26. Susan Eisenberg, "Welcoming Sisters into the Brotherhood," *Sojourner: The Women's Forum* 17 (July 1995): 17–18; and Susan Eisenberg, "Still Building the Foundation: Women in the Construction Trades," *WorkingUSA* (May–June 1998): 23–35.

27. Molly Martin, ed., *Hard-Hatted Women: Life on the Job*, 2d ed. (Seattle: Seal Press, 1997).

28. Barbara Ehrenreich, *Nickel and Dimed: On (Not) Getting By in America* (New York: Henry Holt, 2001).

29. Peter B. Doeringer and Michael J. Piore, *Internal Labor Markets and Manpower Analysis* (Lexington, MA: D.C. Heath, 1971).

30. These are not entirely arbitrary distinctions, data analysis confirms the difference between primary and secondary sector jobs based on very specific job characteristics. See Maury B. Gittleman and David R. Howell, "Changes in the Structure and Quality of Jobs in the United States: Effects by Race and Gender, 1973–1990," *Industrial and Labor Relations Review* 48, no. 3 (1995): 420–40. The authors employed cluster analysis to establish patterns among 621 occupations, according to seventeen measures of job quality. In this bottom-up analysis, they did not assume segmented markets existed, but allowed the data clusters to determine whether SLM Theory accurately depicted labor markets. They found six groups of occupations, grouped into three categories, "a structure that is remarkably consistent with the descriptions found in much of the labor market segmentation literature."

31. David Gordon, Richard Edwards, and Michael Reich, *Segmented Work, Divided Workers: The Historical Transformations of Labor in the United States* (New York: Cambridge University Press, 1982).

32. Claudia Goldin, "Monitoring Costs and Occupational Segregation by Sex: A Historical Analysis," *Journal of Labor Economics* 4, no. 1 (1986): 1–27. See also Jayne Dean, "Sex-Segregated Employment, Wage Inequality and Labor-Intensive Production: A Study of 33 U.S. Manufacturing Industries," *Review of Radical Political Economics* 23, no. 3 (1991): 244–68; and Bulow and Summers.

33. Barbara F. Reskin and Patricia A. Roos, *Job Queues, Gender Queues: Explaining Women's Inroads into Male Occupations* (Philadelphia: Temple University Press, 1990).

34. Ibid., 31–45.

35. Annette Bernhardt, Martina Morris, Mark S. Handcock, and Marc A. Scott, *Divergent Paths: Economic Mobility in the American Labor Market* (New York: Russell Sage Foundation, 2001).

36. Brigid O'Farrell, "Women in Blue Collar and Related Occupations at the End of the Millennium," *Quarterly Review of Economics and Finance* 39 (1999): 699–722.

37. Tilly and Tilly, 281.

38. Sharon H. Mastracci, "Persistent Problems Demand Consistent Solutions: Evaluating Programs to Mitigate Occupational Segregation," *Review of Radical Political Economics* (forthcoming).

39. Hamermesh, 298–300.

40. Ibid., 307.

41. Tilly and Tilly, 293.

42. Ron Baiman, Marc Doussard, Sharon Mastracci, Joe Persky, and Nik Theodore, *Raising and Maintaining the Value of the Illinois Minimum Wage: An Economic Impact Study* (February 2003): www.uic.edu/cuppa/uicued/Publications/EXECSMRY/IllinoisMinimumWage.htm.

43. Hamermesh, 164–66.

44. See National Bureau of Economic Research: www.nber.org/data/morg.html; and Bureau of Labor Statistics: www.bls.gov.

45. In Chapter 4 when consecutive years are used, replications using even and odd years are also done to ensure that the results are robust.

46. Max L. Carey, "How Workers Get Their Training," *BLS Bulletin* 2226 (Washington, DC: U.S. Department of Labor, Bureau of Labor Statistics, March 1985); Alan Eck, "How Workers Get Their Training: A 1991 Update," *BLS Bulletin* 2407 (Washington, DC: U.S. Department of Labor, Bureau of Labor Statistics, August 1992).

47. Shulamit Reinharz, *Feminist Methods in Social Research* (Oxford: Oxford University Press, 1992).

Notes to Chapter 2

1. Robert McAndrews, Coordinator of the Associated General Contractors Apprenticeship Program, interview by Steve Knight on *Construction Affairs*, KIEV 870AM, February 13, 1999: www.constructionaffairs.com/carp_apprent.html.

2. Jennifer Cheeseman Day and Kurt Bauman, "Have We Reached the Top? Educational Attainment Projections of the U.S. Population," Bureau of the Census Population Division, Working paper no. 43 (May 2000): 14.

3. Barbara Ehrenreich, *Nickel and Dimed: On (Not) Getting By in America* (New York: Henry Holt, 2001).

4. The 1962 and 1975 figures are from Louise Kapp Howe, *Pink Collar Workers* (New York: G.P. Putnam's Sons, 1977), 21. Updated information is from annualized 2001 Current Population Survey (CPS) data and can be found at www.stats.bls.gov/cps/home.htm#annual, under Table 11. Some of these occupational titles have changed, for instance, the closest occupational title to "Sewers and stitchers" in the 2001 data is "Textile Sewing Machine Operators."

5. Daniel E. Hecker, "Occupational Employment Projections to 2010," *Monthly Labor Review* (November 2001): 81.

6. E. Schmidt and G. Denhert, "Why Women Should Be in Trades," *Canadian Vocational Journal* 26, no. 2 (August 1990): 11–12.

7. See, for example, ten-year earnings projections for women and men published in the *Monthly Labor Review*, November 2001; earnings averages for male- and female-dominated occupations published by the Bureau of Labor Statistics, annualized 2001 Current Population Survey (CPS) data, which can be found at stats.bls.gov/cps/home.htm#annual, under "Table 11: Employed Persons by Detailed Occupation, Sex, Race, and Hispanic Origin"; see also Barbara Byrd, "Great Work If You Can Get It: Women in the Skilled Trades," in *Squaring Up: Policy Strategies to Raise Women's Incomes in the United States*, ed. Mary C. King, 202 (Ann Arbor: University of Michigan Press, 2001).

8. Robert W. Glover, "Apprenticeship: A Route to the Trades for Women?" in *Job Training for Women: The Promise and Limits of Public Policies,** ed. Sharon L. Harlan and Ronnie J. Steinberg, 283 (Philadelphia: Temple University Press, 1989).

9. Throughout the analysis, the focus has been on government programs and not privately funded ones, because government programs are held to Title IX anti-sex discrimination regulations, so legal recourse exists in the event that publicly funded programs were found to discriminate against women. Policy interventions can cover privately funded proprietary vocational training and education programs interested in increasing the diversity of their students. Proprietary institutions, although important, are not held to sex-equity standards, and they still reach the minority of vocationally trained students, so emphasizing government-funded programs remains at the heart of truly altering patterns of sex segregation in training and employment. See Lois Haignere and Ronnie J. Steinberg, "Nontraditional Training for Women: Effective Programs, Structural Barriers and Political Hurdles," in Harlan and Steinberg, 334.

10. Harlan and Steinberg, 35–36. Emphasis in original. In same book see also Sharon Harlan, "Women and Federal Job Training Policy," 267.

11. Ray Marshall, "The Economics of Discrimination as Applied to Business Development," in *Eli Ginzberg: The Economist as a Public Intellectual*, ed. Eli Ginzberg and Irving Louis Horowitz, 61–106 (Princeton, NJ: Transaction, 2002).

12. Message posted on the Hammering It Out message board, www.hammeringitout.com, May 3, 2001.

13. "Hard-Hatted Women: Challenge Tradition in the Skilled Trades," *Focus on WICS,* Women in Community Service newsletter 3 (Fall 1997): 1.

---

* Further references to this book or articles in this book will be simply "Harlan and Steinberg."

14. Leslie McCall. "Gender and the New Inequality: Explaining the College/Non-College Wage Gap," *American Sociological Review* (April 2000): 234–55.

15. John H. Bishop and Shani Carter, "How Accurate Are Recent BLS Occupational Projections?" *Monthly Labor Review* 114 (October 1991): 37–43.

16. See, among others, Harlan and Steinberg, 24–25; Ruth Sidel, *Women and Children Last: The Plight of Poor Women in Affluent America*, (Middlesex, UK: Penguin Book, 1986) and the National Coalition for Women and Girls in Education, *Invisible Again: The Impact of Changes in Federal Funding on Vocation Programs for Women and Girls* (Washington, DC: NCWGE, 2001).

17. Harlan and Steinberg, 20.

18. Harlan and Steinberg, 40; see also Haignere and Steinberg, 350. Haignere and Steinberg point out that the "necessary support services" for women in these programs increases their cost, which makes them less politically feasible, particularly in tight fiscal environments.

19. Nance Goldstein, "Management Training Strategies in Electronics," in Harlan and Steinberg, 491.

20. Harlan and Steinberg, 13; Marilyn Gittell and Janice Moore, "Denying Independence: Barriers to the Education of Women on AFDC," in Harlan and Steinberg, 445–79.

21. K. Bloomer, J. Finney, and Barbara Gault, "Education and Job Training under Welfare Reform," *Welfare Reform Network News*, no. 9–10 (Washington, DC: Institute for Women's Policy Research, August/September 1997).

22. Among others, see Haignere and Steinberg, 351.

23. Harlan and Steinberg, 12.

24. Elizabeth H. Giese, "Expanding Occupational Choices in Michigan's Secondary Vocational Education," in Harlan and Steinberg, 323.

25. Haignere and Steinberg, 340.

26. Jane Smeaton and Daniel J. Wagner, "Barriers to Enrollment in Post-Secondary VTAE Programs in Wisconsin," Southwest Wisconsin Vocational-Technical Institute, Fennimore, June 1976 (emphasis added).

27. Haignere and Steinberg, 341 (emphasis added).

28. Ibid.

29. See, among others, Harlan and Steinberg, who observed that the skewed attention paid to women in professional and managerial nontraditional roles "obscure[s] many of the ways by which the labor market confines and channels the majority of women into low-status and low-paying clerical, service and blue-collar occupations . . . [and] hinders efforts to improve their status because neither social scientists nor policy makers adequately understand the institutional structures within which the average woman is trained and subsequently employed" (7).

30. Olivia Crosby, "Apprenticeships: Career Training, Credentials, and a Paycheck in Your Pocket," *Occupational Outlook Quarterly* (Summer 2002): 2.

31. Bernard Elbaum, "The Persistence of Apprenticeship in Britain and Its Decline in the United States," in *Industrial Training and Technological Innovation*, ed Howard F. Gospel, 194–212 (London: Routledge, 1991).

32. Glover, 286. See also Chris Tilly and Charles Tilly, "Capitalist Work and Labor Markets," in *The Handbook of Economic Sociology*, ed. N. Smelser and R. Swedberg, 300 (Princeton: Princeton University Press, 1994).

33. Susan Eisenberg, "Welcoming Sisters into the Brotherhood," *Sojourner: The Women's Forum* 17 (July 1995): 17–18. See also Susan Eisenberg, "Still Building the Foundation: Women in the Construction Trades," *WorkingUSA* (May–June 1998): 23–35.

34. Message posted on the Hammering It Out message board, www.hammeringitout. com. May 21, 2001.

35. Robert J. Gitter, "Apprenticeship-trained Workers: United States and Great Britain," *Monthly Labor Review* 117, no. 4 (1994): 38–43.

36. Glover, 285.

37. Ibid., 284.

38. Ibid., 285.

39. McCall.

40. Alan Eck, "Job-related Education and Training: Their Impact on Earnings," *Monthly Labor Review* (October 1993): 32; Max L. Carey, "How Workers Get Their Training," *BLS Bulletin* 2226 (Washington, DC: U.S. Department of Labor, Bureau of Labor Statistics, March 1985); Alan Eck, "How Workers Get Their Training: A 1991 Update," *BLS Bulletin* 2407 (Washington, DC: U.S. Department of Labor, Bureau of Labor Statistics, August 1992).

41. Question 35, "Did you need specific skills or training to obtain you current (last) job?" and Question 38, "Since you obtained your present job did you take any training to improve your skills?" of the Supplement to January 1983 and 1991 Current Population Surveys, see *How Workers Get Their Training* (1985): 58; and *How Workers Get Their Training: A 1991 Update* (1992): 67. If they answered yes to either question, respondents were asked to identify sources of each type of training in subsequent questions.

42. Eck, "Job-related Education and Training," 37.

43. Matthew Mariani, "High-earning Workers Who Don't Have a Bachelor's Degree," *Occupational Outlook Quarterly* (Fall 1999): 9–15.

44. Kristina J. Shelley, "The Future of Jobs for College Graduates," *Monthly Labor Review* (July 1992): 13–21; Daniel E. Hecker, "Reconciling Conflicting Data on Jobs for College Graduates," *Monthly Labor Review* (July 1992): 3–12. See also Daniel E. Hecker, "College Graduates in 'High School' Jobs: A Commentary," *Monthly Labor Review* (December 1995): 28.

45. John Tyler, Richard J. Murnane, and Frank Levy, "Are More College Graduates Really Taking 'High School' Jobs?" *Monthly Labor Review* (December 1995): 18–27.

46. Annette Bernhardt, Martina Morris, Mark S. Handcock, and Marc A. Scott, *Divergent Paths: Economic Mobility in the American Labor Market* (New York: Russell Sage Foundation, 2001).

47. Arlene Dohm and Ian Wyatt, "College at Work: Outlook and Earnings for College Graduates, 2000–10," *Occupational Outlook Quarterly* (Fall 2002): 3–15. See also the National Center for Educational Statistics for the numbers of degrees awarded over time.

48. See Mariani.

49. Hecker, "Reconciling Conflicting Data on Jobs for College Graduates," 11.

50. Shelley, 19.

Notes to Chapter 3

1. National Coalition for Women and Girls in Education, *Invisible Again: The Impact of Changes in Federal Funding on Vocational Programs for Women and Girls* (Washington, DC: NCWGE, 2001).

2. Barbara Byrd, "Great Work If You Can Get It: Women in the Skilled Trades," in *Squaring Up: Policy Strategies to Raise Women's Incomes in the United States*, ed. Mary C. King, 205 (Ann Arbor: University of Michigan Press, 2001).

3. NCWGE, *Invisible Again*; see also NCWGE, *Empowering America's Families* (Washington, DC: NCWGE, 1995).

4. NCWGE, *Invisible Again*, 2.

5. Piedmont Works, A Program of Piedmont Virginia Community College 2001–2002: www.piedmontworks.org.

6. Daniel E. Hecker, "Earnings of College Graduates: Women Compared with Men," *Monthly Labor Review* (March 1998): 62–71.

7. Marlene Kim, "Women Paid Low Wages: Who They Are and Where They Work," *Monthly Labor Review* (September 2000): 29 (emphasis added).

8. Alan Eck, "Job-related Education and Training: Their Impact on Earnings," *Monthly Labor Review* (October 1993): 32.

9. For 1979, 1984, 1989, 1994, and 1999, women comprise a greater portion of both the some-college population and the college-graduate population. See Appendix B for a detailed table of these proportions.

10. William J. Carrington and Bruce C. Fallick, "Do Some Workers Have Minimum Wage Careers?" *Monthly Labor Review* (May 2001): 26 (emphasis added).

11. Harriett B. Presser and Amy G. Cox, "The Work Schedules of Low-Educated American Women and Welfare Reform," *Monthly Labor Review* (April 1997): 25–34.

12. Barbara H. Wootton, "Gender Differences in Occupational Employment," *Monthly Labor Review* (April 1997): 15–24.

13. For the 1999 data, assembler and cook fall out of the top ten employers for women with some post-secondary schooling compared to high school-only women workers, falling to twenty-first and twenty-eighth, respectively.

14. Eck, "Job-related Education and Training."

15. Kim; Wootton.

Notes to Chapter 4

1. Michelle Simko, interviewed in "Hard-Hatted Women: Challenge Tradition in the Skilled Trades," *Focus on WICS*, Women In Community Service newsletter 3 (Fall 1997).

2. In addition to the studies cited here, see A. Bandura, "Self-Efficacy: Toward a Unifying Theory of Behavior Change," *Psychological Review* 84 (1977): 191–215; N.E. Betz, "Counseling Uses of Career Self-Efficacy Theory," *Career Development Quarterly* 41 (1992): 22–26; Barbara Morgan and Victoria Foster, "Career Counseling for Reentry Dual Career Women: A Cognitive Developmental Approach," *Journal of Career Development* 26, no. 2 (Winter 1999): 125–36; Jane L. Swanson and Mary B. Woitke, "Theory into Practice in Career Assessment for Women: Assessment and Interventions Regarding Perceived Career Barriers," *Journal of Career Assessment* 5, no. 4 (Fall 1997): 443–62; Cheryl G. Bartholomew and Donna L. Schnorr, "Gender Equity: Suggestions for Broadening Career Options of Female Students," *School Counselor* 41, no. 4 (March 1994): 245–55; Laurie Stenberg and Jerry Tuchscherer, "Women in Nontraditional Careers: Setting Them Up to Succeed," *Vocational Education Journal* 67, no. 5 (May 1992): 33–35; Christopher A. Borman and Florence Guido-DiBrito, "The Career Development of Women: Helping Cinderella Lose Her Complex," *Journal of Career Development* 12, no. 3 (March 1986): 250–61; Valeri G. Ward, "Career Counseling of Girls and Women: Guidelines for Professional Practice," Canadian Guidance and Counseling Association (1995).

3. This section reflects findings in Sharon H. Mastracci, "Employment and Training Alternatives for Non-College Women: Do Redistributive Policies Really Redistribute?" *Policy Studies Journal* (forthcoming).

4. Natasha A. McLennan and Nancy Arthur, "Applying the Cognitive Information Processing Approach to Career Problem Solving and Decision Making to Women's Career Development," *Journal of Employment Counseling* 36, no. 2 (June 1999): 82–96; Linda Seligman, "Outcomes of Career Counseling with Women," *Journal of the NAWDAC* 44, no. 3 (Spring 1981): 25–32; Patricia L. Romero, "Expanding Career Options: Non-Stereotyped Career Counseling," Irvine Career Planning and Placement Center, California University (1979). Some studies have found there to be no benefit to career counseling on the occupational choice of women in nontraditional fields, but, on closer inspection, these studies focused on *professional* women in NTOs (physicians, dentists, etc.) and found that these women were more influenced and inspired by the occupations of their professional parents, especially their fathers. These higher-socioeconomic-status women had other quasi-counseling resources at their disposal, and, therefore, formal career counseling was far less influential in their decision. In the one study that had a similar finding for blue-collar women, the ten women studied either already possessed or they drew from their families and support systems what formal career counseling would have otherwise provided (Carol J. Auster and Donald Auster, "Factors Influencing Women's Choice of Nontraditional Careers: The Role of Family, Peers, and Counselors," *Vocational Guidance Quarterly* 29, no. 3 [March 1981]: 253–63; C.K. Greene and W.L. Stitt-Gohdes, "Factors That Influence Women's Choices to Work in the Trades," *Journal of Career Development* 23, no. 4 [1997]: 265–78). The bulk of the evidence still supports the assertion that formal career counseling and especially increasing women's self-efficacy has a significant positive impact on women's occupational choices and overall opportunities for economic independence.

5. Robert W. Glover, "Apprenticeship: A Route to the Trades for Women?" In S. Harlan and R. Steinberg, 280. See also, David T. Wearne, "Occupational Choices of Children: Must They Be Traditional?" EDRS Microfiche, January 1991); Auster and Auster. In addition, Faith Dunne found that "rural high school girls face a strong home-versus-career conflict stemming from traditional rural values and myths about women." Education and employment programs located in rural areas must be sensitive to the unique socialization patterns in their areas (Faith Dunne, "They'd Never Hire a Girl: Vocational Education in Rural Secondary Schools," EDRS Microfiche, Dartmouth College Department of Education, 1980).

6. Kate Roy Sullivan and James R. Mahalik, "Increasing Career Self-Efficacy for Women: Evaluating a Group Intervention," *Journal of Counseling & Development* 7 (Winter 2000): 55.

7. Marilyn J. Haring and Karen C. Beyard-Tyler, "Counseling with Women: The Challenge of Nontraditional Careers," *School Counselor* 31, no. 4 (March 1984): 301–9.

8. Sullivan and Mahalik, 57.

9. See anything under the Institutionalist banner. See also, Jane Gaskell, "The Politics of Methodological Decisions: How Social Policy and Feminism Affect the Study of Careers," in *Methodological Approaches to the Study of Career*, ed. R.A. Young and W.A. Borgen, 221–31 (New York: Praeger 1990).

10. Stenberg and Tuchscherer, 33–35.

11. Susan Eisenberg, "Welcoming Sisters into the Brotherhood," *Sojourner: The Women's Forum* 17 (July): 17–18.

12. Barbara Byrd, "Great Work If You Can Get It: Women in the Skilled Trades," in *Squaring Up: Policy Strategies to Raise Women's Incomes in the United States*, ed. Mary C. King, 210 (Ann Arbor: University of Michigan Press, 2001).

13. Lois Haignere and Ronnie J. Steinberg, "Nontraditional Training for Women: Effective Programs, Structural Barriers and Political Hurdles," in Harlan and Steinberg, 339.

14. Louise F. Fitzgerald, "Nontraditional Occupations: Not for Women Only," *Journal of Counseling Psychology* 27, no. 3 (1980): 252–59.

15. Ibid., 258.

16. Haignere and Steinberg, 345.

17. Jill Miller, "Displaced Homemakers in the Employment and Training System," in Harlan and Steinberg, eds., 143–64.

18. Median earnings were used instead of mean earnings to account for the positive skewness of earnings data, and the nominal values in the 1979–1999 CPS-MORG data were deflated using the Bureau of Labor Statistics' Consumer Price Index (CPI) deflator, using 1990 as the index year.

19. Specifically, see Marlene Kim, "Women Paid Low Wages: Who They Are and Where They Work," *Monthly Labor Review* (September 2000): 26–30. Kim defines low wages in several ways, including the poverty level, the poverty level times 1.25, and the poverty level times 1.50.

20. In my interview with labor secretary Alexis M. Herman on December 15, 2000, she indicated that while she was Women's Bureau Director from 1977 to 1981, the 25 percent cutoff emanated from her exploratory data analysis of patterns of occupational segregation over time. The Bureau has published lists of nontraditional occupations for women on a regular basis since that time.

21. As stated earlier, estimations were conducted with all years 1979 to 1999, and repeated with even and odd years to ensure against the remote, yet possible, problem in the CPS-MORGs of double-counting cases in consecutive years. Estimations were repeated with and without controls to ensure robustness of results, as well. Using every other year also reduced the total number of observations by about half, which further underscored the robustness of the results insofar as the results were virtually unchanged by the number of observations used. Results shown are from the estimations using all years. Coefficients in each of the versions (all observations, even years, odd years) were virtually identical. The estimation technique (STATA's dprobit) also allows one to interpret the output directly as probabilities by estimating the effects of dichotomous variables as the discrete change of dummy variables from zero to one. Therefore, the output is interpretable as *percentage point changes in probability* from the baseline probability. Baseline probabilities, the means for all variables, are found in Appendix 4A.

22. The definition of "non-college" used in these estimations includes all workers who did not hold four-year college degrees or who did not complete at least sixteen years of schooling. Two definitions of non-college were used—one that includes only high school graduates and those with some college experience, and one that includes high school dropouts as well. As one might expect, the probability that a high school dropout will earn at least 125 percent of real median earnings is low, so including this group in the non-college definition resulted in lower baseline probabilities of earning at least 125 percent the median income, and the effects of holding a nontraditional job were much smaller. Holding at least a high school diploma raises a worker's chances of earning more money and increases the impact of holding a high-wage nontradi-

tional job. Table 4.2 illustrates the results of using the definition of non-college that includes those without high school diplomas, and, therefore, these are the more conservative estimates.

23. *Sixty-Ninth Annual Report of the Secretary of Labor* (1981): 53.

24. *Seventieth Annual Report of the Secretary of Labor* (1982): 133; *Seventy-First Annual Report of the Secretary of Labor.* (1983): 133.

25. *Seventy-Sixth Annual Report of the Secretary of Labor* (1988): 198.

26. *Seventy-Eighth Annual Report of the Secretary of Labor* (1990): 205; and *Seventy-Ninth Annual Report of the Secretary of Labor* (1991): 221.

27. Sharon Harlan, "Women and Federal Job Training Policy," in Harlan and Steinberg.

28. Brigid O'Farrell, "Women in Blue-Collar and Related Occupations at the End of the Millennium," *Quarterly Review of Economics and Finance* 39 (1999): 699–722.

29. *Non-traditional Employment for Women* (NEW) *Act*, Section 2 (b)(1)(2)(3), Public Law 102-235, as signed on December 12, 1991 (*not* verbatim).

30. In three of its four years, six states received NEW grants (the maximum number allowed in the act); in one year, five states were awarded a grant.

31. *NEW Act* as enrolled, Section 8.

32. This information is based on archives of Roberta V. McKay, the Grant Officer's Technical Representative for the NEW grant program of the Women's Bureau of the U.S. Department of Labor. Archives accessed June 19, 2000.

33. *Women in Apprenticeships and Non-Traditional Occupations Act.* Section 2 (b)(1)(2)(3)(4), Public Law 102-530, as signed on October 27, 1992 (*not* verbatim).

34. Language of *Women in Apprenticeships and Nontraditional Occupations Act*, Public Law 102-530 as enrolled, signed October 27, 1992.

Notes to Chapter 5

1. Policies developed and implemented under Labor Secretary Ray Marshall and Women's Bureau Director Alexis Herman are the earliest *systematic* initiatives to increase women's numbers among nontraditional jobs. See, among others, Sharon H. Mastracci, "The Political Benefits of Protectionism for the Women's Bureau of the U.S. Department of Labor" (unpublished manuscript); Robert W. Glover, "Apprenticeship: A Route to the Trades for Women?" in Harlan and Steinberg, 269–89; Louise B. Haignere and Ronnie J. Steinberg, "Nontraditional Training for Women: Effective Programs, Structural Barriers and Political Hurdles," in Harlan and Steinberg, 336; Barbara Byrd, "Great Work if You Can Get It: Women in the Skilled Trades," in *Squaring Up: Policy Strategies to Raise Women's Incomes in the United States*, ed. Mary C. King, 200 (Ann Arbor: University of Michigan Press, 2001).

2. See also Chris Tilly and Charles Tilly, "Capitalist Work and Labor Markets," in *The Handbook of Economic Sociology*, ed. N. Smelser and R. Swedberg, 303 (Princeton: Princeton University Press, 1994); Susan Eisenberg, "Welcoming Sisters into the Brotherhood," *Sojourner: The Women's Forum* 17 (July 1995): 17–18; and Ruth Sidel, *Women and Children Last: The Plight of Poor Women in Affluent America* (New York: Penguin Books 1986).

3. Glover, "Apprenticeship," 282.

4. Employment policy applications include: Daniel S. Hamermesh and Stephen

J. Trejo, "The Demand for Hours of Labor: Direct Evidence from California," *Review of Economics and Statistics* 82, no. 1 (2000): 38–47; Daniel S. Hamermesh and David Scoones, "Multilevel 'General Policy Equilibria': Evidence from the American Unemployment Insurance Tax Ceiling," NBER working paper W5578 (1996); David Card and Daniel Sullivan, "Measuring the Effect of Subsidized Training Programs on Movements In and Out of Employment," *Econometrica* 56, no. 3 (1998): 497–530; James Heckman and Jeffrey A. Smith, "The Pre-Program Earnings Dip and the Determinants of Participation in a Social Program," NBER working paper W6983 (1999); James Heckman, Hidehiko Ichimura, Jeffrey Smith, and Petra Todd, "Characterizing Selection Bias Using Experimental Data," NBER working paper W6699 (1998).

5. Health care policy applications include: Aaron S. Yelowitz, "The Medicaid Notch, Labor Supply and Welfare Participation," *Quarterly Journal of Economics* 110, no. 4 (1995): 909–39; Jonathan Gruber, "The Incidence of Mandated Maternity Benefits," *American Economic Review* 84, no. 3 (1994): 622–41; Debra Sabatini Dwyer, Olivia S. Mitchell, Robert Cole, and Sylvia K. Reed, "Evaluating Mental Health Capitation Treatment: Lessons from Panel Data," NBER working paper W5297 (1995); A. Bowen Garrett and Sherry Glied, "The Effect of U.S. Supreme Court Ruling *Sullivan v. Zebley* on Child SSI and AFDC Enrollment," NBER working paper W6125 (1997).

6. Tax policy applications include: Martin Feldstein and Daniel Feenberg, "The Effect of Increased Tax Rates on Taxable Income and Economic Efficiency," NBER working paper W5370 (1995); Jonathan Gruber and James Poterba, "Tax Incentives and the Decision to Purchase Health Insurance," MIT working paper series, no. 94-10 (1994).

7. Applications to determine the impact of policy by race or gender include: David Card, "The Impact of the Mariel Boatlift on the Miami Labor Market," *Industrial and Labor Relations Review* 43, no. 2 (1990): 245–57; see also Gruber; Hamermesh and Trejo; and Yelowitz.

8. Thomas Cook and Donald T. Campbell, *Quasi-Experimentation: Design and Analysis Issues for Field Settings* (Chicago: Rand McNally, 1979).

9. See Card. The Mariel boatlift was a series of flotilla from Cuba to Miami in mid-1980. Cuban president Fidel Castro deported hundreds of Cuban men and many women, half of whom stayed in the Miami area permanently. Card measured the impact of this truly exogenous and unanticipated decision on the Miami labor market to determine how similar workers in terms of age, experience, education and training, and race and English fluency were affected by the sudden influx of competitors in local labor markets.

10. Daniel S. Hamermesh, "Review Symposium: Comment," *Industrial and Labor Relations Review* 48, no. 4 (1995): 835.

11. Ibid., 836.

12. In "The Impact of the Mariel Boatlift," Card defined the Mariel boatlift as a "natural experiment" because it was an exogenous event, neither planned nor anticipated by the population it affected. However, sometimes the tag "natural experiment" is inappropriately applied. Hamermesh discussed this when critiquing a certain application of the differences estimator when he observed, "their cases are *neither natural nor experiments*" (Hamermesh, "Review Symposium," 837, emphasis original).

13. Daniel S. Hamermesh, *Labor Demand* (Princeton: Princeton University Press, 1993).

14. As the table on grant recipients will show, WANTO and NEW projects were implemented throughout the United States—urban and rural, poor and wealthier

states—so the difference between women who had access to these services and those who did not can be attributed to the project, and not other factors. Moreover, men throughout the country, within and outside treatment areas were included as controls, too, to further isolate the impact measured to the presence of a grant-funded project.

15. The National Bureau of Economic Research (NBER) prepares CPS data extracts, which are converted to the more STATA file format and include around 50 variables of individualized data for approximately 60,000 individuals age sixteen and above. NBER simplifies variable names and standardizes missing value codes across variables. CPS is the monthly household survey conducted by BLS and is used to measure unemployment and labor force participation rates. Every household entering the survey is interviewed each month for four months, ignored for eight months, then interviewed again for four more months. Questions on earnings and hours are asked only in the fourth and eighth interview—these are called the "outgoing" interviews. New households enter the survey each month, so only one-fourth of them are in an outgoing rotation each month. The "merged outgoing rotation groups" are all the households in an outgoing rotation, merged to create one file for a single year. There is a small chance that a single household appears in consecutive years. Because of this, all the models were run using odd-numbered years, then even-numbered years. The results did not change. BLS and NBER provide weights for use when analyzing these data. Because respondents are not selected for their proportional U.S. representation, using the data without employing weights may result in overrepresenting certain segments of the population if members of those segments happened to be "overinterviewed" with respect to their share of the overall population.

16. In Chapter 6 when consecutive years are used, replications using even and odd years are also done to ensure that the results are robust.

17. For all versions of the model, the R-squared value is low; however, this indicates that numerous factors exist to explain women's employment in NTOs, and among all these factors, these grant programs were small, though important, ones. Because this is a likelihood model, a pseudo R-squared is calculated, which is not quite the same as R-squared in a least squares model. For this reason, F-tests were run to determine whether the effect found could be equal to zero, and the results in all cases confirmed the statistically-significant and positive impacts reported above.

18. Heckman et al.

19. Ibid., 36.

20. Heckman and Smith.

21. Ibid., 21.

22. Recall that the larger grantees that have received multiple grants were excluded from this analysis. Recall that the geographic areas where multiple grant-funded projects were implemented were also excluded from this analysis. It may be assumed that if both multiple-award grantees and multiple-project areas were included, the impact of policy intervention would be even greater.

Notes to Chapter 6

1. Brigid O'Farrell, "The NEW Demonstration Program: Informational Materials for the Workforce Investment Community," report prepared for the Women's Bureau, Women's Research and Education Institute (May 2000): 4.

2. Frances Worthey, interview by author, Waco, TX, June 25, 2001.

3. This chapter draws on Sharon H. Mastracci, "The 'Institutions' in Institution-alization: State-Level Employment and Training Programs for Women in High-Skilled, High-Wage Occupations," *WorkingUSA* 6, no. 4 (Spring 2003): 116–42.

4. Brigid O'Farrell, "The WANTO Technical Assistance Program: Informational Materials for Employers and Unions," report prepared for the Women's Bureau, Women's Research and Education Institute (May 2000); "The NEW Demonstration Program."

5. Vivian Price, *Hammering It Out: Women in the Construction Zone*, 54 min. video, prod. and dir. Vivian Price, Hardhat Video Productions, 2000.

6. Louise Kapp Howe, *Pink Collar Workers* (New York: G.P. Putnam's Sons, 1977).

7. Susan Eisenberg, *We'll Call You If We Need You: Experiences of Women Working Construction* (Ithaca, NY: Cornell University Press, 1998).

8. Molly Martin, ed., *Hard-Hatted Women: Life on the Job*, 2d ed. (Seattle: Seal Press, 1997).

9. Barbara Ehrenreich, *Nickel and Dimed: On (Not) Getting By in America* (New York: Henry Holt, 2001).

10. Dorothy McBride Stetson and Amy Mazur, eds., *Comparative State Feminism* (Thousand Oaks, CA: Sage, 1995), 1–2.

11. Gender Equity Expert Panel, "Exemplary and Promising Gender Equity Programs, 2000," Harilyn Rousso and Mary Wiberg, panel co-chairs, 2000.

12. Robert K. Yin, *Case Study Research: Design and Methods* (Beverly Hills: Sage, 1984), 19.

13. Ibid., 103 (emphasis in original).

14. Ibid., 107.

15. Shulamit Reinharz, *Feminist Methods in Social Research* (Oxford: Oxford University Press, 1992), 164–66.

16. Yin, 78.

17. Annette Bernhardt, Martina Morris, Mark S. Handcock, and Marc A. Scott, *Divergent Paths: Economic Mobility in the American Labor Market* (New York: Russell Sage Foundation, 2001).

18. Annette Bernhardt, Laura Dresser, and Joel Rogers, "Taking the High Road in Milwaukee: The Wisconsin Regional Training Partnership," *WorkingUSA* 5, no. 3 (Winter 2001–2): 109–30; AFL-CIO and Working for America Institute, *High Road Partnerships Report* (Working for America Institute, 2002).

19. Wisconsin Department of Workforce Development, Division of Workforce Excellence, "State of Wisconsin Nontraditional Employment for Women (NEW) Demonstration Project: Final Report" (Madison, WI, March 1998).

20. Roberta V. McKay, *Nontraditional Employment for Women (NEW) Act* Demonstration Program Grants. Archives of the Women's Bureau National Office, Washington, DC accessed June 19, 2000.

21. Brigid O'Farrell, "Women and High-Wage Occupations: What We Know from Research," report prepared for the Women's Bureau of the U.S. Department of Labor, Women's Research and Education Institute (September 1999): 11.

22. Kit Strykowski and Nancy Hoffman (illustrator Keith Ward), "Materials Diskette." Nontraditional Employment for Women Tool Kit for Job Centers, State of Wisconsin Department of Workforce Development, September 1996: 55.

23. Wisconsin Department of Workforce Development, Division of Workforce

Excellence, "State of Wisconsin Nontraditional Employment for Women Demonstration Project: Final Report."

24. Strykowski and Hoffman.

25. Nancy D. Nakkoul, program specialist, Tools for Tomorrow: Women in the Trades, Madison Area Technical College, interview by author, Madison, WI, April 20, 2001.

26. Dane County Job Center, site visit by author, Madison, WI, April 19, 2001; Joy Wiggert, training coordinator, Employment and Training Association, Inc., DCJC, correspondence with author, June 15, 2001; Nakkoul, interview by author, April 20, 2001; and Mary Cirilli, policy analyst, State of Wisconsin Department of Workforce Development, interview by author, Madison, WI, April 18, 2001.

27. Nancy D. Nakkoul, "Nontraditional Occupations for Women. Building the Tool Kit Initiative: 2000 Annual Report and Evaluation," Dane County Job Center and South Central SDA, (June 2000): 12.

28. Nancy D. Nakkoul, Tools Mentoring Project, Tools for Tomorrow: Women in Trades & Technology Program, "Mentor Handbook" (Madison, WI: Madison Area Technical College, 2000).

29. Joel Dresang, "A Perfect Match: Training Center Provides Hands-On Practice Wanted by Employers," *Milwaukee Journal Sentinel*, May 22, 2002.

30. Nakkoul, "Building the Tool Kit Initiative."

31. Cirilli, interview by author, April 18, 2001.

32. Gaylen Lange, workforce development director, Heart of Texas Council of Governments, interviews by author, Waco, TX, October 18, 2000 November 10, 2000, and June 25, 2001.

33. McKay.

34. O'Farrell, "The NEW Demonstration Program," 4.

35. Texas State Technical College at Waco, site visits by author, June 5, 2001 and June 25, 2001.

36. Ibid.; Jerry Reay, instructor, Laser Electro-Optics Department, TSTC Waco, interview by author, Waco, TX, June 5, 2001; Carliss Hyde, director of External Resource Development, TSTC Waco, interview by author, Waco, TX, June 5, 2001; Carol Baker, Texas State Technical College System Statistical Data Reports, October 2000; Women's Resource Center at TSTC Waco, site visits by author, June 5, 2001 and June 25, 2001; and Frances Worthey, director of Women's Resource Center, TSTC Waco, telephone interview by author, June 18, 2001; and interview by author, Waco, TX, June 25, 2001.

37. Gaylen Lange, "A Returns-to-Investment Analysis of Project TExAS: Draft," unpublished manuscript, 2000.

Notes to Chapter 7

1. "Hard-Hatted Women: Challenge Tradition in the Skilled Trades," *Focus on WICS*, Women in Community Service newsletter 3 (Fall 1997): 1.

2. Ibid., 3.

3. Brigid O'Farrell, "The WANTO Technical Assistance Program: Informational Materials for Employers and Unions: Draft," report prepared for the Women's Bureau of the U.S. Department of Labor, Women's Research and Education Institute (May 2000).

4. An interesting perspective on the role of advocacy on the effectiveness of nonprofit organizations can be found in Sharon H. Mastracci, "The Coordinated Assault on Nonprofit Effectiveness: FEC Reforms and Community-Based Partnerships in Workforce Development," unpublished manuscript, 2003.

5. Office of Management and Budget (OMB) Watch. "Executive Summary: Overview of Findings of the Strengthening Nonprofit Advocacy Project," May 28, 2002.

6. Ibid.

7. Ibid.

8. Curtis W. Meadows, Jr., senior lecturer and founder, the Meadows Foundation, interview by author, Austin, TX, March 3, 2001.

9. Sharon L. Harlan and Judith R. Saidel, "Board Members' Influence on the Government-Nonprofit Relationship," *Nonprofit Management and Leadership* 5, no. 2 (1994): 173–96; Judith R. Saidel and Sharon L. Harlan, "Contracting and Patterns of Nonprofit Governance," *Nonprofit Management & Leadership* 8, no. 3 (1998): 243–59.

10. Harlan and Saidel, 175.

11. Ibid.

12. Robert Herman and David Renz, "Nonprofit Organizational Effectiveness: Contrasts Between Especially Effective and Less Effective Organizations," *Nonprofit Mangement and Leadership* 9, no. 1 (1998): 23–38.

13. Ralph M. Kramer, "The Voluntary Agency in a Mixed Economy: Dilemmas of Entrepreneurialism and Vendorism," *Journal of Applied Behavioral Science* 21: 377–91.

14. According to the implementation plan of the Bipartisan Campaign Reform Act, the Federal Election Commission (FEC) had to strengthen "coordination" provisions. Invitations to comment on the proposal were sent September 24, 2002, comments were due on October 11, 2002, the approved version was released December 5, 2002, and the final rules were scheduled for release in December 2002; "Alliance for Justice Criticizes FEC Coordination Rules; New Regulations Threaten Protected Speech," Alliance for Justice, December 5, 2002: www.usnewswire.com; "FEC Considers Coordinated Expenditures," October 23, 2002: www.foxnews.com; "Coordination Defined," Campaign Finance Institute: www.cfinst.org; "Legal Center Weekly Report," Campaign Legal Center, September 13, 2002: www.camlc.org.

15. Saidel and Harlan, 249 (emphasis added).

16. Office of Management and Budget Watch.

17. Evidence that women are especially effective in nonprofit management and advocacy can be found in Kathleen B. Fletcher, "Effective Boards: How Executive Directors Define and Develop Them," *Nonprofit Leadership & Management* 2, no. 3 (1992): 283–93; and in Ronald G. Shaiko, "Female Participation in Association Governance and Political Representation: Women as Executive Directors, Board Members, Lobbyists and Political Action Committee Members," *Nonprofit Management & Leadership* 8, no. 2: 121–39. Mixed evidence of women's effectiveness in nonprofits (and evidence that there is no difference) can be found in Michael O'Neill, "The Paradox of Women and Power in the Nonprofit Sector," in *Women and Power in the Nonprofit Sector*, ed. Teresa Odendahl and Michael O'Neill, 1–16 (San Francisco: Jossey-Bass, 1994); and in Theresa Odendahl and Sabrina Youmans, "Women on Nonprofit Boards," in *Women and Power in the Nonprofit Sector* (San Francisco: Jossey-Bass, 1994), 183–222.

18. O'Farrell, "The WANTO Technical Assistance Program."

19. See for example, Sharon H. Mastracci, "The 'Institutions' in Institutionaliza-

tion: State-Level Employment and Training Programs for Women in High-Skilled, High-Wage Occupations," *WorkingUSA* 6, no. 4 (Spring 2003): 116–42; Dorothy McBride Stetson and Amy Mazur, eds., *Comparative State Feminism* (Thousand Oaks, CA: Sage, 1995); Jeffrey L. Pressman and Aaron Wildavsky, *Implementation* (Berkeley: University of California Press, 1973).

20. Sandra Kerka, "Has Nontraditional Training Worked for Women?" *Myths and Realities, No. 1*, Center on Education and Training for Employment, Ohio State University College of Education (1999): 1.

21. Farar Elliot, Carol Anne Douglas, Bridget Kulla, Amanda Maclay, et al., "United States: President's Plan to Defund Federal Women's Offices," *Off Our Backs* (January/February 2002): 7.

22. "Chao Keeps Women's Bureau Regional Offices Open," *Safety & Health* 165, no. 3: 12.

23. Wider Opportunities for Women (WOW), *Respect That Woman,* 30 min. video, prod. and dir. WOW, 1995.

24. Wider Opportunities for Women, *Workplace Solutions: The Employer Manual* (Washington, DC: WOW, 1996).

25. Ibid.

26. Nancy D. Nakkoul and Lauren Sugerman, *Drafting the Blueprint: A Planning Guide for Achieving Workforce Diversity and Equity in Construction*, prepared for the Great Lakes Tradeswomen Alliance, 1999); Chicago Women in Trades, *Breaking New Ground: Worksite 2000* (Chicago: Chicago Women in Trades, 1992).

27. Nancy Nakkoul and Lauren Sugerman, "WANTO Grant Closeout Materials," prepared for the Great Lakes Tradeswoman Alliance Partner Organizations, EdVentures Unlimited, Inc. September 1, 1999; Lauren Sugerman, "Technical Assistance to Employers and Unions for the Retention of Women in Apprenticeable and Non-Traditional Occupations: Final Report," WANTO, prepared by Chicago Women in Trades, May 13, 1996.

28. Chicago Women in Trades, *Breaking New Ground*, 25.

29. Nakkoul and Sugerman, *Drafting the Blueprint.*

30. Nakkoul and Sugerman, "WANTO Grant Closeout Materials," 30.

31. Ibid., 7.

32. "About TNT:" www.tradeswomennow.org.

33. Lauren Sugerman, "Great Lakes Tradeswoman Technical Assistance Network: Technical Assistance to Employers and Unions for the Recruitment and Retention of Tradeswomen in the Midwest Region," report to the U.S. Department of Labor prepared by Chicago Women in Trades, May 15, 1997; Lauren Sugerman, "Great Lakes Tradeswoman Technical Assistance Network: Technical Assistance to Employers and Unions for the Recruitment and Retention of Tradeswomen in the Midwest Region," report to the U.S. Department of Labor prepared by Chicago Women in Trades, December 5, 1997.

34. Chicago Women in Trades, "Guide for Manufacturing Intern Programs," Draft prepared by the Manufacturing Opportunities for Women Project, December 2000.

35. Lisa Kuklinski, Steve Everett, and the Center for Research on Women and Gender, "Final Report and Evaluation: Manufacturing Opportunities for Women (MOW) Technical Assistance Program," prepared by Chicago Women in Trades MOW Team.

36. Alice Dan, director, and Janise Hurtig, research scientist, Center for Research on Women and Gender, University of Illinois Chicago, interview by author, Chicago, IL, April 20, 2001.

37. Nakkoul and Sugerman, "WANTO Grant Closeout Materials," 26.

38. Ibid., 33.

39. Chicago Women in Trades, "CWIT Calls for Legislature to Support Job Opportunities Initiative," *Nuts & Bolts* (Spring 2001).

40. Nakkoul and Sugerman, "WANTO Grant Closeout Materials," 12 (emphasis original).

41. Ibid., 17.

42. Ibid., 22.

43. Julie Nyland, "Issue Networks and Nonprofit Organizations," *Policy Studies Review* (Summer 1995): 198.

44. Ibid., 200.

45. Nakkoul and Sugerman, "WANTO Grant Closeout Materials," 3.

Notes to Chapter 8

1. Lauren Sugerman, "Challenging Sex Segregation in the Workplace: Women Working in Male-Dominated Jobs in Cuba, Nicaragua and South Africa," paper presented at the Institute for Women's Policy Research Conference, Washington DC, June 8, 2001.

2. Vivian Price, "Lessons of Affirmative Action for Women in the U.S. Highway Construction Industry," paper presented at the Institute for Women's Policy Research Conference, Washington, DC, June 8, 2001.

3. Dorothy McBride Stetson and Amy Mazur, eds. *Comparative State Feminism* (Thousand Oaks, CA: Sage, 1995).

4. James K. Galbraith, *Created Unequal: The Crisis in American Pay* (New York: Free Press, 1998). Specifically, see his rationale for examining industries rather than occupations or race and gender categories on pp. 50–59.

5. Shirley Dex and Heather Joshi, "Careers and Motherhood: Policies for Compatability," *Cambridge Journal of Economics* 23, no. 5 (1999): 641–59.

Notes to Appendix

1. Women's Bureau, *Directory of Non-Traditional Training and Employment Programs Serving Women* (Washington, DC: U.S. Government Printing Office, 1991); *The Women's Bureau: A Voice for Working Women* (Washington, DC: U.S. Government Printing Office, 1988); *Women's Bureau: Meeting the Challenges of the 80s* (Washington, DC: U.S. Government Printing Office, 1985).

2. Women's Bureau, "Nontraditional Occupations for Women in 1999," February 1999: www.dol.gov/wb (July 6, 2000); and "Nontraditional Occupations for Women in 1998," February 1998.

3. Wider Opportunities for Women, Women in Nontraditional Occupations and Apprenticeships (WANTO), WANTO Grant Home Page: www.workplace solutions.org/about/grantees.cfm (May 11, 2000), and checked regularly thereafter.

4. Status reports and final reports submitted to Roberta McKay, Grant Officer's Technical Representative of the Women's Bureau, accessed files on June 20, 2000.

5. U.S. Bureau of the Census, "American Fact Finder," www.factfinder.census.gov, first accessed July 15, 2000. MSAs were cross-referenced with JTPA SDAs as necessary to ensure treatment areas were properly defined.

Bibliography

AFL-CIO and Working for America Institute. *High Road Partnerships Report.* Working for America Institute, 2002: www.workingforamerica.org/documents/HighRoadReport/highroadreport.htm.

Albelda, Randy. "Nice Work if You Can Get It: Segmentation of White and Black Women Workers in the Postwar Period." *Review of Radical Political Economics* 17 (1985): 72–85.

———. "Occupational Segregation by Race and Gender, 1958–1981." *Industrial and Labor Relations Review* 39 (1986): 404–11.

Anderson, Betty. (NTO Specialist, U.S. Department of Labor Women's Bureau.) Interview by author, Washington, DC, July 16, 2001.

Angrist, Joshua D., and Jinyong Hahn. "When to Control for Covariates? Panel-Asymptotic Results for Estimates of Treatment Effects." NBER technical working paper 241, National Bureau of Economic Research, Cambridge, MA, 1999.

Anoa'i, Suataute. (Training Coordinator, Century Housing Corporation.) Telephone interview by author, November 21, 2000.

Arrow, Kenneth. "Models of Job Discrimination." In *Racial Discrimination in Economic Life*, ed. A.H. Pascal, 83–102. Lexington, MA: D.C. Heath, 1972.

———. "Some Mathematical Models of Race in the Labor Market." In *Racial Discrimination in Economic Life*, ed. A.H. Pascal, 187–204. Lexington, MA: D.C. Heath, 1972.

———. "The Theory of Discrimination." In *Discrimination and Labor Markets*, ed. O.C. Ashenfelter and A.E. Rees, 3–33. Princeton: Princeton University Press, 1973.

Ashenfelter, Orley. "Discrimination and Trade Unions." In *Discrimination and Labor Markets*, ed. O.C. Ashenfelter and A.E. Rees, 88–112. Princeton: Princeton University Press, 1973.

Ashenfelter, Orley C., and Robert J. LaLonde. *The Economics of Training Volume II: Empirical Evidence.* Cheltenham, UK: Edward Elgar, 1996.

———, eds. *The Economics of Training Volume I: Theory and Measurement.* Cheltenham, UK: Edward Elgar, 1996.

Auster, Carol J., and Donald Auster. "Factors Influencing Women's Choice of Nontraditional Careers: The Role of Family, Peers, and Counselors." *Vocational Guidance Quarterly* 29, no. 3 (March 1981): 253–63.

Baiman, Ron; Marc Doussard; Sharon Mastracci; Joe Persky; and Nik Theodore. *Raising and Maintaining the Value of the Illinois Minimum Wage: An Economic Impact Study*: www.uic.edu/cuppa/uicued/Publications/EXECSMRY/IllinoisMinimumWage.htm (February 2003).

Baker, Carol. Texas State Technical College System Statistical Data Reports. October 2000.

Bandura, A. "Self-Efficacy: Toward a Unifying Theory of Behavior Change." *Psychological Review* 84 (1977): 191–215

Barbash, Jack. "A Department to Protect Workers' Equity." *Monthly Labor Review*. Special issue: "The Labor Department at 75" (1988): 3–9.

Barsby, Steve L. *Cost-Benefit Analysis and Manpower Programs*. Lexington, MA: Lexington Books, D.C. Heath, 1972.

Bartholomew, Cheryl G., and Donna L. Schnorr. "Gender Equity: Suggestions for Broadening Career Options of Female Students." *School Counselor* 41, no. 4 (March 1994): 245–55.

Becker, Gary S. *The Economics of Discrimination*. Chicago: University of Chicago Press, 1957.

———. "Nobel Lecture: The Economic Way of Looking at Behavior." *Journal of Political Economy* 101 (1993): 385–409.

Beller, Andrea H. "Changes in the Sex Composition of U.S. Occupations, 1960–1981." *Journal of Human Resources* 20 (1985): 235–49.

Ben-Porath, Yoram. "The Production of Human Capital in the Life Cycle of Earnings." In *The Economics of Training, Volumes I and II*, ed. O.C. Ashenfelter and R.J. LaLonde, Vol. 1, 57–64. Cheltenham UK: Edward Elgar, 1996.

Bergmann, Barbara R. "Sex Discrimination in Wages: Comment." In *Discrimination and Labor Markets*, ed. O.C. Ashenfelter and A.E. Rees, 152–54. Princeton: Princeton University Press, 1973.

———. "Occupational Segregation, Wages and Profits When Employers Discriminate by Race or Sex." *Eastern Economic Journal* 1, nos. 2/3 (April/July 1974): 103–10.

———. "Becker's Theory of the Family: Preposterous Conclusions." *Challenge* 39 (1996): 9–12.

Berik, Gunseli, and Cihan Bilginsoy. "Do Unions Help or Hinder Women in Training? Apprenticeship Programs in the United States." *Industrial Relations* 39, no. 4 (October 2000): 600–24.

Bernhardt, Annette; Laura Dresser; and Joel Rogers. "Taking the High Road in Milwaukee: The Wisconsin Regional Training Partnership." *WorkingUSA* 5, no. 3 (Winter 2001–2): 109–30.

Bernhardt, Annette; Martina Morris; Mark S. Handcock; and Marc A. Scott. *Divergent Paths: Economic Mobility in the American Labor Market*. New York: Russell Sage Foundation, 2001.

Bernstein, Susan R. *Managing Contracted Services in the Nonprofit Agency: Administrative, Ethical and Political Issues*. Philadelphia: Temple University Press, 1991.

Bertaux, Nancy E. "The Roots of Today's 'Women's Jobs' and 'Men's Jobs': Using the Index of Dissimilarity to Measure Occupational Segregation by Gender." *Explorations in Economic Theory* 28 (1991): 433–59.

Betz, N.E. "Counseling Uses of Career Self-Efficacy Theory." *Career Development Quarterly* 41 (1992): 22–26.

Beyer, S., and A. Finnegan. "The Accuracy of Gender Stereotypes Regarding Occupations." Paper presented at the annual meeting of the American Psychological Association, Chicago, IL 1997.

Bhola, Jackie. (Policy Analyst, Women's Bureau National Office.) Telephone interview by author, April 3, 2001.

———. Interview by author, Baltimore, MD, July 17, 2001.

Bianchi, Suzanne M., and Nancy Rytina. "The Decline in Occupational Sex Segregation during the 1970s: Census and CPS Comparisons." *Demography* 23 (1986): 79–86.

Bischoff, Dolores. (Equal Opportunity Specialist, Women's Bureau Region VI.) Interview by author, Dallas, TX, December 20, 1999.

———. Interview by author, Baltimore, MD, July 17, 2001.

Bishop, John H., and Shani Carter. "How Accurate Are Recent BLS Occupational Projections?" *Monthly Labor Review* 114 (October 1991): 37–43.

Blackburn, Robert M.; Janet Siltanen; and Jennifer Jarman. "The Measurement of Occupational Gender Segregation: Current Problems and a New Approach." *Journal of the Royal Statistical Society Series A* 158 (1995): 319–31.

Blau, Francine D., and Andrea H. Beller. "Trends in Earnings Differentials by Gender, 1971–1981." *Industrial and Labor Relations Review* 41 (1988): 513–29.

Blau, Francine D., and Wallace E. Hendricks. "Occupational Segregation by Sex: Trends and Prospects." *Journal of Human Resources* 24 (1979): 197–210.

Bloch, Farrell E., ed. *Evaluating Manpower Training Programs*. Greenwich, CT: JAI Press, 1979.

Bloomer, K.; J. Finney; and Barbara Gault. "Education and Job Training under Welfare Reform." *Welfare Reform Network News*, no. 9–10 (August–September, 1977). Washington, DC: Institute for Women's Policy Research.

Boris, Eileen, and Michael Honey. "Gender, Race and the Politics of the Labor Department." *Monthly Labor Review* 111 (1988): 26–36.

Borman, Christopher A., and Florence Guido-DiBrito. "The Career Development of Women: Helping Cinderella Lose Her Complex." *Journal of Career Development* 12, no. 3 (March 1986): 250–61.

Bossio, Dale; Kathy Hayes; and J. Hirschberg. "Occupational Segregation in the Multidimensional Case: Decomposition and Tests of Significance." *Journal of Econometrics* 61 (1994): 161–71.

Buckley, John E. "Rankings of Full-Time Occupations, by Earnings, 2000." *Monthly Labor Review* (March 2002): 46–61.

Bulow, Jeremy I., and Lawrence H. Summers. "A Theory of Dual Labor Markets with Application to Industrial Policy, Discrimination and Keynesian Unemployment." *Journal of Labor Economics* 4 (1986): 376–413.

Burnette, Suzanne. (Policy Analyst, Women's Bureau National Offices.) Interview by author, Washington, DC, January 10, 2000.

Butler, Linda. (Project Manager, Tradeswomen of Purpose/Women in Non-Traditional Work, Inc.) Telephone interview by author, August 14, 2000.

Byrd, Barbara. "Great Work if You Can Get It: Women in the Skilled Trades." In *Squaring Up: Policy Strategies to Raise Women's Incomes in the United States*, ed. Mary C. King, 200–225. Ann Arbor: University of Michigan Press, 2001.

Card, David. "The Impact of the Mariel Boatlift on the Miami Labor Market." *Industrial and Labor Relations Review* 43, no. 2 (1990): 245–57.

Card, David, and Daniel Sullivan. "Measuring the Effect of Subsidized Training Programs on Movements In and Out of Employment." *Econometrica* 56, no. 3 (1988): 497–530.

Carey, Max L. "How Workers Get Their Training." *BLS Bulletin* 2226. Washington, DC: U.S. Department of Labor, Bureau of Labor Statistics, March 1985.

Carrington, William J., and Bruce C. Fallick. "Do Some Workers Have Minimum Wage Careers?" *Monthly Labor Review* (May 2001): 17–27.

Chasse, John Dennis. "The American Association for Labor Legislation: An Episode in Institutionalist Policy Analysis." *Journal of Economic Issues* 25 (1991): 799–828.

Cheeseman Day, Jennifer, and Kurt Bauman. "Have We Reached the Top? Educational Attainment Projections of the U.S. Population." Working paper no. 43, Bureau of the Census, Population Division, May 2000.

Chen, Nancy. (Regional Administrator, Women's Bureau Region V.) Telephone interviews by author, December 10, 1999 and May 18, 2000.

Chicago Women in Trades. *Building Equal Opportunity: Six Affirmative Action Programs for Women Construction Workers*. Chicago: CWIT, n.d.

————. *Breaking New Ground: Worksite 2000*. Chicago: CWIT, 1992.

————. *Tools for Success: A Manual for Tradeswomen*. Chicago: CWIT, 1997.

————. *Tradeswomen of Tomorrow: An Educator's Guide to Nontraditional Career Awareness for Girls*. Chicago: CWIT 1999.

————. Site visit by author, Chicago, IL, May 25, 2000.

————. "Guide for Manufacturing Intern Programs." Draft prepared by Manufacturing Opportunities for Women Project, December 2000.

————. *Nuts & Bolts*. Chicago: CWIT, 2001.

Cirilli, Mary. (Policy Analyst, State of Wisconsin Department of Workforce Development.) Telephone interview by author, November 8, 2000.

————. Interview by author, Madison, WI, April 18, 2001.

Corcoran, Mary E., and Paul N. Courant. "Sex-Role Socialization and Occupation Segregation: an Exploratory Investigation." In *Female Labor Force Participation and Development*, ed. I. Sirageldin et al., 378–94. London: JAI Press, 1990.

Craig, Christine; Elizabeth Garnsey; and Jill Rubery. "Labor Market Segmentation and Women's Employment: A Case-Study from the United Kingdom." *International Labour Review* 124 (1985): 267–80.

Craig, Christine; Jill Rubery; Roger Tarling; and Frank Wilkinson. "Economic, Social and Political Factors in the Operation of the Labour Market." In *New Approaches to Economic Life*, ed. Bryan Roberts, 97–137. Manchester: Manchester University Press, 1985.

Crockett, Delores. (Regional Administrator, Region IV and Regional Coordinator, U.S. Department of Labor Women's Bureau.) Interview by author, Baltimore, MD, July 17, 2001.

Crosby, Olivia. "Apprenticeships: Career Training, Credentials, and a Paycheck in Your Pocket." *Occupational Outlook Quarterly* (Summer 2002).

Cuda, Carol Ann. *The Development of a Training Program to Prepare Women for a Career in Non-Traditional Employment*. Pittsburgh: University of Pittsburgh, 1986.

Dan, Alice. (Director, Center for Research on Women and Gender, University of Illinois at Chicago.) Interview by author, Chicago, April 20, 2001.

Dane County Job Center. Site visit by author, Madison, WI, April 19, 2001.

Dean, Jayne. "Sex-Segregated Employment, Wage Inequality and Labor-Intensive Production: A Study of 33 U.S. Manufacturing Industries." *Review of Radical Political Economics* 23, no. 3 (1991): 244–68.

Deutsch, Joseph; Yves Fluckinger; and Jacques Silber. "Measuring Occupational Segregation." *Journal of Econometrics* 61 (1994): 133–46.

Doeringer, Peter B., and Michael J. Piore. *Internal Labor Markets and Manpower Analysis*. Lexington, MA: D.C. Heath, 1971.

Dohm, Arlene, and Ian Wyatt. "College at Work: Outlook and Earnings for College Graduates, 2000–10." *Occupational Outlook Quarterly* (Fall 2002): 3–15.

Dorion, Denise J., and Garry F. Barrett. "Inequality in Male and Female Earnings: The Role of Hours and Wages." *Review of Economics and Statistics* 78 (1996): 410–20.

Drago, Robert. "Divide and Conquer in Australia: A Study of Labor Segmentation." *Review of Radical Political Economics* 27 (1995): 25–70.

Dresang, Joel. "A Perfect Match: Training Center Provides Hands-On Practice Wanted by Employers." *Milwaukee Journal Sentinel*, May 22, 2002.

Dugger, William M. "Radical Institutionalism: Basic Concepts." *Review of Radical Political Economics* 20 (1988): 1–20.

———. *Underground Economics: A Decade of Institutionalist Dissent.* Armonk, NY: M.E. Sharpe, 1992.

Duncan, O.D., and B. Duncan. "A Methodological Analysis of Segregation Indexes." *American Sociological Review* 20 (1955): 210–17.

Dunne, Faith. "They'd Never Hire a Girl: Vocational Education in Rural Secondary Schools." EDRS Microfiche, Dartmouth College Department of Education,1980.

Durkheim, Emile. *The Division of Labor in Society.* New York: Free Press, [1993] 1997.

Eck, Alan. "How Workers Get Their Training." *BLS Bulletin* 2226, U.S. Department of Labor, Bureau of Labor Statistics, Washington, DC, February 1985.

———. "How Workers Get Their Training: A 1991 Update." *BLS Bulletin* 2407, U.S. Department of Labor, Bureau of Labor Statistics, Washington, DC, August 1992.

———. "Job-related Education and Training: Their Impact on Earnings." *Monthly Labor Review* (October 1993): 32–44.

Ehrenreich, Barbara. *Nickel and Dimed: On (Not) Getting By in America.* New York: Henry Holt, 2001.

Eisenberg, Susan. *We'll Call You If We Need You: Experiences of Women Working Construction.* Ithaca, NY: Cornell University Press, 1998.

———. "Welcoming Sisters into the Brotherhood." *Sojourner: The Women's Forum* 17 (July 1995): 17–18.

———. "Still Building the Foundation: Women in the Construction Trades." *WorkingUSA* (May–June 1998): 23–35.

Elbaum, Bernard. "The Persistence of Apprenticeship in Britain and its Decline in the United States." In *Industrial Training and Technological Innovation*, ed. Howard F. Gospel, 194–212. London: Routledge, 1991.

Elliot, Farar; Carol Anne Douglas; Bridget Kulla; Amanda Maclay, et al. "United States: President's Plan to Defund Federal Women's Offices." *Off Our Backs* (January/February 2001): 7.

England, Paula. "Failure of Human Capital Theory to Explain Occupational Sex Segregation." *Journal of Human Resources* 22 (1982): 354–69.

———. "Wage Appreciation and Depreciation: A Test of Neoclassical Economic Explanations of Occupational Sex Segregation." *Social Forces* 62 (1984): 726–43.

———. "Occupational Segregation: Rejoinder." *Journal of Human Resources* 20 (1985): 441–43.

———. "A Feminist Critique of Rational-Choice Theories: Implications for Sociology." *American Sociologist* 20 (1989): 14–28.

Feldstein, Martin, and Daniel Feenberg. "The Effect of Increased Tax Rates on Taxable Income and Economic Efficiency: A Preliminary Analysis of the 1993 Tax Rate Increases." NBER working paper W5370, National Bureau of Economic Research, Cambridge, MA, November 1995.

Fitzgerald, Louise F. "Nontraditional Occupations: Not for Women Only." *Journal of Counseling Psychology* 27, no. 3 (1980): 252–59.

Fletcher, Kathleen B. "Effective Boards: How Executive Directors Define and Develop Them." *Nonprofit Management & Leadership* 2, no. 3 (1992): 283–93.

Folbre, Nancy. "The Unproductive Housewife: Her Evolution in Nineteenth-Century Economic Thought." *Signs: Journal of Women in Culture and Society* 16 (1991): 463–84.

———. "Socialism, Feminist and Scientific." In *Beyond Economic Man*, ed. Marianne Ferber and Julie Nelson, 94–110. Chicago: University of Chicago Press, 1993.

———. *Who Pays for the Kids?* New York: Routledge, 1994.

Fuchs, Victor R. "A Note on Sex Segregation in Professional Occupations." *Explorations in Economic Research* 2 (1975): 105–11.

Galbraith, James K. *Created Unequal: The Crisis in American Pay.* New York: Free Press, 1998.

Gaskell, Jane. "The Politics of Methodological Decisions: How Social Policy and Feminism Affect the Study of Careers." In *Methodological Approaches to the Study of Career*, ed. R.A. Young and W.A. Borgen, 221–31. New York: Praeger, 1990.

Gelb, Joyce, and Marian Leif Palley. *Women and Public Policies.* Princeton: Princeton University Press, 1982.

Gershuny, Jonathan. "Technology, Social Innovation and the Informal Economy." *Annals of the American Academy of Political and Social Sciences* 493 (1987): 47–63.

Giese, Elizabeth H. "Expanding Occupational Choices in Michigan's Secondary Vocational Education." In *Job Training for Women*, ed. S. Harlan and R. Steinberg, 316–32. Philadelphia: Temple University Press, 1989.

Gitter, Robert J. "Apprenticeship-trained Workers: United States and Great Britain." *Monthly Labor Review* 117, no. 4 (1994): 38–43.

Gittleman, Maury B., and David R. Howell. "Changes in the Structure and Quality of Jobs in the United States: Effects by Race and Gender, 1973–1990." *Industrial and Labor Relations Review* 48, no. 3 (1995): 420–40.

Glover Robert W. "Apprenticeship: A Route to the Trades for Women?" In *Job Training for Women*, ed. S. Harlan and R. Steinberg, 269–89. Philadelphia: Temple University Press, 1989

Goldberg, Arthur J. "Reflections of Eight Former Secretaries." *Monthly Labor Review*. Special issue: "The Labor Department at 75" (1988): 37–56.

Goldin, Claudia. "Monitoring Costs and Occupational Segregation by Sex: A Historical Analysis." *Journal of Labor Economics* 4, no. 3 (1986): 1–27.

Goldstein, Nance. "Management Training Strategies in Electronics." In *Job Training for Women*, ed. S. Harlan and R. Steinberg, 491. Philadelphia: Temple University Press, 1989.

Gordon, David; Richard Edwards; and Michael Reich. *Segmented Work, Divided Workers: The Historical Transformations of Labor in the United States*. New York: Cambridge University Press, 1982.

Greenberg, David; Robert H. Meyer; and Michael Wiseman. "Multisite Employment and Training Program Evaluations: A Tale of Three Studies." *Industrial and Labor Relations Review* 47 (1994): 679–91.

Gruber, Jonathan. "The Incidence of Mandated Maternity Benefits." *American Economic Review* 84, no. 3 (1994): 622–41.

Gruber, Jonathan, and James Poterba. "Tax Incentives and the Decision to Purchase Health Insurance." MIT working paper series, no. 94-10 (1994).

Haas, Peter J., and John Giambruno. "Fiscal Management in Government-Funded Nonprofit Organizations." *Nonprofit Management & Leadership* 4, no. 3 (1994): 317–29.

Hamermesh, Daniel S. *Economic Aspects of Manpower Training Programs: Theory and Policy.* Lexington, MA: Heath Lexington Books, 1971.

———. *Labor in the Public and Nonprofit Sectors.* Princeton: Princeton University Press, 1975.

———. *Labor Demand.* Princeton: Princeton University Press, 1993.

———. "Review Symposium: Comment." *Industrial and Labor Relations Review* 48, no. 4 (1995): 835–38.

Hamermesh, Daniel S., and Albert Rees. *The Economics of Work and Pay,* 4th ed. New York: Harper and Row, 1988.

Hamermesh, Daniel S., and David Scoones. "Multilevel 'General Policy Equilibria': Evidence from the American Unemployment Insurance Tax Ceiling." NBER working paper W5578, National Bureau of Economic Research, Cambridge, MA, May 1996.

Hamermesh, Daniel S., and Stephen J. Trejo. "The Demand for Hours of Labor: Direct Evidence from California." *Review of Economics and Statistics* 82, no. 1 (2000): 38–47.

"Hard-Hatted Women: Challenge Tradition in the Skilled Trades." *Focus on WICS.* Women In Community Service newsletter 3 (Fall 1997).

Haring, Marilyn J., and Karen C. Beyard-Tyler. "Counseling with Women: The Challenge of Nontraditional Careers." *School Counselor* 31, no. 4 (March 1984): 301–9.

Harlan, Sharon. "Women and Federal Job Training Policy." In *Job Training for Women,* ed. S. Harlan and R. Steinberg, 55–90. Philadelphia: Temple University Press, 1989.

Harlan, Sharon L., and Judith R. Saidel. "Board Members' Influence on the Government-Nonprofit Relationship." *Nonprofit Management & Leadership* 5, no. 2 (1994): 173–96.

Harlan, Sharon L., and Ronnie J. Steinberg, eds. *Job Training for Women: The Promise and Limits of Public Policies.* Philadelphia: Temple University Press, 1989.

Harper, Harriett J. (Policy Analyst, Women's Bureau National Office.) Interview by author, Washington, DC, January 10, 2000.

Hartmann, Heidi I. "The Family as the Locus of Gender, Class and Political Struggle: The Example of Housework." *Signs: Journal of Women in Culture and Society* 6 (1981): 366–94.

Heart of Texas Workforce Development Board. Site visit by author, Waco, November 10, 2000.

———. Site visit by author, Waco, June 5, 2001.

Hecker, Daniel E. "Reconciling Conflicting Data on Jobs for College Graduates." *Monthly Labor Review* (July 1992): 3–12.

———. "College Graduates in 'High School' Jobs: A Commentary." *Monthly Labor Review* (December 1995): 28.

———. "Earnings of College Graduates: Women Compared with Men." *Monthly Labor Review* (March 1998): 62–71.

———. "Occupational Employment Projections to 2010." *Monthly Labor Review* (November 2001): 57–84.

Heckman, James J., and Jeffrey A. Smith. "The Pre-Program Earnings Dip and the Determinants of Participation in a Social Program: Implications for Simple Program Evaluation Strategies." NBER working paper W6983, National Bureau of Economic Research, Cambridge, MA, 1999.

Heckman, James, et al. "Characterizing Selection Bias Using Experimental Data." NBER working paper W6699, National Bureau of Economic Research, Cambridge, MA, 1998.

Herman, Alexis. Telephone interview by author, December 15, 2000.

———. Quoted in dissemination products for the WANTO technical assistance program, developed by Brigid O'Farrell, 2000.

Herman, Robert D. *The Jossey-Bass Handbook of Nonprofit Leadership and Management.* San Francisco: Jossey-Bass, 1994.

Hodgkinson, Virginia A.; M.S. Weitzman; Christopher M. Toppe; and Stephen M. Noga. *Nonprofit Almanac: Dimensions of the Independent Sector 1992–1993.* San Francisco: Jossey-Bass, 1992.

Home Builders Institute (HBI). *Opening New Doors to the American Dream: A Video about Careers and Opportunities in the Home Building Industry, Especially Opportunities for Women.* 9 min. video, prod. and dir. Home Builders Institute, n.d.

Howe, Gail. (Chicago Women in Trades.) Interview by author, Chicago, IL, May 25, 2000.

Howe, Louise Kapp. *Pink Collar Workers.* New York: G.P. Putnam's Sons, 1977.

Hoyman, Michele. "Female Participation in the Informal Economy: A Neglected Issue." *Annals of the American Academy of Political and Social Sciences* 493 (1987): 64–82.

Humphries, Jane. "The Sexual Division of Labor and Social Control: an Interpretation." *Review of Radical Political Economics* 23 (1991): 269–96.

———. *Gender and Economics.* Cambridge, UK: Edward Elgar, 1995.

Hurtig, Janise. (Senior Research Scientist, Center for Research on Women and Gender, University of Illinois at Chicago.) Interview by author, Chicago, IL, April 20, 2001.

Hutchens, Robert M. "Segregation Curves, Lorenz Curves and Inequality in the Distribution of People across Occupations." *Mathematical Social Sciences* 21 (1991): 31–51.

Hwang, Sean-Shong, and Kevin M. Fitzpatrick. "The Effects of Occupational Sex Segregation and the Spatial Distribution of Jobs on Commuting Patters." *Social Science Quarterly* 73 (1992): 550–64.

Hyde, Carliss. (Director of External Resource Development, Texas State Technical College Waco.) Telephone interview by author, May 31, 2001.

———. Interview by author, Waco, TX, June 5, 2001.

Hydrick, Blair. *Records of the Women's Bureau of the Department of Labor, 1918–1965.* Chicago: Center for Research Libraries, 1986.

Inez, Camille C. (Project and Web Site Manager, Wider Opportunities for Women.) Interview by author, Washington, DC, March 14, 2001.

Ivey, Laura. (Researcher, Home Builders' Institute.) Telephone interview by author, August 8, 2000.

Jackson, Mary. (Project Manager, International Union of Operating Engineers.) Telephone interview by author, November 7, 2000.

Karmel, T., and M. Maclachlan. "Occupational Sex Segregation: Increasing or Decreasing?" *The Economic Record* 64 (1988): 187–95.

Kerka, Sandra. "Has Nontraditional Training Worked for Women?" *Myths and Realities, No. 1.* Center on Education and Training for Employment, Ohio State University College of Education, 1999.

Kim, Marlene. "Women Paid Low Wages: Who They Are and Where They Work." *Monthly Labor Review* (September 2000): 26–30.

Kruse, Julie. (Assistant Director, Chicago Women in Trades.) Interview by author, Chicago, IL, May 25, 2000.

Kreutz, Eileen. *In for a Change: A Curriculum Guide for Pre-Apprenticeship Training*. Chicago: Chicago Women in Trades, 1995.

Kuklinski, Lisa. (Policy Director, Chicago Women in Trades.) Interview by author. Chicago, IL, May 25, 2000.

Kuklinski, Lisa, and Steve Everett. "Final Report and Evaluation: Manufacturing Opportunities for Women (MOW) Technical Assistance Program." Prepared by Chicago Women in Trades MOW Team, n.d.

Kuttner, Robert. *Everything for Sale: The Virtues and Limits of Markets*. New York: Knopf, 1997.

Lange, Gaylen. (Workforce Development Director, Heart of Texas Council of Governments.) Interviews by author, Waco, October 18, 2000, November 10, 2000, and June 25, 2001.

———. "Returns-to-Investment Analysis of Project TExAS: Draft." Unpublished manuscript, 2000.

Leung, Yuk-Hi Patrick. An Evaluation of a Non-Traditional Job Training Program for Women in Ohio. An evaluation of a pilot project conducted by PREP-Ohio, Ohio State University, Columbus, OH, 1986.

Levine, Ruth E. "Occupational Segregation by Gender: Relevance to Labor Supply and Fertility Relationships." *Research in Human Capital and Development* 6 (1990): 17–25.

Lewis, Donald E., and Brett Shorten. "Occupational Segregation, Labour Force Participation and the Relative Earnings of Men and Women." *Applied Economics* 23 (1991): 167–77.

Lyle, Beverly. (Regional Administrator, Women's Bureau Region VI.) Interview by author, Dallas, TX, December 20, 1999.

Mackey, Wade C. "Comparative Success in Recruiting Women into Non-Traditional Occupations: A Greater El Paso Analysis." EDRS Microfiche, El Paso Community College, 1992.

Madden, Janice Fanning. "A Spatial Theory of Sex Discrimination." *Journal of Regional Science* 17 (1977): 369–80.

Madden, Janice F., and Michelle J. White. "Spatial Implication of Increases in the Female Labor Force: A Theoretical and Empirical Synthesis." *Land Economics* 56 (1980): 432–46.

March, James G., and Johan P. Olsen. "The New Institutionalism: Organizational Factors in Political Life." *American Political Science Review* 78 (1984): 734–49.

Mariani, Matthew. "High-earning Workers Who Don't Have a Bachelor's Degree." *Occupational Outlook Quarterly* (Fall 1999): 9–15.

Marshall, Ray. "Economics of Racial Discrimination." *Journal of Economic Literature* 12 (1974): 849.

———. (Secretary of the U.S. Department of Labor, 1977–1981.) Interviews by author throughout 1999–2001.

———. "The Economics of Discrimination as Applied to Business Development." In *Eli Ginzberg: The Economist as a Public Intellectual*, ed. Eli Ginzberg and Irving Louis Horowitz, 61–106. Princeton, NJ: Transaction, 2002.

Marshall, Ray, and Virgil L. Christian, Jr. *Employment of Blacks in the South: A Perspective on the 1960s*. Austin: University of Texas Press, 1991.

Martin, Molly, ed. *Hard-Hatted Women: Life on the Job*, 2d ed. Seattle: Seal Press, 1997.

Massey, Doreen. *Spatial Divisions of Labor: Social Structures and the Geography of Production*. New York: Methuen, 1984.

Mastracci, Sharon H. "The Political Benefits of Protectionism for the Women's Bureau of the U.S. Department of Labor." Unpublished manuscript, n.d.

———. "The Coordinated Assault on Nonprofit Effectiveness: FEC Reforms and Community-Based Partnerships in Workforce Development." Unpublished manuscript, 2003.

———. "The 'Institutions' in Institutionalization: State-Level Employment and Training Programs for Women in High-Skilled, High-Wage Occupations." *WorkingUSA* 6, no. 4 (Spring 2003): 116–42.

———. "Persistent Problems Demand Consistent Solutions: Evaluating Programs to Mitigate Occupational Segregation by Gender." *Review of Radical Political Economics* (forthcoming).

———. "Employment and Training Alternatives for Non-College Women: Do Redistributive Policies Really Redistribute?" *Policy Studies Journal* (forthcoming.)

Maynard, Rebecca A. "Evaluating Employment and Training Programmes: Lessons from the USA." *International Journal of Manpower* 14 (1993): 94–104.

Mazur, Amy, and Dorothy McBride Stetson. "Conclusion: The Case for State Feminism." In *Comparative State Feminism*, ed. Stetson and Mazur, 272–90. Thousand Oaks, CA: Sage, 1995.

McAndrews, Robert. (Coordinator of the Associated General Contractors Apprenticeship Program.) Interview by Steve Knight on *Construction Affairs* KIEV 870AM, February 13, 1999: www.constructionaffairs.com/carp_apprent.html.

McCall, Leslie. "Gender and the New Inequality: Explaining the College/Non-College Wage Gap." *American Sociological Review* (April 2000): 234–55.

McLennan, Natasha A., and Nancy Arthur. "Applying the Cognitive Information Processing Approach to Career Problem Solving and Decision Making to Women's Career Development." *Journal of Employment Counseling* 36, no. 2 (June 1999): 82–96.

McKay, Roberta V. *Nontraditional Employment for Women (NEW) Act* Demonstration Program Grants. Archives of the Women's Bureau National Office, Washington, DC, accessed June 19, 2000.

———. (Grant Officer's Technical Representative and Non-Traditional Initiatives Director, Women's Bureau National Offices.) Interviews by author, Washington, DC, January 11, 2000, June 19 and 20, 2000.

———. Telephone interview by author, May 18, 2000.

Meadows, Jr., Curtis W. (Senior Lecturer and Founder, the Meadows Foundation.) Interview by author, Austin, TX, March 3, 2001.

Milkman, Ruth, and Eleanor Townsley. "Gender and the Economy." In *The Handbook of Economic Sociology*, ed. N. Smelser and R. Swedberg, 600–19. Princeton: Princeton University Press, 1994.

Miller, Paul W. "The Wage Effect of the Occupational Segregation of Women in Britain." *Economic Journal* 97 (1987): 885–96.

Mincer, Jacob. "Labor Force Participation of Married Women: A Study of Labor Supply." In *Aspects of Labor Economics*, ed. H.G. Lewis, 211–53. Princeton: Princeton University Press, 1962.

Mincer, Jacob, and Solomon Polachek. "Family Investments in Human Capital: Earnings of Women." *Journal of Political Economy* 82 (1974): S76–S108.

Monguko, Maurice Y., and William J. Pammer, Jr. "The Impact of Targeted Partnership Grants on Minority Employment." In *African Americans and Post-Industrial Labor Markets*, ed. James B. Stewart, 359–69. New Brunswick, NJ: Transaction, 1997.

Morgan, Barbara, and Victoria Foster. "Career Counseling for Reentry Dual Career Women: A Cognitive Developmental Approach." *Journal of Career Development* 26, no. 2 (Winter 1999): 125–36.

Morris, Darlene. Technology Profiles Texas State Technical College, Waco. Institutional Effectiveness Research and Planning, Waco, August 1997.

Mullahy, John. "Interaction Effects and Difference-in-Difference Estimation in Loglinear Models." NBER technical working paper 245, National Bureau of Economic Research, Cambridge, MA, 1999.

Murray, Vic, and Bill Tassie. "Evaluating the Effectiveness of Nonprofit Organizations." In *The Jossey-Bass Handbook of Nonprofit Leadership and Management*, ed. Robert D. Herman, 303–29. San Francisco: Jossey-Bass, 1994.

Nakkoul, Nancy D. "Nontraditional Occupations for Women. Building the Tool Kit Initiative: 2000 Annual Report and Evaluation." Dane County Job Center and South Central SDA, June 2000.

———. Tools Mentoring Project. Tools for Tomorrow: Women in Trades and Technology Program. "Mentor Handbook." Madison, WI: Madison Area Technical College, 2000.

———. (Program Specialist, Tools for Tomorrow: Women in the Trades. Madison Area Technical College.) Interview by author, Madison, WI, April 20, 2001.

Nakkoul, Nancy, and Lauren Sugerman. WANTO Grant Closeout Materials. Prepared for the Great Lakes Tradeswomen Alliance Partner Organizations by EdVentures Unlimited, Inc., 1999.

———. *Drafting the Blueprint: A Planning Guide for Achieving Workforce Diversity and Equity in Construction.* Prepared for the Great Lakes Tradeswoman Alliance, 1999.

National Coalition for Women and Girls in Education. *Empowering America's Families.* Washington, DC: NCWGE, 1995.

———. *Invisible Again: The Impact of Changes in Federal Funding on Vocational Programs for Women and Girls.* Washington, DC: NCWGE, 2001.

Nontraditional Employment for Women Act. Public Law 102-235, enacted December 12, 1991.

Nyland, Julie. "Issue Networks and Nonprofit Organizations." *Policy Studies Review* (Summer 1995): 198–218.

Oaxaca, Ronald. "Sex Discrimination in Wages." *Discrimination and Labor Markets*, ed. O.C. Ashenfelter and A.E. Rees, 124–50. Princeton: Princeton University Press, 1973.

Odendahl, Teresa, and Michael O'Neill, eds. *Women and Power in the Nonprofit Sector.* San Francisco: Jossey-Bass, 1994.

O'Farrell, Brigid. "Women in Blue Collar and Related Occupations at the End of the Millennium." *Quarterly Review of Economics and Finance* 39 (1999): 699–722.

———. "Women and High-Wage Occupations: What We Know from Research." Report prepared for the Women's Bureau of the U.S. Department of Labor, Women's Research and Education Institute, September 1999.

————. "The NEW Demonstration Program: Informational Materials for The Workforce Investment Community: Draft." Report prepared for the Women's Bureau of the U.S. Department of Labor, Women's Research and Education Institute, May 2000.

————. "The WANTO Technical Assistance Program: Informational Materials for Employers and Unions: Draft." Report prepared for the Women's Bureau of the U.S. Department of Labor, Women's Research and Education Institute, May 2000.

————. (Scholar-in-Residence, Women's Resource and Education Institute.) Telephone interview by author, November 9, 2000.

————. Interview by author, Washington, DC, July 16, 2001.

O'Farrell, Brigid; Marie Sandy; Kristin Watkins; Lisa Dragoni; and Cindy Marano. *Workplace Solutions: The Union Manual.* Prepared for Wider Opportunities for Women, n.d.

Office of Management and Budget (OMB) Watch. "Executive Summary: Overview of Findings of the Strengthening Nonprofit Advocacy Project." May 28, 2002: www.ombwatch.org/article/articleprint/769/-1/101.

Oi, Walter Y. "Labor as a Quasi-Fixed Factor." In *The Economics of Training, Volumes I and II*, ed. O.C. Ashenfelter and R.J. LaLonde, Vol. 1, 33–50. Cheltenham UK: Edward Elgar, [1962] 1996.

Olsen, Susan L. (IT Program Coordinator, Workforce 2000.) Telephone interview by author, November 10, 2000.

Orlans, Harold, ed. *Nonprofit Organizations: A Government Management Tool.* New York: Praeger Scientific, 1980.

Palomba, Catherine A., and Neil A. Palomba. "Occupational Segregation and Earnings Differentials by Sex: A Simultaneous Model." *Review of Business and Economic Research* 17 (1982): 45–51.

Peck, Jamie. *Workplace: The Social Regulation of Labor Markets.* New York: Guilford Press, 1996.

Phelps, Edmund S. "The Statistical Theory of Racism and Sexism." *American Economic Review* 62 (1972): 659–61.

Phillips, Collis. (Division Director, Women's Bureau National Office.) Interview by author, Washington, DC, January 10, 2000.

————. Interview by author, Washington, DC, July 16, 2001.

Polachek, Solomon W. "Occupational Segregation: Reply." *Journal of Human Resources* 20 (1985): 444.

Polachek, Solomon W. "Occupational Segregation: A Defense of Human Capital Predictions." *Journal of Human Resources* 20 (1985): 437–40.

Presser, Harriett B., and Amy G. Cox. "The Work Schedules of Low-Educated American Women and Welfare Reform." *Monthly Labor Review* (April 1997): 25–34.

Pressman, Jeffrey L., and Aaron Wildavsky. *Implementation.* Berkeley: University of California Press, 1973.

Price, Vivian. *Hammering It Out: Women in the Construction Zone.* 54 min. video, prod. and dir. Vivian Price, Hardhat Video Productions, 2000.

————. Web site with online bulletin board, links, and electronic resources for NTO women: www.hammeringitout.com.

————. "Lessons of Affirmative Action for Women in the U.S. Highway Construction Industry." Paper presented at the Institute for Women's Policy Research Conference, June 8, 2001.

Puma, Michael J., and Nancy R. Burstein. "The National Evaluation of the Food Stamp Employment and Training Program." *Journal of Policy Analysis and Management* 13 (1994): 311–30.

Reay, Jerry. (Instructor, Laser Electro-Optics Department, Texas State Technical College, Waco.) Interview by author, Waco, June 5, 2001.

Reich, Robert. (U.S. Secretary of Labor, 1993–1997.) Interview by author, Austin, TX, February 6, 2001.

Reinharz, Shulamit. *Feminist Methods in Social Research*. Oxford: Oxford University Press, 1992.

Reskin, Barbara F., and Irene Padavic. *Women and Men at Work*. Thousand Oaks, CA: Pine Forge Press, 1994.

Reskin, Barbara F., and Patricia A. Roos. *Job Queues, Gender Queues: Explaining Women's Inroads into Male Occupations*. Philadelphia: Temple University Press, 1990.

Romero, Patricia L. "Expanding Career Options: Non-Stereotyped Career Counseling." Irvine Career Planning and Placement Center, California University, 1979.

Rosen, Sherwin. "Learning and Experience in the Labor Market." In *The Economics of Training, Volumes I and II*, ed. O.C. Ashenfelter and R.J. LaLonde, Vol. 1, 65–81. Cheltenham UK: Edward Elgar, 1996.

Sagen, Deborah Ann. *Safeguarding Women's Interests, Promoting Women's Welfare: an Administrative History of the Women's Bureau, 1963–1968*. Austin, TX: LBJ School of Public Affairs, 1984.

Saidel, Judith R., and Sharon L. Harlan. "Contracting and Patterns of Nonprofit Governance." *Nonprofit Management & Leadership* 8, no. 3 (1998): 243–59.

Saint-Paul, Gilles. *Dual Labor Markets: A Macroeconomic Perspective*. Cambridge: MIT Press, 1996.

Schmidt, E., and G. Denhert. "Why Women Should Be in Trades." *Canadian Vocational Journal* 26, no. 2 (August 1990): 11–12.

Seligman, Linda. "Outcomes of Career Counseling with Women." *Journal of the NAWDAC* 44, no. 3 (Spring 1981): 25–32.

Shelley, Kristina J. "The Future of Jobs for College Graduates." *Monthly Labor Review* (July 1992): 13–21

Sidel, Ruth. *Women and Children Last: The Plight of Poor Women in Affluent America*. Middlesex, UK: Penguin Books, 1986.

———. *Keeping Women and Children Last: America's War on the Poor*. New York: Penguin Books, 1996.

Simon, Herbert A. "Theories of Decision-Making in Economic and Behavioral Sciences." *American Economic Review* 49 (1959): 253–83.

Sirageldin, Ismail; Alan Sorkin; and Richard Frank, eds. *Female Labor Force Participation and Development*. London: JAI Press, 1990.

Skocpol, Theda. *Protecting Soldiers and Mothers: The Political Origins of Social Policy in the United States*. Cambridge: Harvard University Press, 1995.

Smeaton, Jane, and Daniel J. Wagner. "Barriers to Enrollment in Post-Secondary VTAE Programs in Wisconsin." Southwest Wisconsin Vocational-Technical Institute, Fennimore, June 1976.

Smelser, Neil J., and Richard Swedberg, eds. *The Handbook of Economic Sociology*. Princeton: Princeton University Press, 1994.

Smith, Steven Rathgeb. "Managing the Challenges of Government Contracts." In *The Jossey-Bass Handbook of Nonprofit Leadership and Management*, ed. Robert B. Herman, 325–40. San Francisco: Jossey-Bass, 1994.

Spriggs, William E. and Rhonda M. Williams. "A Logit Decomposition Analysis of Occupational Segregation: Results for the 1970s and 1980s." *The Review of Economics and Statistics* 78(1996): 348–55.

Statham, Anne; Eleanor M. Miller; and Hans O. Mauksch, eds. *The Worth of Women's Work: A Qualitative Synthesis*. Albany: State University of New York Press, 1988.

Stegelin, Dolores A., and Judith Frankel. "Families of Employed Mothers in the United States." In *Families of Employed Mothers: An International Perspective*, ed. Judith Frankel, 237–61. New York: Garland, 1997.

Stenberg, Laurie, and Jerry Tuchscherer. "Women in Nontraditional Careers: Setting Them Up to Succeed." *Vocational Education Journal* 67, no. 5 (May 1992): 33–35.

Stetson, Dorothy McBride. "The Oldest Women's Policy Agency: The Women's Bureau in the United States." In *Comparative State Feminism*, ed. Stetson and Amy Mazur, 254–70. Thousand Oaks: Sage, 1995.

Stetson, Dorothy McBride, and Amy Mazur, eds. *Comparative State Feminism*. Thousand Oaks, CA: Sage, 1995.

Strykowski, Kit, and Nancy Hoffman. "Materials Diskette" (and Illustration by Keith Ward). Nontraditional Employment for Women Tool Kit for Job Centers, State of Wisconsin Department of Workforce Development, September 1996.

Sugerman, Lauren. "Technical Assistance to Employers and Unions for the Retention of Women in Apprenticeable and Non-Traditional Occupations: Final Report, WANTO." Prepared by Chicago Women in Trades, May 13, 1996.

———. "Great Lakes Tradeswoman Technical Assistance Network: Technical Assistance to Employers and Unions for the Recruitment and Retention of Tradeswomen in the Midwest Region." A Report to the U.S. Department of Labor prepared by Chicago Women in Trades, May 15, 1997.

———. "Great Lakes Tradeswoman Technical Assistance Network: Technical Assistance to Employers and Unions for the Recruitment and Retention of Tradeswomen in the Midwest Region." A Report to the U.S. Department of Labor prepared by Chicago Women in Trades, December 5, 1997.

———. *Challenging Sex Segregation in the Workplace*. Electronic slide show of preliminary results of fieldwork in Cuba, Nicaragua, and South Africa. Reprinted April 16, 2001.

———. (Director, Chicago Women in Trades.) Interview by author, Chicago, April 20, 2001.

———. "Challenging Sex Segregation in the Workplace: Women Working in Male-Dominated Jobs in Cuba, Nicaragua, and South Africa." Paper presented at the Institute for Women's Policy Research Conference, Washington, DC, June 8, 2001

Sullivan, Kate Roy, and James R. Mahalik. "Increasing Career Self-Efficacy for Women: Evaluating a Group Intervention." *Journal of Counseling & Development* 7 (Winter 2000): 54–61.

Swanson, Jane L., and Mary B. Woitke. "Theory into Practice in Career Assessment for Women: Assessment and Interventions Regarding Perceived Career Barriers." *Journal of Career Assessment* 5, no. 4 (Fall 1997): 443–62.

Texas State Technical College at Waco. Site visit by author, Waco, June 5, 2001.

Thomas, John Clayton. "Program Evaluation and Program Development," In *The Jossey-Bass Handbook of Nonprofit Leadership and Management*, ed. Robert D. Herman, 342–65. San Francisco: Jossey-Bass, 1994.

Thomas, Sue. *How Women Legislate*. New York: Oxford University Press, 1994.

———. *Women and Elective Office: Past, Present and Future*. New York: Oxford University Press, 1998.

Tilly, Chris, and Charles Tilly. "Capitalist Work and Labor Markets." In *The Handbook of Economic Sociology*, ed. N. Smelser and R. Swedberg, 283–311. Princeton: Princeton University Press, 1994.

Tyler, John; Richard J. Murnane; and Frank Levy. "Are More College Graduates Really Taking 'High School' Jobs?" *Monthly Labor Review* (December 1995): 18–27.

U.S. Department of Labor. *Sixty-Ninth Annual Report of the Secretary of Labor*. Washington, DC: U.S. Government Printing Office, 1981.

―――. *Seventieth Annual Report of the Secretary of Labor*. Washington, DC: U.S. Government Printing Office, 1982.

―――. *Seventy-First Annual Report of the Secretary of Labor*. Washington, DC: U.S. Government Printing Office, 1983.

―――. *Seventy-Second Annual Report of the Secretary of Labor*. Washington, DC: U.S. Government Printing Office, 1984.

Vartanian, Dorothy. Telephone interview by author, October 18, 2000.

Veblen, Thorstein. *The Theory of the Leisure Class*. New York: Penguin Books [1899] 1967.

Wagman, Barnet. "Occupation, Power and the Origins of Labor Segmentation in the U.S., 1870–1910." *Review of Radical Political Economics* 27 (1995): 1–24.

Wallace, Phyllis A. "Employment Discrimination: Some Policy Considerations." *Discrimination and Labor Markets*, ed. O.C. Ashenfelter and A.E. Rees, 155–75. Princeton: Princeton University Press, 1973.

Walstadt, Jane. (Policy Analyst, Women's Bureau National Offices.) Interview by author, Washington, DC, January 10, 2000.

Ward, Valeri G. "Career Counseling of Girls and Women: Guidelines for Professional Practice." Canadian Guidance and Counseling Association, 1995.

Watts, Martin. "Divergent Trends in Gender Segregation by Occupation in the United States: 1970–1992." *Journal of Post-Keynesian Economics* 17 (1995): 357–75.

Wearne, T. David. "Occupational Choices of Children: Must They Be Traditional?" EDRS Microfiche, January 1991.

Weisbrod, Burton A. *The Nonprofit Economy*. Cambridge, MA: Cambridge University Press, 1988.

―――. "The Future of the Nonprofit Sector: Its Entwining with Private Enterprise and Government." *Journal of Policy Analysis and Management* 16 (1997): 541–55.

Wider Opportunities for Women (WOW). *Respect That Woman*. 30 min. video, prod. and dir. WOW, 1995.

―――. Site visit by author, Washington, DC, March 14, 2001.

Wiggert, Joy. (Training Coordinator, Dane County Job Center.) Interview by author, Madison, WI, April 19, 2001.

―――. Correspondence with author, June 15, 2001.

Williams, Jennifer Dingledine. *The "Gender Gap" Differences between Men and Women in Political Attitudes and Voting Behavior in the 1980s*. Washington, DC: Congressional Research Service, 1989.

Wisconsin Department of Workforce Development, Division of Workforce Excellence. "State of Wisconsin Nontraditional Employment for Women Demonstration Project: Final Report." Madison, WI, March 1998.

―――. Site visit by author, Madison, WI, April 19, 2001.

―――. "DWD Secretary Recognizes Work of Task Force: Task Force Goal Is to Attract Women to Male-Dominated Jobs." Press release, May 1, 2001, available at: www.dwd.state.wi.us/dwd/newsreleases/2001/3926_536.htm.

White, Michelle J. *Nonprofit Firms in a Three Sector Economy*. COUPE Papers on Public Economics. Washington, DC: Urban Institute, 1981.

Woman in Industry Service. *First Annual Report of the Director of the Woman in Industry Service.* Washington, DC: U.S. Government Printing Office, 1919.

Women in Apprenticeships in Non-traditional Occupations Act. Public Law 102-530, enacted October 27, 1992.

Women's Bureau, U.S. Department of Labor. *Handbook on Women Workers.* Washington, DC: U.S. Government Printing Office, 1956.

———. *Women's Bureau: Meeting the Challenges of the 80s.* Washington, DC: U.S. Government Printing Office, 1985.

———. Microfilm. Records of the Women's Bureau of the Department of Labor, 1918–1965. Frederick, MD: University Publications of America, 1986.

———. *The Women's Bureau: A Voice for Working Women.* Washington, DC: U.S. Government Printing Office, 1988.

———. Draft of WANTO cover memo to Congress and the press, dated May 9, 2000.

———. Site visits by author, January 10, 11, and 12, 2000, June 19, 2000, and July16, 2001.

Women's Resource Center at Texas State Technical College, Waco. Site visit by author, June 5, 2001.

Wootton, Barbara H. "Gender Differences in Occupational Employment." *Monthly Labor Review* (April 1997): 15–24.

Worthey, Frances. (Director of the Women's Resource Center, Texas State Technical College, Waco, TX.) Telephone interview by author, June 18, 2001.

———. Interview by author, Waco, June 25, 2001.

Yelowitz, Aaron S. "The Medicaid Notch, Labor Supply and Welfare Participation." *Quarterly Journal of Economics* 110, no. 4 (1995): 909–39.

Yin, Robert K. *Case Study Research: Design and Methods.* Beverly Hills: Sage, 1984.

Zald, M.N. *Organizational Change: The Political Economy of the YMCA.* Chicago: University of Chicago Press, 1970.

Index

About the Author

Sharon Mastracci is an assistant professor of Public Administration at the University of Illinois at Chicago (UIC). She sits on the faculty board of the Center for Research on Women and Gender and is a faculty affiliate of the UIC Center for Urban Economic Development. She researches employment outcomes by industry and occupation for non-college women and men, non-traditional occupations, and intergovernmental service delivery strategies involving the third sector.